For Harry and Ligia

Series preface

The Americas have been unique for the mingling and intermixing of peoples from the world's continents – Native Americans, Africans, Asians, Europeans – most as newcomers, whether enslaved, indentured or free. With race and ethnicity now commanding loyalties as never before, overriding commitment to established nation states, the experience of the Americas has come to assume a new significance for the insights it provides into the dynamics of race relations.

Few scholars of Latin America and the Caribbean can have been uninfluenced by the seminal studies of Professor Hoetink for whom the Caribbean, with its variants in race relations, is a laboratory where hypotheses can be tested. It is an honour to be able to publish such a distinguished and challenging collection by international experts on the region reflecting, as they do, the pan-Caribbean approach of Professor Hoetink, an Associate Fellow of the Centre in its early palmy days; he himself has a rare command of the comparative and interdisciplinary approach without which Caribbean Studies, as an academic discipline, lacks a rationale. He is also a specialist in the rarely studied history of the Dominican Republic on which he contributed essays to previous volumes in this series – *Labour in the Caribbean* and *Intellectuals in the Caribbean.*

It is appropriate that after the editor's theoretical introduction the first chapter should include two South American thinkers, one Hispanic, José Carlos Mariátegui, and the other a less well known untranslated Brazilian, Paulo Prado, who, like his better known contemporary Gilberto Freyre, was obsessed by the consequences of miscegenation. In the past, too little attention has been paid in the anglophone Caribbean to the 'Other America': the majority of Caribbean peoples, for whom Spanish is their main language, relate to the cultural universe of Latin America rather than to their English, French or Dutch-speaking neighbours. However, one of the many strengths of this collection is the inclusion of essays on the too-little known cases of the Dutch Caribbean and Guyane.

What unites these essays, to quote from Professor Oostindie's masterly editorial introduction is the 'shared interest in identifying the underlying and ever-shifting significance of ethnicity as a potent factor in shaping both intimate relations and the politics and even international dimensions of Caribbean societies'. The complex interweaving of economic, historical and cultural variables, transcending linguistic boundaries, is well illustrated in this collection. It is a worthy tribute to one of the giants of Caribbean scholarship.

Alistair Hennessy

Warwick University Caribbean Studies

Series Editors: Alistair Hennessy and Gad Heuman

Contents

The contributors

Michiel Baud is Associate Professor at the Department of Social History, Erasmus University Rotterdam, the Netherlands. He teaches Latin American history. He has published many articles on the social history of the Dominican Republic. His books are *Historia de un sueño: Los ferrocarriles públicos en la República Dominicana, 1880–1930* (1993), *Peasants and Tobacco in the Dominican Republic, 1870–1930* (1995) and *Etnicidad como estrategía en América Latina y el Caribe* (1996, co-authored).

Colin Clarke is a University Lecturer in Geography at Oxford University, UK, and an Official Fellow of Jesus College. He has taught at the Universities of Toronto and Liverpool, where he was, until 1981, Reader in Geography and Latin American Studies. He has carried out numerous field investigations in Mexico and the Caribbean, and has published more than ten books. He is the author of *Kingston, Jamaica: Urban Development and Social Change, 1692–1962* (1975), *East Indians in a West Indian Town: San Fernando, Trinidad, 1930–1970* (1986), and editor of *Society and Politics in the Caribbean* (1991).

Franklin W. Knight is Leonard and Helen R. Stulman Professor of History and Director of the Latin American Studies Program at the Johns Hopkins University, Baltimore, USA. He authored *Slave Society in Cuba during the Nineteenth Century* (1970), *The African Dimension of Latin American Societies* (1974), *The Caribbean: The Genesis of a Fragmented Nationalism* (1978; 2nd rev. ed. 1990), and co-edited *Africa and the Caribbean: Legacies of a Link* (1979), *The Modern Caribbean* (1989), and *Atlantic Port Cities: Economy, Culture and Society in the Atlantic World, 1650–1850* (1991).

Anthony P. Maingot is Professor of Sociology at Florida International University, Miami, USA. He is a co-author of *A Short History of the West Indies,* now in a fourth edition (1987). His most recent books are *Small Country Development and International Labor Flows: Experiences in the Caribbean* (1991), and *The United States and the Caribbean: Challenges of an Asymmetrical Relationship* (1994). He is the editor of a special issue on

'Trends in US Relations' of *The Annals of the American Academy of Political and Social Science* (1994), and also editor of *Hemisphere*.

Sidney W. Mintz is Wm. L. Straus Jr. Professor of Anthropology, Johns Hopkins University, Baltimore, USA. He has conducted fieldwork in Puerto Rico, Jamaica, Haiti and Iran, and has taught at Yale, Princeton, the Collège de France, the University of Munich, and elsewhere. Professor Mintz's publications include *The People of Puerto Rico* (with others, 1956), *Worker in the Cane* (1960), *Caribbean Transformations* (1974), *Sweetness and Power* (1985), and (with Richard Price) *The Birth of African-American Culture* (1992; original ed. 1976).

Richard Morse graduated from Princeton and took a doctorate in History at Columbia University. His academic appointments include Columbia, the University of Puerto Rico, Yale, Stanford, and the Woodrow Wilson Center in Washington, DC. Two central themes of Morse's scholarship are the comparative urban history of the Americas, and Latin American thought and culture. He has published some sixty books and articles, including *El espejo de Próspero* (1982) and *New World Soundings. Culture and Ideology in the Americas* (1989). Richard Morse is based in Washington, DC, USA.

Gert J. Oostindie directs the Department of Caribbean Studies at the KITLV/Royal Institute of Linguistics and Anthropology in Leiden and is Professor of Caribbean Studies at Utrecht University, the Netherlands. He is managing editor of the *New West Indian Guide*. His research interests are history, international relations, and ethnicity, with a focus on the Dutch Caribbean and Cuba. His publications include *Roosenburg en Mon Bijou. Twee Surinaamse plantages, 1720–1870* (1989), *Etnicidad como estrategía en América Latina y el Caribe* (1996, co-authored) and, as editor, *Fifty Years Later. Capitalism and Antislavery in the Dutch World* (1995).

Richard Price's books include *First-Time* (1983; winner of the Elsie Clews Parsons Prize) and *Alabi's World* (1990; winner of the Albert Beveridge Award, the Gordon K. Lewis Award and the J.I. Staley Prize). **Sally Price** is the author of *Co-Wives and Calabashes* (1984; winner of the Hamilton Prize) and *Primitive Art in Civilized Places* (1989). Their most recent jointly-authored books are *Equatoria* (1992), *On the Mall* (1994), and *Enigma Variations* (1995). They live in rural Martinique but spend each fall semester at the College of William & Mary, where Richard Price is Dittman Professor of American Studies, Anthropology, and History, and Sally Price is Dittman Professor of American Studies and Anthropology.

Angel G. Quintero Rivera is Professor at the Social Science Research Center of the University of Puerto Rico. He received his PhD from the London School of Economics (1976). He has published extensively on the historical sociology of Puerto Rico, particularly on labor history and class relations and struggles, and more recently, on the sociology of culture. Among his nine books and many more articles are *Workers' Struggle in Puerto Rico* (1976), 'The Rural Urban Dichotomy in the Formation of Puerto Rico's Cultural Identity' (*New West Indian Guide*, 1988), and a chapter in the *Cambridge History of Latin America* (1986).

Acknowledgements

In editing this book I have collected a mass of debts. First and foremost, I would like to thank all contributing authors for helping me make this book something better than a *Festschrift* of miscellaneous papers. *Ethnicity in the Caribbean* has a genuine focus, and I feel it is a book worthy of the scholar we all wanted to honor, Harry Hoetink. I also thank the contributors, either for their patience with my insistent queries and suggestions, or for leaving me with nothing to request at an early stage. I am grateful that over the last years, their friendship to Harry seems to have spilled over to me as well.

Earlier versions of the contributions by Richard M. Morse, Sidney W. Mintz, Anthony P. Maingot, Richard and Sally Price, and Franklin W. Knight were presented at a conference in January, 1993, organized on the occasion of Hoetink's retirement as a Professor of Anthropology from Utrecht University. The articles by Michiel Baud, Angel Quintero Rivera, Colin Clarke, and myself were subsequently written on request. I should express my thanks to Geert A. Banck for organizing this conference with me, and to Kootje Willemse of the Department of Anthropology for her logistic support. I note with gratitude the financial support given to the conference by Utrecht University, the KNAW/Royal Netherlands Academy of Arts and Sciences in Amsterdam, the KITLV/Royal Institute of Linguistics and Anthropology in Leiden, and KabNA/Netherlands Cabinet of Antillean and Aruban Affairs, the Hague.

In the final, sometimes tedious, technical stages of editing, I was cheerfully and efficiently assisted by Marco Last. Peter Mason helped to smooth remaining stylistic inelegancies in some of the non-native speakers' contributions. It was a pleasure working with both of them.

Professor Alistair Hennessy, formerly of Warwick University, might just as well have been a contributor to this book. I am not even particularly certain why he is not, and I know the blame is on me. Anyway, his enthusiasm about the project was very welcome, and I am delighted that the English edition of the book is published in 'his' series.

Finally, I should thank Harry for bearing with this project in his own special way: slightly embarrassed, flattered, and worried at the same time, and trying hard – and successfully – not to interfere. As always, his few careful comments were salutary.

The subtitle to this book is 'Essays in Honor of Harry Hoetink', yet the dedication also bears the name of his wife, Ligia Espinal de Hoetink. This is not just a token of my personal appreciation, which I know is shared by all contributors. It is also a way of expressing an awareness of how the life and works of a former outsider, who in his recent book on *Santo Domingo y el Caribe* could legitimately refer to 'nuestro país', became inextricably and happily intertwined with this gracious *dominicana,* herself engaged in the liberating act of trespassing frontiers too.

GO

Harry Hoetink in the 1960s

CHAPTER 1 | Introduction: ethnicity, as ever?

Gert Oostindie

Race and often biologized conceptions of ethnicity have been potent factors in the making of the Americas. They were so, more often than not in the most blatant forms of racism and racial antagonism, throughout the centuries of post-Columbian exploration and colonization. They remain crucial factors in the contemporary Americas, even if far more ambiguously than before. This collection of essays addresses the workings of ethnicity in a part of the Americas where, from the early days of empire through today's post-colonial limbo, this phenomenon has arguably remained in the center of public society as well as private life. The essays deal with various parts of the Caribbean and cover various periods of its history. Both the variety of themes and periods discussed and the authors' interest in providing a comparative perspective to their contributions are in line with the intellectual explorations of the Dutch scholar for whom these essays were written, Professor Harry Hoetink.

Ethnicity is a central theme in the scholarly writings of Harry Hoetink, from his early work on preindustrial Curaçao through his seminal studies on slavery and race relations in the Caribbean and the Americas at large to his later work. His early comparative work on race relations was characterized not only by theoretical sophistication, but equally by a subtle inclusion of his own experiences in the region. Both his 1962 *De gespleten samenleving in het Caraïbisch gebied*, translated as *The Two Variants in Caribbean Race Relations* (1967), and *Slavery and Race Relations in the Americas* (1973) were highly acclaimed studies. The references made to the conceptual reflections and tools developed in these books by the contributors to the present collection testify to the continuing relevance of Hoetink's work for the analysis of ethnicity in the present-day Americas.

Slavery and race relations

In *The Two Variants in Caribbean Race Relations* as well as *Slavery and Race Relations in the Americas*, Hoetink questioned many commonplaces from the prevailing sociological analyses of 'race relations' in the Americas, and introduced fresh insights into this field of study. Two of these contributions should be summarized, both to put Hoetink's work into proper perspective and to help the reader of this collection in appreciating the use made of these concepts by authors in this book. The first is his theorizing of the linkages between slavery and race relations; the second is the concept of the somatic norm image.

Scholarly concern with comparative race relations had assumed increasing importance in the US since the 1940s. Concern over the enduring dichotomy in American society between white and black informed the perspective of scholars such as Tannenbaum, who contrasted the supposedly relaxed racial relations in Latin America with the sad realities of their own world. For Tannenbaum and later American scholars, notably Elkins, there was a distinct relation between contemporary race relations and the divergent colonial experiences of slavery in the various parts of the Americas. The alleged harshness or mildness of slavery in a given colony was related to the religious and cultural backgrounds as well as the political traditions of the various metropoles exploiting slaves in the New World. Moreover, a direct linkage was proposed between the nature of slavery in any particular colony or group of colonies and the contemporary and subsequent record of race relations. Where slavery was allegedly mild, as in the Iberian Americas, race relations were supposed to be fluid and relaxed; the cleavage between white and black was easily bridged. For the Anglo-Saxon and Dutch colonies, the opposite was held to be true.

The scholarly fate of such theorizing seemed sealed within a relatively short time. In the academic debate, the Caribbean functioned as a crucial frame of reference and indeed as a laboratory for preparing and testing hypotheses. First, there was the empirical falsification of the idea that slavery in the Iberian colonies had always been mild. Not only had this interpretation been based more upon the letter than upon the actual implementation of slave codes such as the *Siete partidas*, but historical research made it increasingly clear that, for instance, slavery in the booming Cuban economy of the early nineteenth century hardly differed in severity from eighteenth-century slavery on Jamaican or Suriname sugar estates. Among the scholars contributing to the present collection, both Sidney W. Mintz and Franklin W. Knight played an important role in this debate. Mintz (1958) introduced the concept of a systadial analysis, that is, the cross-colonial, 'same-stage' comparison of systems of slavery. Knight, in his pioneering *Slave Society in Cuba in the Nineteeenth Century* (1970), helped to destroy the myth of a benevolent slavery in the booming Spanish colony.

In these discussions, Hoetink introduced the Dutch Caribbean as a laboratory-like test case of the theory linking metropolitan cultures to New

World slavery, and the nature of slavery in a particular colony to its contemporary and subsequent race relations.[1] The Dutch plantation colony on the Wild Coast of the Guianas, Suriname, had long held a reputation for presenting the worst in New World slavery.[2] The Dutch trading post of Curaçao, a tiny Caribbean island off the Venezuelan coast, held the opposite acclaim. This contrast by definition falsified the claim for a predominantly metropolitan determination of New World slavery, suggesting instead the predominance of economic function and geographical characteristics in determining the severity of slavery.

Moreover, as Hoetink demonstrated, race relations in these two Dutch colonies failed to conform to the Tannenbaum–Elkins logic. Whereas the large proportion of free blacks and coloreds in Curaçao and the contrasting low proportion in Suriname might seem to fit the theory, the record of race relations did not. The conspicuous thing about the the free Afro-Curaçaoan population during slavery was not so much its size. The high frequency of manumissions corresponded primarily to the whimsicality of a commercial economy in which during the frequent slumps a calculation of present costs of maintaining slaves set against the possible future gains to be made from them induced many slave holders to opt for manumitting their bonded labor. The more remarkable point is that the high proportion of free Afro-Curaçaoans served to imbue the local white elite with a sense of distrust and menace which only strengthened the racial barriers. After Emancipation, and in fact right up to the 1960s at least, 'color' would continue to be a crucial marker in Curaçaoan society.

Manumission figures in Suriname remained low throughout the eighteenth century, an indication of the economic rationality of plantation slavery in the colony. Whereas this seemed to underline the bad reputation of Suriname slavery, the other side of the equation was provided by better rather than slimmer chances of upward social mobility for free blacks and coloreds. It would again be difficult to construe a causality between slavery type and racial relations. Rather, the proportion of the various color groups dominated the outcome. During slavery, the small white elite started to tolerate and even co-opt free coloreds, thus hoping to establish a buffer between themselves and the slave masses. After Emancipation, the demise of the plantation colony and the resultant further depletion of the white population only served to enlarge the chances of Afro-Surinamers to reach the higher echelons of colonial society, particularly through the colonial educational system. Again, the previous experience of slavery was not the major explanatory factor for subsequent race relations.

The somatic norm image

The various contributions to this debate served to falsify the theory of a necessary and 'logical' relationship between metropolitan cultures and types of slavery, and between types of slavery and subsequent race relations. Yet they did not necessarily address, much less explain, the enigma conceded by most observers: the generally greater fluidity of color distinctions in the Iberian Americas compared to the rigidity of the non-Hispanic Americas. In this context, Hoetink's concept of 'somatic norm image' was a truly innovative infusion to the debate.

A truth often lost on North American observers, socialized into a rigid two-tier view of race relations which considered all persons not defined as 'white' by phenotype as 'black', Hoetink emphasized time and again the socially construed psychological dimension to perceptions and definitions of 'race':

> One and the same person may be considered white in the Domin-
> ican Republic or Puerto Rico, and 'coloured' in Jamaica,
> Martinique, or Curaçao; this difference must be explained in
> terms of socially determined somatic norms. The same person
> may be called a 'Negro' in Georgia; this must be explained by the
> historical evolution of social structure in the Southern United
> States (1967:xii).

By analyzing the divergent patterns of race relations *within* the Caribbean and Latin America, he helped to undermine the then prevailing tendency to consider precisely 'such anomalies as the North American socioracial di-chotomy'[3] as the yardstick whereby the significance of ethnicity in the Americas should be measured. Analytically, he introduced the distinction between socioracial structure and the character of race relations. Once historically established under the influence of economic and demographic factors, the hierarchy as defined in the socioracial structure was resistant to change. The racially as well as socioeconomically dominant group would see to its permanence out of sheer self-interest. This permanence applied to *all* multiracial societies, and would continue to do so – 'only their rationalizations adapt themselves to the fashions of the times' (1973:55). From this perspective, the US experience might be interpreted as unique in that it developed a two-tier (white-black) socioracial structure instead of the three-tier variants (white-colored-black) or virtual racial continuums emerging over time elsewhere in the Americas. Yet all these socioracial structures concurred in the resilience of their socioracial hierarchies. Structurally, then, Brazil or Cuba were not as fluid as American observers had held them to be.

Yet according to Hoetink, the character of race relations *did* change from one place and period to another. Here, one could indeed discern a contrast of a kind between the Anglo-Saxon or Northern European variants on the one hand and the Latin variant on the other. Cultural ingredients such as religion, shared ideas regarding community, and modes of cultural communication all determined the character of daily racial contact. The Latin American variant indeed boasted a far greater social skill in downplaying the significance of race and color differentiations. Instead of the American experience of virtual segregation and dual cultures, Latin America had developed a wide array of cultural expressions and institutions symbolically bridging the racial divide between two opposite poles now linked by substantial numbers, if not a majority, of intermediate groups. As such, its social atmosphere was indeed more fluid and amenable; yet below this deceptively relaxed surface, a hierarchical socioracial structure with its corresponding racist conception of white supremacy remained in place.

In *The Two Variants in Caribbean Race Relations*, Hoetink discerned three ideal-typical variants of race relations in the Americas. The most rigid, two-tier variant belonged to the US alone. Most of the non-Hispanic Caribbean had developed a three-tier variant, in which the colored group held an intermediate position. The Latin variant, finally, was characterized by its racial continuum. Departing from the presumption that all segmented Caribbean societies tended towards homogenization, in which ultimately racial factors as such would no longer determine social structure, Hoetink predicted two divergent future scenarios for the region. One option would be homogenization through the elimination of the racially distinct – white – minority; a long-term process. In a three-tiered society, elimination of the white segment would not produce instant homogeneity: the remaining tiers would again be faced with various future scenarios. The alternative option was homogenization through the gradual mingling of racial groups and cultures. The latter option implied both biological miscegenation and probably greater cultural acculturation. His prediction was clear enough: 'The Iberian type tends to homogenization through mingling, the North-West European one to homogenization through the elimination of the dominant segment' (1967:175).

Before attempting to evaluate these scenarios in the light of subsequent history, two more ingredients to the theoretical apparatus developed in *The Two Variants in Caribbean Race Relations* and *Slavery and Race Relations in the Americas* should be introduced. In an effort to escape from the socially relevant, but analytically untenable concept of 'race', Hoetink introduced the concept of somatic norm image, defined as 'the complex of physical (somatic) characteristics which are accepted by a group as its norm and ideal' (1967:120). The product of socialization, the somatic norm image guides an individual in a segmented society in his or her everyday dealings with other individuals who may have different physical characteristics. This socialization has been structured in an historical context of both intersegmentary acculturation and a continuing racial hierarchy. A society's somatic norm image therefore, according to Hoetink, tends to reflect the preferences of the dominant segment which in time and to a certain extent become accepted by the lower segments as well. Hoetink argued that segmented societies are characterized by varying measures of somatic distance, that is, degrees of difference subjectively experienced between the dominant somatic norm image and the physical appearance of different groups in society (including one's own). Hoetink used both concepts to explain why, in his opinion, the Latin American process of ethnic homogenization could and indeed did proceed via biological and cultural mingling. An absence of racism among the Euro-Latin elites would be a poor explanation: Iberian whites, Hoetink maintained, tended to entertain much the same racial prejudices as their Caribbean counterparts of North-west European origin. Yet the somatic norm image did diverge between the two white groups, as did, consequently, attitudes towards part of the nonwhites. In the North-west European variant, the social definition was such that members of the group defined as 'light coloreds' were generally not accepted as marriage partners. In the Iberian variant, in contrast, a slightly darker norm emerged, mainly under the influence of Iberian-European standards of beauty which in turn had incorporated pre-*conquista* Mediterranean and particularly Moorish contributions. The resulting higher grade of acceptance as whites of individuals who would have been defined as 'light coloreds' by the North-west Europeans created a white elite with comparatively more intimate, socially accepted, relations with part of the intermediate group.[4] This process in turn stimulated not only the emergence of a continuum of 'racial types' but equally the process of cultural transfers. Therefore, even if the somatic distance between white and black was large in both the North-west European and the Iberian variants, the latter's fluidity in the white–colored spectrum could conceivably allow for an ultimate homogenization of this type of segmented society. There was indeed more to the Iberian variant than a significantly greater social skill in interracial contacts alone. The lesser somatic distance in the Iberian world allowed for a somewhat easier, and socially acceptable, crossing of the color divide. From the divergences in this sphere of intimate relations emerged the wider societal contrast between the variants of American race relations.

Caribbean ethnicity revisited

The concepts of the 'somatic norm image' and 'somatic distance' provided challenging – if in a sense speculative and therefore debatable – theoretical tools to move back and forward from the origins of Caribbean colonialism to the contemporary Americas, and particularly from the macro-perspective of national cultures to the private lives of citizens in such variegated roles as intellectuals, parents, or lovers. Yet as the Caribbean has changed enormously over the past decades, one may well wonder about the contemporary significance of both Hoetink's first work and his later writings, in which he pondered some of the new characteristics of the postwar Caribbean, particularly the dynamics of 'decolonized politics' and the impact of Caribbean migrations.

Perhaps the most persistent and worrying cases of ethnic division in the Caribbean continue to be the three societies characterized by an African-Asiatic pluralism. Whereas these countries were not discussed in *The Two Variants in Caribbean Race Relations*, Hoetink later included the particular cases of Guyana, Suriname and Trinidad as *sui generis* in the region.[5] In *Slavery and Race Relations in the Americas*, he was extremely prudent regarding the future role of ethnicity in these societies (1973:95–6). In the mid-1980s, his views were more outspoken and rather pessimistic:

> So far, mutual suspicion, negative stereotyping, and a sense of indentity nurtured by what is distinctive in each group rather than by what they have in common have proved hard to overcome (1985b:75).

From the perspective of the mid-1990s, the cases of Guyana, Suriname and Trinidad indeed seem to have confirmed in the most glaring terms the weight of a continuing ethnic pluralism. A measure of acculturation may be evident in all of these three nations. Yet it is still difficult to discern, beyond the persistence of ethnic divides, processes of genuine cultural homogenization, much less significant biological mingling. It is not just the divergence in historical trajectories and even cultural traditions which serves to separate the African and Asiatic ethnic groups from one another. A traditional mixture of stereotypes and truths concerning each group's socioeconomic orientations and, consequently, potential for social mobility has continued to aggravate the divide. Subsequent scholarship may have stressed the colonial origins of ethnic division and its continuing manipulation for electoral and other less applaudable purposes, yet an emphasis on the processes of antagonistic ethnogenesis cannot ignore the reality of an enduring and potentially explosive ethnic divide in these three nations.[6] Ironically, these three cases, and possibly the more recent case of Belize with its creole versus *latino* antagonisms, demonstrate the continuing weight of ethnicity in the Americas even more dramatically than the African-European cases which dominate Hoetink's analyses.

The continuing importance of ethnicity elsewhere in the Caribbean might be taken as a demonstration of the futility of earlier optimisms regarding the presumed declining significance of race. Even if the once heated debates on the plural or segmented societies in the Caribbean have withered, it is hard to deny that such concepts have retained much of their earlier heuristic – arguably, as opposed to explanatory – validity. Even so, the record of race relations has inspired other, more optimistic conclusions too.

At the level of individual Caribbean states, the past decades have witnessed a change of discourse towards the emphasis on local or regional unicity rather than on the traditionally acclaimed Western models. This by definition implies changes in ethnic rhetoric and practice as well. Black politicians now dominate government in virtually all but the Hispanic Caribbean nations. Their national pantheons now feature heroes from slave revolts through leaders of anti-colonial resistance to contemporaries such as the late Bob Marley. Postwar decolonization and the search for nationhood have indeed stimulated the positive commitment to Afro-Caribbean culture.

One may wonder though about the depth and range of such processes. Clearly one witnesses contradictory developments and open-ended negoti-ations. Thus, the rhetorical emancipation of the Afro-Caribbean state and its cultural legacy has developed in an ambivalent context. On the one hand, since Garvey, *négritude*, decolonization, and Black Power, both black politics and the African American cultural legacy have become fundamen-tal to Caribbean life and self-esteem. Yet at the same time, there is a consistent drive to remain firmly embedded in the Western, and particularly US orbit. Obviously, a sensible pragmatism dictates this policy.[7] Yet pre-cisely this predicament of emphasizing unicity while remaining fully within the realm of the West, with all its imperial and ethnic connotations, does little to boost the former. The Haitian case has not helped. To the previous history of mismanagement, brutality, and the continuing relevance of color, the most recent chapters of this tragic story have added the factor of a historically remarkable US intervention. As this time the North Americans intervened in favor of the good guy – Aristide – against the bad ones, this move even more than most earlier 'neocolonial' US interventions in the region served to enhance the painful realization of the Caribbean's post-colonial dependency.

Nor do the Hispanic Caribbean cases allow for easy generalizations. In all of these three nations, white elites continue to be of crucial importance in the economy, culture, and politics. Yet there is no longer a question of an exclusively white elite, and, moreover, the strict delineation of what is 'white' is probably less to the point in an Hispanic Caribbean context. Whereas both the Dominican and Puerto Rican elites have tended to empha-size their Hispanic antecedents, one may surmise different subtexts. In the Dominican case, this discourse should certainly be interpreted in the con-text of the traditional antagonism towards the neighboring black republic of

Haiti. It is a' moot point whether one may discern at the same time a confirmation of an internal hierarchization along socioracial lines in such a discourse. In Puerto Rico, the project of *hispanidad* is predominantly directed towards the US, to which the island is subordinated in a Commonwealth construction. If we take the continuing predominance of Spanish over American English as a yardstick, elite policy and popular practice have dovetailed nicely. At the same time, the scant attention paid to the African contribution to Puerto Rican culture, at least until very recently, serves not only to illustrate a wider Latin American tendency to value European over US markers, but equally to underline the island's subordination in the American cultural universe with its problematic attitude towards African American culture. But then again, it is evident that comparatively, the Afro-American element is simply less present in the Puerto Rican population than in the Dominican Republic or Cuba.

On the level of national self-definition, revolutionary Cuba with its large population of African descent has been the only Hispanic Caribbean nation formally recognizing the African heritage in its national culture. Castro's concept of Cuba as *afrolatino* corresponded not only to the renewed effort at nation-building and the revolution's reaching out to the Caribbean and Africa, but arguably also to his program of positioning Cuba as an antipode to the US. In this context the North American racial record was a moot point indeed. Yet beyond the rhetoric, one cannot ignore the sad fact that during the entire revolutionary period, the contribution of black Cubans to the new elites has been extremely limited. Revolutionary politics therefore, whatever the rewards for the black Cubans, remained controlled by their white fellow citizens. There is an ironic – though unfinished – contrast here with the more conservative Dominican Republic. The same black politician mentioned by Hoetink in the mid-1980s as a candidate still widely considered to be not-presidential because of his partly Haitian origin would nearly win the Dominican elections of 1994.[8]

If these last observations underscore what have by now become fashionable criticisms of the Cuban revolution, there is a deeper reality beyond this. The debate on Cuba's racial policies remains open to many interpretations. Yet perhaps more than to the failure of the revolutionary leadership, the persistence of a socioracial hierarchy testifies to the resilience of such structures and mentalities which not even a would-be totalitarian state can dismiss. To quote from personal experience, it was frightening to hear, on the beaches of Cojímar during the mid-1994 crisis, Cubans leaving the island on their ramshackle *balsas* and others staying behind ridiculing and cursing one another in the most blatantly racist terms – as if, indeed, all the rhetoric and genuine policies of the revolution had not made any difference, or worse.

*

In recent decades, encompassing attempts at defining the national heritage have also been made by intellectuals stressing the creole nature of Caribbean society. Metaphorically, the concept of *créolité* as elaborated particularly in the French Caribbean is the synthesis of the European-African, imperialist-colonized antagonism. It emphasizes both the unique and newly-created character of Caribbean culture and the contributions made to this cultural genesis by all ethnic groups historically represented in the process. Parallels may be found in the ideas of such West Indian intellectuals as Stuart Hall and Rex Nettleford or, on another level, in the social and even political significance of Papiamentu as the vernacular of all social classes and ethnic groups in Curaçao.

These concepts of creolization and creole culture have become very popular in modern Caribbean studies. The praise of cultural acculturation and the reminders of a tradition of miscegenation recall Hoetink's theorizing on the ultimate homogenization of racial groups and cultures in the Hispanic Caribbean. In the non-Hispanic Caribbean, biological homogenization would only follow the elimination – through its departure – of the leading white elite; a process of cultural homogenization in contrast might well be underway long before that phase. The ascendancy of the concept of creole culture, precisely in the non-Hispanic Caribbean, seems to illustrate a scenario in which the gradual elimination of the once-dominant white segment stimulates ethnic acculturation. Concepts such as *créolité* indeed originated mostly in societies where the white elite had already lost its previously dominant position, or had eliminated itself by departure. The contemporary efforts of intellectuals of various ethnic backgrounds to substitute creole culture for earlier counter-discourses such as *négritude* therefore seems to address the project of bringing together the remaining colored and black segments of the local population no less than the attempt to insert the local culture as a unique entity into the outside cultural world.

From this suggestion, it is but a step towards the next caveat regarding the 'praise of creole culture'.[9] It has become somewhat fashionable to portray Caribbean cultures as having been in the forefront of cultural globalization for centuries. Yet whereas the observation may be correct and whereas the resultant cultures and their internationally marketed highlights have indeed made a disproportional impact around the world, the specter of cultural globalization, US-style, seems not particularly promising. Paradoxically, at a time when elements of specific Caribbean cultures – a range of musical styles, prose and poetry, the region's contributions to the ideologies of the South, – boost a hitherto unthinkable prestige, the very foundations of these cultures are being progressively undermined.

Whereas 'purity' is not the relevant concern here, the various Caribbean countries' capacities to maintain some of their cultural unicity is. In this context, ethnicity and race relations re-enter the picture: the gradual though uneven insertion of the entire Caribbean into a 'global' culture still dominated in this hemisphere by its American variety may well have implications for the ways in which race and ethnicity are conceptualized.[10] In spite of the impressive broadening of the ethnic make-up of the US, its rigid, two-tier stratification of black-and-white relations has remained painfully in place, as has a mixed opinion of African American culture. The West Indian diaspora in the US has gone through a long history of negotiating a niche of its own in, or preferably beyond, this traditional dichotomy. Other Caribbean migrants in the US have since gone through similar ordeals, certainly not always successfully. Today, the increasing exposure to the US, through migrations and such media as television, educational standards and business may bring home this pressure to the Caribbean itself. The endurance of the hard-won Caribbean unicity, including its specific and by North American standards still flexible race relations, may well be put to the test again.

These and several other themes have been discussed time and again in the enormous literature on ethnicity in the Americas and the Caribbean in particular. Yet one notes that recent scholarship has been reluctant to use sociopsychological concepts such as Hoetink's concept of the somatic norm image, and in many cases hesitates to detail the continuing – yet arguably changing – everyday discourse of 'race' and color.[11]

One may speculate why. Few would deny the persistent legacy of a past which shaped the logic of hierarchies of beauty, the perverse ideal of *mejorar la raza,* and the discomforting vocabulary linking 'race' with behavior, as in the Papiamentu saying, *Stop di hasi kos di bo koló.*[12] It is in his analyses of such phenomena that one senses Hoetink's fascination with the deep structures of ethnicity and his interest in the continuing enigma of the origins and contemporary workings of the varying somatic norm images characterizing societies as seemingly close in geographic and historical terms as those in plantation America at large, and even within the Caribbean proper. If many scholars, presumed insiders and outsiders alike, now generally eschew such reflections, there may be an interest in avoiding the field where one may be seen to loose track of political correctness – in fact, some critics once upheld the absurd claim that the concept of the somatic norm image was racist (Hoetink, 1973:197). Yet it may also be because the seemingly unending daily discourse on race and beauty is still too embarrassing to the academic, and Fanon's reasoning of black internalization of white racism still more relevant than one might be prepared to acknowledge.

The persistence of ethnicity

Even though he is one of those exceptional Caribbeanists bringing a truly comparative perspective to his work, Hoetink did allow for a distinct geographic bias in his writings – not coincidentally, one in line with his personal biography. The Dutch Caribbean, and particularly Curaçao, where as a secondary school teacher he taught geography in the 1950s, was his first chosen specialization. In the mid-1990s, his 1958 study of pre-industrial Curaçao is still considered the best introduction to the subject, and he continues to be acknowledged as one of the few intellectuals able to mediate between Antillean and Dutch cultures.

From Curaçao, Hoetink moved to Puerto Rico and briefly to the US mainland, and eventually to his native Netherlands where he worked for two decades at Dutch institutions of higher learning. His second geographic focal point, however, would be yet another Caribbean country, namely the Dominican Republic (Hoetink, 1982, 1985a). Personal motivation – his wife Ligia Espinal is *dominicana* – need not be emphasized too much in an introduction of this kind, any more than other personal dimensions of his biography. Suffice it to state that through his writings on the country, particularly his classic *El pueblo dominicano*, he not only managed to win broad confidence within the Dominican Republic as an intellectual speaking out for his *segunda patria*, but through this work, he also substantially helped to bring the country more into the spotlights of Caribbean and Latin American studies. Formerly, this rightful place seemed denied to the Dominican Republic as if by a conspiracy in which all history and all modern scholars concurred: no history dominated by slavery as was wont for Caribbean countries; a struggle for independence too hesitant and too uneventful in comparison to neighboring Haiti, and actually fought mostly against this heroic neighbor; a present deemed not spectacular enough in contrast to revolutionary Cuba and not as schizophrenic as its other Spanish Caribbean relative, Puerto Rico; a country, in sum, unduly ignored in much writing on the Caribbean (and, incidentally, Latin America as well). Hoetink's efforts to help the Dominican Republic attain its rightful place in Caribbean and Latin American studies also reflect an empathy which very few 'outsiders' have been able to replicate.

In all of his work – and even when the term was still *avant la lettre* – Hoetink has been an interdisciplinary scholar, combining insights and methodologies from the historical and sociological sciences with a keen interest in literature and the arts. At the same time, his oeuvre – still in progress – reflects an intellectual endeavor to pose the pertinent questions and to offer tentative suggestions rather than to come up with final verdicts. His generalizations, such as, indeed, the concept of somatic norm image, are of the most prudent type. In the same vein, he consistently criticized both the unwarranted lumping together of all non-Western countries under such delusive labels as 'the Third World', and the thoughtless application of theories and concepts derived from Western sociology to these cultures.[13] Or, to cite another theoretical concern, while invariably emphasizing the historical dimension to contemporary issues, he eschews the illusion of linearity. It was precisely in this spirit that he strongly questioned the sociological optimism about the declining significance of race and ethnicity so fashionable in the 1960s and 1970s.[14] Time would tell indeed.

Hoetink's first published works addressed issues hotly debated in the Americas, but rather subdued in Europe. Ethnicity was relatively 'cold' in Western Europe, and the specter of American race relations seemed far afield from the realities of Europe. Today much of this has changed, and with it, easy optimisms have been shattered. The disintegration of the former Communist bloc of Eastern Europe has brought about in a dramatic way the resilience of the ethnic factor in international and domestic politics. Moreover, the contemporary issue of ethnic minorities in Western Europe has caused an avalanche of so-called ethnic studies. Whatever the strands of this boom – ranging from supposedly straight empiricism to an obsession with the issue of 'constructions' or 'inventions' of ethnicity – 'race' and ethnicity have definitely been reconfirmed as central concerns of the social sciences today. This has had the ironic effect that whereas initially the expatriate Hoetink's analyses of ethnicity were underestimated by many a Dutch scholar, today an early concept such as the somatic norm image has been conceptually 'translated' for the analysis of ethnic minorities in the Netherlands (Gowricharn, 1993).

Certainly this brief discussion does not pretend to cover, much less to discuss in a satisfactory way, all of Hoetink's oeuvre. Of the themes neglected here, suffice to mention his further theorizing on the divergence in phases of colonization and slave imports and the varying consequences to the development of creole cultures (1979, 1985b), or his writings on the impact of the extraordinary phenomenon of migration on Caribbean nationalisms and ethnicity (1985b).

It should be clear, though, both that ethnicity continues to be a crucial factor in the Caribbean – as in the Americas and the world at large – and that Hoetink's writings may still inspire critical enquiry into this phenomenon. The persistence of ethnicity in itself confirms his early objections against the sociological optimism regarding the declining significance of race and somatic differences. At the same time, in contemporary scholarship one notes a move away from the micro-levels and sociopsychological dimensions of ethnicity towards the, in a way less unsettling, study of phenomena such as the relations between ethnicity and national identity, and the 'invention' and engineering of ethnicity for strategic purposes. In fact, the present collection is no exception to this rule.

On this book

This collection of essays was written by a disparate group of scholars, all close to Hoetink. Most are old friends from his Caribbean decades, a few are friends made later in life and graduates turned colleagues – in several ways, they illustrate his intellectual biography. In their contributions, they honor both a prominent scholar and his subtle and wide-ranging approach to the study of Afro-American and particularly Caribbean ethnicity.

In 'Race, culture and identity in the New World,' Richard M. Morse discusses five seminal Latin American and Caribbean identity essays. Three were published in 1928: Mariátegui's *Siete ensayos de interpretación de la realidad peruana*, Price-Mars's *Ainsi parla l'oncle*, and Prado's *Retrato do Brasil*. These three essayists all aimed at uncovering the blockages keeping their nations from the 'normal' development they sought to achieve, that is, following the model of the industrialized world while retaining their distinctive national or regional cultures. Yet their thoughts on ethnicity differed markedly. Mariátegui, in accordance with his Marxist leanings, thought little of *indigenismo* and was harsh on the presumed Afro-Peruvian primitivism. Price-Mars departed from an opposite position, 'ripping off the *masque blanc* from the *peau noire* long before the terms were coined'. In Prado, Morse uncovers an affinity with Catholic traditions rather than with modernism, and at the same time an emphasis on the shared character of all Brazilians rather than on their alleged ethnic tripartition. The two later essayists discussed reflected further on the uniqueness of their national cultures. Ortiz's *Contrapunteo cubano del tabaco y azúcar* (1940) construed the Cuban condition from the demands of the country's two leading crops, while at the same time uncovering the dazzling variety of ethnic and cultural ingredients making up the *cocción* of *cubanía*. Finally, González' *El país de cuatro pisos* (1980) argued against the asphyxiating post-colonial condition of Puerto Rican culture, and for a 're-Caribbeanization' of the island's cultural consciousness, in which the hitherto suppressed African contribution would be more adequately represented. In a postscript to this essay, Morse stresses the renewed importance of the Latin American identity essay, arguing, with Paz, '[t]he essayist does not colonize, he discovers'.

With the contribution by Sidney W. Mintz, 'Ethnic difference, plantation sameness', the focus shifts from the Latin American context to the Caribbean proper. Mintz returns to one of the themes fundamental both to Hoetink's writings and his own: the consequences for the genesis of specific ethnicities of the region's uneven development towards a series of plantation economies. In a broad historical analysis, Mintz analyzes both the major migration moves linked to the plantation complex and the fate of various ethnic groups on the margins of this system. The latter include the Barbadian Redlegs, the Puerto Rican *jíbaros*, and the Maroons. Other 'marginal' and ethnically distinct groups such as the Jews, the Portuguese, and the Lebanese were often there precisely because they were functional to the system. Mintz argues that only systadial (same-stage) analyses may help to explain the differential patterns of ethnic insertion in societies characterized by 'plantation sameness'. While admitting the continuing and often divisive weight of ethnicity in the Caribbean, he stresses the remarkably peaceful ways in which Caribbean ethnicities are played out. Mintz suggests that the absence, for virtually all Caribbean ethnic groups – all migrants, after all – of a *Blut und Boden* mystique may help to explain the low level of interethnic hostility.

No doubt, the Haitian Revolution has written some of the most dramatic chapters in Caribbean slavery, ethnic relations, and decolonization. In 'Haiti and the terrified consciousness of the Caribbean', Anthony P. Maingot analyzes how the specter of the slave revolution and the subsequent existence of the free black state of Haiti haunted not only Europeans and Americans, but also, and particularly, whites in the region. From Miranda through Bolívar to the majority of Cuban intellectuals in the nineteenth century and beyond, Haiti inspired nothing but racially based distrust. Yet, Maingot argues, the postwar decolonization of the non-Hispanic Caribbean has turned the tables. In spite of the shift of power towards the black majority, the small pockets of whites still living in islands such as Jamaica, Trinidad, and Martinique remain firmly tied to their native countries. Their feeling of security should be credited to the policies of the new black leadership. Contrary to the fears embodied in the terrified consciousness inspired by the myths surrounding Haiti, the new leaders of the non-Hispanic Caribbean have chosen the path of racial tolerance, democracy, and non-violence. In choosing this 'more conservative path to liberation', Maingot concludes, they have set an example for much of the world: 'Decolonization without terrified consciousness should be the metaphor for the twenty-first century.'

In 'Museums, ethnicity, and nation-building', Richard and Sally Price focus on France's Overseas Departments in the Caribbean, exploring how, in a context of continued dependence on the metropole, these ex-colonies negotiate their 'national' identities and represent their ethnic make-up. They argue that in both Martinique and Guadeloupe – relatively homogeneous societies in terms of ethnicity – identity politics are played out in the context of a polarity formed by France's largely successful *mission civilatrice* on the one hand, and the celebration of a folklorized past (what

Glissant has referred to as *le culturel*) on the other. In Guyane, the third of France's territories in the Caribbean, a long-standing ethnic pluralism has mushroomed even more in recent years through a flood of immigrants, both legal and illegal, largely from Brazil, Haiti, and Suriname. The Prices analyze the ideologically charged task of defining an ethnic identity in Guyane, by looking at plans for a state-run museum in the capital and pointing to the celebration of ethnic difference in its vitrines even as assimilationist programs, notably *francisation*, are hard at work to eradicate those very differences in people's daily lives. Their digressions to consider museum depictions of two other plural socieites (Belize and Suriname) allow them to contextualize and broaden their insights about ethnicity and nation-building in the Caribbean.

Franklin W. Knight's 'Ethnicity and social structure in contemporary Cuba' is the first of three articles specifically focusing on the Hispanic Caribbean. In reviewing the dearth of solid studies on race and ethnicity in contemporary Cuba, Knight highlights both continuities and contrasts with the colonial epoch and the period of the *pseudorrepública*. The revolution-ary government made a concerted effort to improve the situation of the lowest strata of the population. As these were disproportionally black, Afro-Cubans benefitted greatly from the Revolution. Moreover, racial discrim-ination was officially prohibited. In a quasi-totalitarian state, such policies could indeed be put into effect in public life, even if critics have argued that discrimination persisted. As for its incursions in private life, Knight argues that the state was not successful in removing race considerations from daily intercourse, nor for that matter gender or class. Even if critical in relation to the achievements of the communist regime, Knight voices par-ticular caution regarding the present situation of instability and the effects of a possible transition. Not only may a future regime be less prepared to support the still predominantly Afro-Cuban lower orders of society, but a return to Cuba of the exiled community could disclose worrisome contrasts not solely in the respective social and economic realities and aspirations, but equally in their somatic norm images and perceptions of somatic distance.

In ' "Constitutionally white": the forging of a national identity in the Dominican Republic', Michiel Baud discusses ideologies of Dominican nationhood and the specific significance of ethnicity in this discourse. The Dominican case shares many elements of the wider Latin American prob-lem of nation-building as seen from the perspective of the elites, particu-larly their ambivalence between a drive towards modernization and a nostalgia for traditional society, and their identification with European models and ethnicity in spite of the actual ethnic heterogeneity of the population. In the Dominican case, the dominant ideology emphasizes *hispanidad* coupled to anti-Haitianism. Thus the extant ethnic heterogeneity and socioracial inequality is downplayed, and the domestic tensions are externally projected. Yet, argues Baud, popular agreement with this construction of *dominicanidad* is not as strong as both the elites and many observers suggest. He hypothesizes that instead, lower-class Dominicans are well aware of the socioracial inequality within their own society, and do not share the virulent anti-Haitianism propagated within elite circles, particularly those around the conservative President Joaquín Balaguer.

Angel G. Quintero Rivera's paper, 'The somatology of manners: class, race and gender in the history of dance etiquette in the Hispanic Caribbean', addresses the process of the formulation of national identity from another, at first sight strictly cultural, perspective. In comparing the development of Hispanic Caribbean etiquette in the nineteenth century to similar processes in Europe, Quintero discloses an important extra dimension to the upper-class formulation of good manners and civility, that is, the 'somatization' of etiquette. While in Europe table manners occupied a central role in the coding of etiquette, the Hispanic Caribbean plantocracy focused on the body, especially on the public act of body movement and proximity *par excellence*: dancing in couples. This project aimed at formulating etiquette by excluding the African element in local culture, with a particular view to isolating white women from Afro-Caribbean culture, and black and colored men specifically. A striking expression of this biased forging of Puerto Rican identity may be found in the elite's abhorrence of – as well as deep fascination with – the 'voluptuousness' of the *danza* and above all the *merengue*. In distancing themselves from this music and the corresponding dancing and intimacy, Hispanic Caribbean elites attempted to emphasize their own respectability. The contrast with successful currents in recent Puerto Rican culture is dramatic. Today, Quintero argues, there is a provocative emphasizing of precisely those features of Puerto Rican popular culture which for centuries were discarded as tasteless. The modern counterdiscourse highlights the previously subdued dimensions of race and gender in Puerto Rican culture, ferociously refusing to conform to exclusive standards of civility.

The same interest in culture as a factor in the process of nation-building informs Colin Clarke's 'Jamaican decolonization and the development of national culture'. Yet as Clarke focuses on the period of decolonization and independence, he discloses the emergence of a national culture based on local elements, rather than one imagined as derived from metropolitan standards. Post-independence Jamaica has been haunted by economic hardship, massive emigration, and political violence. Yet in spite of this – and to a degree perhaps because of these crises – Jamaica's achievements in the field of culture have been impressive. From a culture defined as parochial and imitative of British standards, contemporary Jamaican culture evolved as innovative, plural, and also successful beyond its own territory, as is witnessed in the world-wide reputation of reggae music. Discussing the development in the plastic and the performing arts, Clarke emphasizes the new dynamism connected to the old antagonisms of 'up-town' versus 'down-town', standard-English versus Creole, European versus Afro-Jamaican, tutored versus untutored, and Culture versus 'slackness'. The novel cross-fertilization between the two could only have been possible through a consistent effort to decolonize the minds of artists and the general population alike. This, Clarke argues, is precisely what the independent state has helped to procure.

Finally, in my own contribution, 'Ethnicity, nationalism and the exodus: the Dutch Caribbean predicament', I return to the hesitant search for national identity in the Caribbean. Much in line with Hoetink's writings on the former Dutch colonies, my focus on Dutch Caribbean experiences ultimately serves to address a wider problem, that is, the interplay of ethnicity, nation-building, and the frustrating experiences of the exodus from the Caribbean and decolonization in the region. The failure of independence in Suriname has strengthened the Antillean and Aruban determination to remain within the fold of their former colonizer. The exodus to the Netherlands further underlines the narrow parameters left to nationalist rhetorics in either of the former colonies. In view of continued economic and political dependency, Dutch Caribbean nationalism expresses itself mostly – and ambiguously – in the sociocultural field, struggling for a measure of individual identity between an increasingly US-dominated regional culture and a metropolitan culture as strongly present as ever. The regional parallels are obvious.

Geographically, then, the book deals with all parts of the Caribbean, yet looks beyond the region to include such themes as the writings of the Peruvian Mariátegui, the significance of the Caribbean diaspora, and the continuing impact of metropolitan linkages. The essays span a period from the initial European colonization right through today's paradoxical balance sheet of decolonization. The topics addressed vary from the international repercussions of Haiti's black revolution to race in revolutionary Cuba, from Puerto Rican dance etiquette through a *musée imaginaire* in Guyane to Jamaica's post-independence culture.

This is a spoonful indeed. Yet beyond this variety, each of the authors displays a shared interest in identifying the underlying and ever shifting significance of ethnicity as a potent factor in shaping both intimate relations and the public and even international dimension of Caribbean societies. As such, the authors attempt to honor Harry Hoetink by addressing the kind of enigmas that he has contemplated and so elegantly discussed himself over the past nearly four decades. Implicitly, they all demonstrate that in the Caribbean as in the Americas at large, no matter how much this 'culture area' has changed over the past decades, ethnicity remains a crucial concern, as ever, if not always the same.

Notes

1 See particularly Hoetink (1967, 1973).
2 On the pedigree and validity of this reputation, see Oostindie (1993).
3 Hoetink, 1973:55. In fact, one would be hard-pressed to find another candidate in this category. Not even South Africa under apartheid held a two-tier racial hierarchy.
4 Of course, sexual relations *outside* marriage, transgressing socioracial borders, were frequent in all these societies.
5 In the Dutch original, Hoetink (1962:6) briefly mentioned these cases. These remarks were subsequently 'lost in translation'.
6 For example, Williams (1991:185). 'This lack of cultural distinctiveness, on the one hand, leads [Guyanese] to comment that, culturally, "Awl ahwee a Doogla [mixed]." On the other hand, it results in intense and intriguing manipulations directed at claiming group ownership [of particular cultural ingredients of Guyanese culture]. . . . Consequently, in an ideal world, [they] conclude, Guyanese should simply be proud of their cultural diversity. . . . That such tolerance and sharing are considered difficult to achieve they attribute to fear and hostility resulting from centuries of racism and discrimination, to current manipulations by such external forces as the US Intelligence Agency, and to the actions of the national elite which, they claim, does everything it can to keep "mati at mati throat" in order to maintain their privileges.'
7 On a geopolitical level as well as at the level of individual social mobility. Of course, the emphasis on Western values has traditionally been strongest in the middle and upper classes, but has 'filtered down' continuously.
8 This candidate, Peña, claimed to be defeated only by fraud. Eventually, the contending parties agreed on a new round of elections.
9 On *créolité*, see Burton (1993).
10 Hoetink's concept of the world's future as one segmented society included some ideas inherent in subsequent theorizing on cultural globalization (Hoetink, 1967:141–7). Yet his theorizing of this phenomenon may have been marked too much by the overpowering influence of the West, and particularly the US, at the time. He speculated that as the world would become more tightly knit together, a process of cultural homogenization was inevitable and was likely to result in the global adoption of a – possibly somewhat modified – Western somatic norm image. On both empirical and conceptual grounds, this reasoning may be questioned. Today, the world-wide dominance of the West is less complete than may have been thought some decades ago, and seems to be eroding. Moreover, wheras in specific parts of the world – such as, indeed, the Caribbean – globalization seems to set the conditions for a particular (US-style) homogenization, the world as a whole continues to be characterized by 'cultural complexities' (Hannerz, 1992). Coupled to the defiance of Western/white dominance in the South, among the non-white population in the US and Europe, and perhaps most significantly in the increasingly powerful Asian states, these phenomena are not likely to result in the adoption of one shared concept of culture, much less one somatic norm image. Either way, after *The Two Variants in Caribbean Race Relations* Hoetink did not elaborate on the concept of the world of the future as a segmented society.
11 See however, for example, Austin-Broos (1994).
12 'Don't behave according to your [dark] color.'

13 For example, 'the ideal-typical Western homogeneous society, which unfortunately keeps producing the conceptual framework for the sociological analysis of completely different types of society;' (Hoetink, 1973:121; cf. Hoetink, 1967:127 and *passim*, 1981, 1987:51). In this effort to emphasize cultural specificity, Hoetink gladly draws on such distinguished theorists from the Western canon as Weber and Ortega y Gasset to illustrate his case against an overly simplifying sociology.

14 For example, 'The sociologist's exposure of racial prejudices as mere myths will not put an end to their psycho-social reality, nor will his diagnosis of these prejudices as a mere defense mechanism spell their doom. On the contrary . . . optimism is not the most natural reaction to the race problem' (Hoetink, 1967:68; cf. Hoetink, 1965, 1973:210).

References

Austin-Broos, D.J.,1994, 'Race/Class: Jamaica's Discourse of Heritable Identity', *New West Indian Guide/Nieuwe West-Indische Gids*, Vol. 68, Nos 3 and 4, pp. 213–33.

Burton, R., 1993, 'Ki Moun Nou Ye? The Idea of Difference in Contemporary French West Indian Thought'. *New West Indian Guide/Nieuwe West-Indische Gids*, Vol. 67, Nos 1 and 2, pp. 5–32.

Gowricharn, R., 1993, 'Remodelling the Moral Order in the Netherlands', *International Journal of Social Economics*, Vol. 20, No. 12, pp. 50–64.

Hannerz, U., 1992, *Cultural Complexity*, New York: Columbia University Press.

Hoetink, H., 1958, *Het patroon van de oude Curaçaose samenleving. Een sociologische studie*, Assen: Van Gorcum.

——— 1962, *De gespleten samenleving in het Caribisch gebied. Een bijdrage tot de sociologie der rasrelaties in gesegmenteerde maatschappijen*, Assen: Van Gorcum.

——— 1965, *Het nieuwe evolutionisme*, Assen: Van Gorcum/Prakke & Prakke. [Inaugurele rede, Nederlandse Economische Hogeschool, Hogeschool voor Maatschappijwetenschappen te Rotterdam.]

——— 1967, *The Two Variants in Caribbean Race Relations. A Contribution to the Sociology of Segmented Societies*, London: Oxford University Press. [Translated from *De gespleten samenleving in het Caribisch gebied*, 1962. Also published in paperback as *Caribbean Race Relations. A Study of Two Variants*, London/New York: Oxford University Press 1971.]

——— 1973, *Slavery and Race Relations in the Americas. Comparative Notes on Their Nature and Nexus*, New York: Harper.

——— 1979, 'The Cultural Links', in Crahan, M.E. and Knight, F.W. (eds), *Africa and the Caribbean. The Legacies of a Link*, Baltimore: Johns Hopkins University Press, pp. 20–40.

——— 1981, 'Het einde van "de Derde Wereld" ', *Amsterdams Sociologisch Tijdschrift*, Vol. 8, No. 1, pp. 90–103.

——— 1982, *The Dominican People 1850–1900. Notes for a Historical Sociology*, Baltimore: Johns Hopkins University Press. [Orig., in Spanish, 1971.]

——— 1985a, 'The Dominican Republic 1850–1930', In Bethell, L. (ed.), *The Cambridge Latin American History*, Vol. V. Cambridge: Cambridge University Press, pp. 287–307.

——— 1985b, ' "Race" and Color in the Caribbean', in Mintz, S.W. and Price, S. (eds), *Caribbean Contours*, Baltimore: Johns Hopkins University Press, pp. 55–84.

——— 1987, 'De spanning tussen afhankelijkheid en onafhankelijkheid in de "derde wereld" ', in van Beek, W.E.A. *et al.* (eds), *Sociologisch en Antropologisch Jaarboek*. Arnhem: Van Loghum Slaterus, pp. 49–60.

Knight, F.W., 1970, *Slave Society in Cuba in the Nineteeenth Century,* Madison: University of Wisconsin Press.

Mintz, S.W., 1958, 'Labor and Sugar in Puerto Rico and Jamaica', *Comparative Studies in Society and History,* Vol. 1, No. 3, pp. 273–83.

Oostindie, G.J., 1993, 'Voltaire, Stedman and Suriname Slavery', *Slavery & Abolition,* Vol. 14, No. 2, pp. 1–34.

Williams, B.F., 1991, *Stains on My Name, War in My Veins; Guyana and the Politics of Political Struggle,* Durham: Duke University Press.

CHAPTER 2

Race, culture and identity in the New World: five national versions

Richard M. Morse

Harry Hoetink's seminal *Two Variants in Caribbean Race Relations* enhanced my understanding of Caribbean societies – and of social science in general – by questioning the easy dichotomies that were applied to research on race at the time. This paper offers an opportunity to continue our dialogue. I have chosen to examine some Latin American identity essays – three published in 1928, one in 1940, and a fifth one in 1980, appended here as a grace note. All but one deal with the Caribbean and Brazil and all are pertinent to the 'ethnic' concerns of this book. The geographic exception is Mariátegui's *Siete ensayos* which makes a useful comparative point. My second purpose is to examine the identity essay as a genre that, however influential in its day, was seen by the 1950s and 1960s as 'impressionistic' or 'literary' save for those texts having a strong political thrust. Today, however, the science–literature split is losing its reputation as an Occam's razor, and in closing I will suggest how Latin American 'identity', however immersed it may seem in local culture, is not at the rim of Western culture but participates in its unfolding (Stabb, 1967; Earle and Mead, 1973; Leite, 1983).

My selection of five writers was arbitrary but has acquired a rationale of sorts. The founder of the modern identity essay who signalizes the shift from *pensadores* of the nineteenth-century intellectual establishment to iconoclastic essayists infected with modernism is often taken to be José Carlos Mariátegui. The book that launched Mariátegui's international reputation in 1928 appeared, however, in the same year as two comparable collections of essays by a Haitian and a Brazilian, both of an earlier generation and both with different prescriptions for their countries of origin. These works offer a vigorous challenge to the comparativist.

Economics and ethnicity: Mariátegui and Price-Mars

We start, then, with Mariátegui (Peru, 1894–1930), Jean Price-Mars (Haiti, 1876–1969), and Paulo Prado (Brazil, 1869–1943). The three men had

comparable diagnostic intentions but were headed toward different conclusions. All three started with a view of countries whose beginnings had
been exploitative and sanguinary and whose 'emancipatory' nineteenth
century had been in large part a mirage. They envisioned nations that were
not yet nations. They hankered not for blueprints or formulae but for
grounds of understanding. They shared an evolutionary view of world
history but with a sense that their particular societies had been blocked
at inception by the mix of incongruent forces unleashed by European
conquest.

The first two of the trio each achieved his reputation with a book of
seven essays: *Siete ensayos de interpretación de la realidad peruana*
(Mariátegui) and *Ainsi parla l'oncle* (Price-Mars).[1] Both helped to
launch, or were later invoked by, international movements, respectively
third-world Marxism and Negritude, although as the latter movement took
shape, Price-Mars never tried to specify inherent traits of black people.
He hoped they would be absorbed into, not differentiated within,
mankind. Thus Price-Mars argued the assimilation of Haitians to the
human condition while Mariátegui demonstrated the peculiar historical
conditioning of Andean America. The paradox was that Price-Mars
required cultural specificity to clinch his universalist argument while
Mariátegui invoked universal principles to show the uniqueness of his
case.

When their books appeared Price-Mars was a pillar of the Haitian
establishment. A physician, former inspector general of public instruction,
and minister to Paris, he had published an indictment of the Haitian elite
(*La vocation de l'élite*, 1919) for having provoked the US occupation of
1915 and for being guilty of *Bovarysme collectif* at a time when Mariátegui,
at the threshold of his 'Radicalization', had been reporting the doings of
Lima's high society under the sobriquet 'Juan Croniqueur'. The latter's
political activity and his exile to Italy would soon form his socialist explanation of why the Peruvian elite had not, in four centuries, assumed its
appointed economic function. Price-Mars had attributed his country's woes
to the 'puerile vanity' of his elitist peers in promoting the 'rancid' idea that
'the Gauls are our ancestors'. As for his country's heritage, he wrote, 'eight-
tenths of it is a gift from Africa'. For Peru, Mariátegui came to see the
'Indian problem' as a false issue.

Born to an impoverished family, crippled in childhood, and forced to
work at fourteen, Mariátegui knew the belly of the Peruvian monster, and
during his European exile (1919–23) he moved into the larger belly of the
Western one. The secret of his intellectual *prise* lies in his Italian sojourn.
He had arrived thinking of Marxism as 'confused, heavy, and cold'; only in
Italy did he have the 'revelation'. A clue to the fragmentation of his
opinions in Europe is his fascination with modernist art. Surrealism

particularly intrigued him for splintering the solid bourgeois world to expose its meretricious ideals.

Mariátegui's changed outlook owed much to the vitalist Marxism that he absorbed under Croce, whose denial that Marxism had laid bare the iron laws of history inspired the young Peruvian. For Croce, Marxism was persuasive as praxis but not as science. Mariátegui then proceeded to Croce's own teacher, Labriola; to Sorel and Pareto; and to Marxist sympathizers like Gramsci, Gobetti, and the Russian revolutionaries. Postwar socialist journals and congresses steered him toward revolutionary communism rather than revisionism. His choice was braced by the fascist march on Rome (1922), which symbolized for him the political bankruptcy of capitalism and recalled the attitudes of South American elites. The task, he saw, was no longer to 'catch up' with Europe but to expose the crepuscular spirit of bourgeois life as expressed by Anatole France, D'Annunzio, and Proust and to embrace the cause of *el hombre matinal,* of peoples receptive to a 'multitudinous myth' wherever it could be found (Mariátegui, 1972).

Mariátegui thus questioned whether Peru had really experienced a national history as a sequential transcending of stages. What aggravated the problem was that 'progressive' spokesmen construed the unassimilability of the vast indigenous population as a challenge for educational policy, humanitarianism, or recognition of 'human rights'. By suspending the ethnic definition of the 'Indian problem' he linked it directly to the 'land question', shifting it from a problem of tutelage to a revolutionary agenda. The solution did not lie, he felt, in the 'Zionism' of servile races, Indian or black. This for him was sheer mysticism. Although Indian militants might win leadership over their fellows, an autonomous Indian state would not be a classless society but one with all the contradictions of a bourgeois state. However sensitive Mariátegui was to the Indian presence in the poetry of César Vallejo, he saw the national problem as social and economic, not racial. Only the struggle of Indians, workers, and peasants, he wrote, allied with the mestizo and white proletariat against the feudal, capitalist regime could permit the free unfolding of indigenous racial characteristics and institutions with collective tendencies. This might eventually unite Indians of different countries across present boundaries that divided ancient racial groups and lead to political autonomy for their race. For Mariátegui not only did the ethnic argument offer no foothold for political diagnosis, but the Afro-Peruvian, he felt, had brought fetishistic sensualism to Catholic worship, 'exuding from every pore the primitivism of his African tribe', while he corrupted the Indians with his 'false servility and exhibitionist, morbid psychology'.

The starting point of Price-Mars was not the 'land question', for impoverished though the Haitian masses might be, the country had experienced its 'agrarian revolution' with the expulsion of the French and become a nation of peasants. The economic issue was not land but fiscal and social exploitation and cultural oppression. *Ainsi parla l'oncle* opens with the question, 'What is folklore?' For Price-Mars the term 'folklore' (coined in 1846) had less innocuous connotations than it may for modern readers; for him it referred to the realm of belief, not to exotic practices and colorful artifacts. His insistence on folklore reflected his conviction that the root cause of Haitian stagnation was that its ancestral heritage was a broken mirror giving off a 'reduced image of human nature'. His argument responded in part to the cultural nationalism provoked by the American occupation, but in larger measure to the general Western view, shared by the Haitian elite, that African and Afro-American culture was primitive and barbarous. *Ainsi parla l'oncle* was to an extent provoked by Price-Mars's 1915 encounter in Paris with Gustave Le Bon, whose books had for years influenced Latin American intellectuals, and who deplored race mixing. Price-Mars took him to task and Le Bon challenged him to write the book.

For Price-Mars, Haitian rehabilitation must necessarily find its ethnic premise. Because the elite 'donned the old frock of Western civilization' after 1804, ignoring or suppressing the African transplants and syncretisms of the people, Price-Mars accused them of denying their country the binding force of shared symbolism so conspicuous in the Greco-Roman world and in modern Africa: hence the importance of Haitian creole, that promised to be the vehicle for a national literature, or of voodoo – ridiculed by sensationalist travelers as fetishism or even cannibalism – which Price-Mars defended as a religion that reached no less mystical heights than did Christianity. Language and faith betokened a new social form arising from confused mores and beliefs. At the moment it was a mere chrysalis, yet one to which 'philosophers and brave men pay heed'. Price-Mars traced Haitian culture to the highest African civilizations. If one were to compare Africans with Europeans and Americans, he wrote, one would not find the former to be the closest to barbarism or the farthest from a higher social ideal. Mariátegui, in all the sufferings of his short life, perhaps never experienced the humiliation of Price-Mars when, as a black intellectual heading the Haitian mission to the St Louis World Fair of 1904, he visited the Deep South of the United States. *Ainsi parla l'oncle* expresses visceral emotion in closing with the ancient adage: 'There is nothing ugly in the house of my father.'[2]

The ghost of Catholicism: Prado

Mariátegui and Price-Mars both built from reputable contemporary sources, neo-Marxist thought and racial anthropology. The intellectual inspiration for Paulo Prado's *Portrait of Brazil, Essay on Brazilian Sadness*, the third of the 1928 landmarks, is more diffuse (Prado, 1944; Levi, 1987:130–7). Scion of a Paulista family of planters, politicians, and entrepreneurs, Prado was drawn to life in Europe and exhibited, contemporaries remarked, traits of dilettantism and neurasthenia. He won credentials as a historian, however, under the tutelage of João Capistrano de Abreu and was a discerning patron of São Paulo's exultant vanguardist movement of 1922. Yet Prado's *Portrait of Brazil* reveals little of the modernity of Mariátegui and Price-Mars or of the modernism of the Paulista avant-garde. His text requires two readings, both linking it to less fashionable modes of inquiry. On the first, it shows affinity to late-positivist essays that deplored the anemia and languor of mixed-race populations. A closer reading brings to light a more venerable, Catholic frame of reference.

The first chapter, 'Luxúria' (lust), describes tropical seductiveness and scenes of 'pure animality'. Documents told Prado that one third or more of the cases brought to the Holy Office in Bahia in 1591–92 featured shameless sins of 'sexual hyperesthesia'. The second chapter addresses the more tyrannical passion of 'Cobiça' (covetousness). Here Prado evokes visions of El Dorado and Potosí that 'volatilized' the social instincts and anarchic individualism of deportees, castaways, and mutineers. Emblematic were the bandeirantes, whose energy and ambition lacked mental or moral basis. 'What wealth, holy Lord, is that' – in Prado's quote from Pombal – 'whose possession brings on the ruin of the State?'

The third chapter, 'Tristeza' (sadness), is the hinge of the book and will detain us again later. It opens with the classic contrast of the morally hygienic spirit of the New England and Virginia colonists with the despotic, demoralized life of the Portuguese in Brazil. Sexual excess (*post coitum animal triste*) and the mirage of easy wealth stamped the Brazilian psyche with abulia and melancholia. A chapter on 'Romanticism' claims that in the era of independence Brazil's 'sickness' was displaced to the new ruling and intellectual classes as a pathological 'romantic illness' that found central loci in the new law schools of Recife and São Paulo. In Europe, Prado felt, romanticism was a passing fashion, while in Brazil it created *tristeza* by its 'concern with human misery, the contingency of events, and above all . . . the desire to find happiness in an imaginary world'. In a 'Post-scriptum' Prado confessed that he disregarded the *Bovarysme* of São Paulo (a key term for Price-Mars as well) and composed his book (in contrast to Mariátegui) as an impressionist version of the forces of history without cubic masses of data and chronology. Only mental images were to remain. His national history was rooted not in the ubiquitous racial conflict of America but in the intimacy of miscegenation (an anticipation of Gilberto Freyre). While denying Gobineau's presumption of racial inequality, however, he saw the 'hybrid vigor' of race-crossing as limited to the early generations.[3] The closing off of social opportunities condemned the population to somatic deficiency and congenital indolence – qualities that, ironically, preserved the unity of Brazil's vast territory. For the four republican decades after 1889, Prado concludes, politicians had danced on this bloated and atrophied body. All was imitative, from political structures to 'spontaneous' flashes of genius. The two solutions he envisioned were War, which might bring a 'providential hero,' or Revolution, which might banish the chimeras of the colonial past.

Thus far I have rendered Prado's argument *ad literam*. What follows is a reading perhaps more adequate to the text and to the author's subjacent intentions. We may start by comparing the first sentence of Prado's book with that of Mariátegui's *Siete ensayos* (which affirms that the schism in Peruvian history is best seen as economic, thus demolishing at a stroke the specious *indigenismo* of the elite) and with Price-Mars's *Ainsi parla l'oncle* (whose 'What is folklore?' was to be answered by a critical inventory of distinctive Haitian oral traditions, legends, songs, riddles, customs, ceremonies, and beliefs – thus ripping off the *masque blanc* from the *peau noire* long before the terms were coined). Here is Paulo Prado's initial sentence: 'In a radiant land lives a sad people.' First, note that he speaks of 'a sad people' and not 'three sad races' in the phrase from a sonnet of the fin-de-siècle poet Olavo Bilac and used as a title by a US literary historian of Brazil (Haberly, 1983). Prado sees Brazil not as an ethnic mosaic but as a nation that collectively experiences a state of spiritual dryness. Second, Prado's sentence implicitly refers us to the first salvo of Rousseau's *Social Contract*: 'Man was born free, and he is everywhere in chains.' Rousseau addressed a state of external oppression, Prado a state of soul. From these clues we recognize that Prado's first two chapters, 'Lust' and 'Covetousness' – two of the deadly sins – point toward theological and moral issues that transcend the fixation of commentators on genes, race, heredity, sanitation, and scientific determinism.

As per the book's subtitle, Prado's third chapter, 'Sadness,' is his pivot. Sadness does not figure in the modern repertory of the seven capital sins; its nearest equivalent is sloth. Yet the genealogy of sloth shows that it merges with medieval acedia, which once counted as a 'deadly' sin and included both mental or spiritual states (listlessness, loathing, slackness of mind) and qualities of behavior (torpor, negligence, idleness) (Wenzel, 1967). Sadness (*tristitia*) was sometimes synonymous with acedia, although it emphasized the spiritual condition of dryness, disgust, or *taedium*. By the late Middle Ages, with the spread of moral theology to the common folk, acedia lost its theological force, yielding primacy in the roster of capital vices to sloth and to an emphasis on 'external' manifestations of indolence. By the time of the Renaissance, acedia and its theological component of *tristitia* were secularized under the atmospheric term 'melancholy' – much in the fashion that Prado derived the *mal romântico* (romantic illness) from colonial 'sadness'.

Prado's attempt to recover the moral premises of Brazil's Catholic society, inspired by his reading of Inquisition documents, was part of a general project of fellow Paulista modernists who had recognized the significance for Brazil of Europe's transition from the late Middle Ages to early modernity. The difference was that while Prado sought, perhaps subconsciously, the medieval therapy for *tristitia*, his younger cohorts, Mário de Andrade and Oswald de Andrade – who achieved notoriety in the Modern Art Week of 1922 – looked ahead to Montaigne, Rabelais, and a Renaissance therapy (M. de Andrade, 1972; O. de Andrade, 1972). Prado held to *tristitia* as a theological, 'internal' aspect of acedia while Mário and Oswald addressed 'external' or behavioral aspects. Thus Mário adopted the Portuguese word *preguiça* (from the Latin *pigritia*) or 'indolence' to designate a Brazilian lack of firm character or aptitude for modern, disciplined life, but also praised it as idleness propitious for cultivating the arts and as a tropical antidote to a technified, consumerized society. Oswald gave an even more positive accent to *ócio* ('leisure', from the Latin *otium*), stressing its denials in the forms of *negócio* ('business', from *nec-otium* or not-leisure) and *sacerdócio* (from *sacerdotium* or 'priesthood'). Oswald's 'way out' was the transition from technical to natural life, or from civilization to culture.[4]

Paulo Prado's 'way out' returns us to historical origins and to the corrective for acedia. His therapy was perhaps confusedly expressed. Yet it prefigures the contribution of his compatriot Paulo Freire, whose conscientization would, a generation later, challenge the passive *tristitia* of the people with psychological and even theological empowerment, presenting a culturally and sociologically rooted version of 'education' in contrast to the utilitarian and manipulative 'schooling' of the industrial West. Freire's starting point was surely one sad people, not three sad races.

Caribbean counterpoints: Ortiz and González

The analytic strategies of the three 1928 essayists are similar in their common recognition of 'blockages' against the 'civilizing' forces of nineteenth-century Western evolution, respectively: socioeconomic exploitation, racial intolerance, and collective spiritual dryness or abulia. They emphasize a need for productive, more egalitarian societies to 'catch up' to normal development processes of industrial countries without sacrifice of distinctive national or regional culture. Certain subsequent writers who have entertained similar hopes cast the issue not so much as a coming to terms with 'problems' than as specifying the self-givenness of identity itself. That is, identity becomes a processual structure and not a goal, or a problem in unfolding self-recognition rather than in achievable self-transcendence. Examples of such studies, more 'expressive' than instrumental, include the Argentine Ezequiel Martínez Estrada's *Radiografía de la pampa* (1971[1933]), the Mexican Octavio Paz's *El laberinto de la soledad* (1985[1950]), and the Cuban José Lezama Lima's *La expresíon americana* (1957). I choose two Caribbean authors for attention, however, who amplify our Caribbean perspective without reaching the dazzling personal universe of Lezama. They are Fernando Ortiz (1881–1969) and José Luis González (b. 1926).

Ortiz published *Contrapunteo cubano del tabaco y azúcar* in 1940.[5] It presented a general statement of his thesis on the counterpoint of tobacco and sugar with a frequently expanded appendix on 'The ethnography and transculturation of Havana tobacco and the beginnings of sugar in America'. Again we have a book that needs two readings, in this case to explicate a counterpoint. On the first we find the starting point to be not Caribbean history conceived as a political and cultural invasion of an exotic periphery. Instead, Ortiz features two agricultural crops (one indigenous, one transplanted) that define the native landscape of every Cuban. He starts with an experienced Cuban 'reality' still to be specified rather than with conflictive impositions upon it. He deduces his Cuban story not from ideologies of control and exploitation but from biotic requirements of two forms of vegetation. Tobacco and sugar are defined not as the currency of capitalist exchange but as products of Cuban soil that in themselves dictate institutional arrangements and ways of life. Ortiz builds from the land and its fruits (as did the early Marx and Engels in the *German Ideology*), not from human contrivances.

There is, then, a ludic and poetic ingredient in Ortiz's counterpoint because it originates as a fact of nature and not a creation of maleficent forces. The initial contrast embraces many subordinate ones. From germination to human consumption, Ortiz observes, tobacco and sugar are radically opposed. One is graminaceous, the other solanaceous; one grows from cuttings, the other from seeds; one is needed for its stalk and not its leaves, the other for its foliage and not its stalk; sugar is ground for juice, tobacco is dried out; one is white and odorless, the other dark and aromatic. 'Always in contrast! Food and poison, waking and drowsing, energy and dream, delight of the flesh and delight of the spirit, sensuality and thought, . . . medicine and magic, reality and deception, virtue and vice.' Sugar is homogeneous; in a box of cigars no two are alike. Sugar nourishes; tobacco poisons. From here Ortiz allowed himself even bolder ruminations. For instance, tobacco with its hairy, sunbrowned leaves is masculine, boasting and swaggering like an oath of defiance, while sugar with its smooth leaves and the eternal refining process to whiten it is feminine. Or: sugar as the mother of alcohol might be Dionysian and tobacco Apollonian with its fallacious beauties and poetic inspirations. Or again, Ortiz asks: might Freud have wondered whether sugar, destined for the stomach, was narcissistic and tobacco, focused on the loins and reproduction, was erotic?

Under this tapestry lay clear consciousness of what Mariátegui would have seen as economic infrastructure. Ortiz was aware that in the 'tobacco and sugar industry the same four factors are present: land, machinery, labor, and money'. He recognized the implications of intensive versus extensive cultivation, the use of skilled immigrants versus slaves; the small holding versus the oppressive plantation; the universal market for tobacco and the single one for sugar: national sovereignty against colonialism. In short, sugar 'passed into anonymous, corporative, distant, dehumanized, all-powerful hands, with little or no sense of responsibility', while tobacco 'created a middle class, a free bourgeoisie' without the extremes of slaves and masters, proletariat and rich. The noise of sugar's boiling-vats drowned the human voice, while in quiet tobacco workshops workers could be read aloud to (often from progressive tracts) as they performed their tasks. The traditional settings of rural idyl and urban cauchemar were, in an important sense, reversed.

Ortiz was eventually taken to task by Juan and Verena Martínez Alier for supplementing his 'propaganda of the *colonos* against the *hacendados* (who had denied them the blessing of Cuban nationality)' with propaganda 'against the proletariat (who were seen as an omen of socialist revolution, a threat more ominous for bearing traces of racism)'. Whatever the grounds of the charge, it seems a carping one to make against a man of large erudition and immense cultural understanding who had devoted thousands of pages to legitimizing the presence of the African tradition in Cuba, who joined political battle to win acceptance of Afro-Cuban performances in the university, and who wrote a 700-page volume to interpret the significance of the hurricane in the popular myth and symbology of the Caribbean and Middle America.[6]

Structural-economic determination was not fundamental for Ortiz. In fact there was perhaps *no* 'foundation' to his argument. And here begins the second reading of *Cuban Counterpoint*, taking a clue once more from opening sentences. If Mariátegui dismissed any plane save the economic for interpreting the schism caused by the Spanish conquest, Ortiz drew on a jovial Spanish poet of the Middle Ages, the Archpriest of Hita (1283?–1350?), who personified Carnival and Lent in unforgettable verses, cleverly imbuing the assertions and rebuttals of their satirical contest with the 'ills and benefits that each has conferred on mankind'. Like Paulo Prado he had recourse to the Iberian tradition. But unlike Prado, who found purchase in persistent 'sinful' categories of moral behavior, he called to mind the 'mocking verse' of the *Libro de Buen Amor* (Ruiz, 1978[1343]) with its

'Pelea que ovo Don Carnal con Doña Quaresma' (Battle of Lord Flesh-Season and Lady Lent) serving as his precedent 'to personify dark tobacco and "high yellow" sugar'. Lacking authority as a poet or priest to conjure up creatures of fantasy, wrote the disingenuous Ortiz, he himself had merely set down 'in drab prose, the amazing contrasts I have observed in the two agricultural products on which the economic history of Cuba rests'.

Unlike the early documents of Paulo Prado, the *Libro de Buen Amor* is far from being a righteous exegesis and condemnation of sin. It is permeated with parody, irony, and ambiguity. Its spirited praise of fleshly pleasures, whether or not written tongue in cheek, conveys the scope and turbulence of medieval life. The intent of the Archpriest has been widely debated, starting from the ambiguous statement of it in his own introduction: ' . . . to whoever would understand . . . salvation and do good works in the love of God, and also to whoever may desire foolish worldly love, . . . this book can say truly to each: *Intellectum tibi dabo, e cetera*, I will give thee understanding, and the rest.'

Pérez Firmat examines Ortiz's thought and sensibility, attempting to show that his appreciation of Cuban culture and society depends less on analyzing historical ingredients and stages than on understanding the processual formation of the nation's vernacular underpinning. His key notion is 'the fermentation and turmoil that *precedes* synthesis', his two key terms being 'transculturation' (translational displacements that generate vernacular culture) and *ajiaco* (a metaphor for the outcome of displacements). The world *ajiaco* itself – a simmering stew – is onomastic, for it combines the African name for an Indian condiment (*ají* or green pepper) with the Spanish suffix *-aco*. The *ajiaco* is never finished, changes incessantly with the addition of fresh ingredients, has no central core of flavor and substance, and changes in taste and consistency depending on whether one dips from the bottom or the top. It is not the *crisol* or 'melting pot' of North America, taken from the metaphor of metal foundries, with its outcome of fusion. (Like Brazil's Gilberto Freyre, Ortiz anticipated by decades the US shift from the melting-pot myth to that of cultural pluralism.) Here the image is unending *cocción* (literally concoction), implying indefinite deferral or a 'no-ser-*siempre*-todaviá' (a state of always not-yet).

The idea just expressed is caught in the difference between the words *cubanidad*, implying defined civil status, and *cubanía*, an open-ended spiritual condition of desire which is given even to those who simply want it. Indeed Ortiz's own work is a prime example of his metaphor, a vast body of texts all falling short of finality and synthesis, creating doubt whether one is reading *about* Cuba or *experiencing* Cuban culture first hand. An outstanding case is *Cuban Counterpoint* with its proliferating appendices. All this, Pérez Firmat suggests, refers back to Ortiz's original counterpoint between the European *contrapunto*, or initial 'point', furnished by the debate between Carnival and Lent in the *Libro de Buen Amor*, and the *contrapunteo,* or '*counter*-point', of Cuba. History itself, at least as he most deeply sensed it, is thus a constant simmer, not an itinerary nor even a dialectic.

Ortiz's engaging manner of pictorializing invisible forces at play in a complex and changing society (national identity in motion we might call the effect) invites comparative reference to a similar technique used just forty years later by the Dominican-born Puerto Rican novelist and social critic José Luis González with his image of the four-storeyed house in his 1980 book *El país de cuatro pisos y otros ensayos* (Flores, 1984; Maldonado Denis, 1982). He in effect arrives at the 'simmer' of Ortiz, but in Puerto Rico the succession of Spanish and varied forms of US domination since the nineteenth century has been too asphyxiating to allow the full blossoming of a spirit equivalent to *cubanía*. González therefore addresses the prevalent versions of Puerto Rican 'national culture' in the traditional Hispanic and modernizing American interpretations as masks for elite ideologies.[7] The reason is that in the absence of a popular independence movement the formation of a nation was left to political and juridical arrangements that produced a national culture dichotomously defined by the dominant class. Popular culture was disparaged as 'folklore' while the group González sees as culturally most important, the Afro-Puerto Ricans, were held to be virtually insignificant.

The stratification of cultural vision leads González to the corrective metaphor of Puerto Rico as a house of four storeys. This device suspends the search for a static national identity by presenting four sociocultural ingredients in historical order, with a popular, mestizo, and above all Afro-Antillean society at the bottom. Above it lies a stratum of expatriates from the Spanish American independence wars enlarged by Europeans and a subsequent 'mezzanine' of Corsicans, Majorcans, and Catalans. Next comes the US occupation that provides, especially in the 1930s to 1950s, an alternative to the classic Spanish model for 'guided identity'. And finally comes the fourth floor, constructed from late-blooming US capitalism welded to the opportunist populism of contemporary Puerto Rico. At first this architectonic structure may seem an elaboration of the basic dualism of oppressors and oppressed. The question, however, is not who is on top but what upholds the structure. In addition, these 'floors' do not compose a fixed portrait but represent forces of living history that have operated, some in neglected or clandestine fashion, through centuries. For González a critical point came in recent years when pseudo-industrialization and the pseudo-autonomous political formula reached a dead end, with marginalization of citizens, the demoralizing false benevolence of the colonial power, the rise of delinquency and criminality, and institutionalized demagogy.

Here the structural metaphor of González takes on some of the fluidity of Ortiz's *ajiaco*. He feels that the dismantled culture of the Puerto Ricans 'on top' is replaced not by a somewhat discredited Americanization but by permeation by the ever more visible culture of Puerto Ricans 'from below'. Similarly the elitist myth of the stalwart Hispanic peasant (*jíbaro*) yields to the reality of the Afro-Antillean populace. Puerto Rico's 'special relationship' with the United States having lost its mystique, the 'simmering' process extends outward to the neighboring Antilles as well as vertically in the island society. French and English can be seen not simply as imperial languages but as Antillean or creolized ones that serve the needs of decolonization. Recovery of its popular culture implies a re-Caribbeanization of Puerto Rico, to give it a custom-made regional identity rather than a 'Latin' or 'Anglo-' American one that is ready-made.

A postscript on Latin American identity

For anyone who aspired in the 1920s to 1940s to understand something of Latin American life and society the 'identity' essays of those years were an obvious starting point. Many *pensadores* of the nineteenth century had been distinguished essayists; and whatever their shortcomings, these re- flected not the limitations of the genre but intellectual and political con- straints of the age. The latter included preconceptions of race and ethnicity that skewed the vision of national or regional identity; an ethos of posi- tivism that was less scientific than scientistic; and a climate of political paternalism that inhibited flights of literary imagination. Nonetheless, the charge that the essay is by nature impressionistic or opinionated is mis- leading. And if its prestige faded with the triumph of social science in Latin American academic life in the 1950s, it has risen again in the postmodern climate. Octavio Paz justifies the essay as being often more persuasive than the scholarly treatise, adducing Ortega y Gasset as a foremost practi- tioner whose ruminations on identity were an intellectual beacon for the 1920s, 1930s, and beyond. The essay's prose flows fresh, never in a fixed channel, writes Paz, always equidistant from the treatise and the aphorism, two forms of congealment. The essayist does not colonize, he discovers (1984).

One might consider the identity essay not as a premature application of science to society but as a tribute to the innate kinship of humanities and science. This leads us to recognize that the texts just examined came at the brink of a split similar to the one Lepenies (1988) posits for eighteenth- century Europe. In *Between Literature and Science* he shows for France,

England, and Germany that during the Enlightenment no sharp division of literature and science had yet occurred. Lepenies identifies Buffon (1707–88), whose *Histoire Naturelle* attained 250 popular editions, as the last European scholar whose reputation rested more on stylistic enticement than on research. He was a prototype for Latin American *pensadores* of a century later whose world had not yet split into 'two cultures'. In Europe the encroachment of science (for example, encyclopedism or English economics) was countered by a romantic reaction that emphasized the sanctity of the self and Wordsworthian lyricism in England, and in German historicity, community, and the spirit. In England the confrontation of the two cultures has been periodically renewed: between Coleridge and Bentham, then Matthew Arnold and T.H. Huxley, then F.R. Leavis and C.P. Snow.

Octavio Paz offers an explanation of why the literature–science split failed to occur in Latin America after independence at the time of its appearance in Europe. Paz holds that the Iberian world could not yet produce modern literature because it had no modern age, 'neither critical reason nor bourgeois revolution', to provoke the process. Spanish romanticism was superficial and sentimental, and Spanish America could only imitate Spain. The romantic urge to 'unite life and art', Paz argues, was postponed in Latin America until the modernist age, whose impulses were akin to those of original romanticism. Like romanticism, the modernism or avant-gardism that took over Latin America was not merely an esthetic and a language but also a political world view, a life-style. 'The urge to change reality appears among the Romantics just as it does in the avant-garde, and in both cases it branches off in opposite yet inseparable directions – magic and politics, religious temptation and revolutionary temptation' (1974:103). As for science, Paz holds that positivism in nineteenth-century Latin America was not the outlook of a liberal bourgeoisie concerned with industrial and social progress but instead, 'an ideology and a belief' and not a culture of science. He therefore concludes that the European binomial of literature-science, or romanticism-positivism, was postponed here for a century: 'Positivism is the Spanish American equivalent of the European Enlightenment, and modernism was our Romantic reaction' (1974:168).

What was needed to establish the literature–science dichotomy in Latin America was not simply intellectual awareness, which was not absent, but a sociology of diffusion favorable to creativity. Only since the 1920s has Latin America produced literary establishments of international caliber and linkage, and only since the 1950s has it groomed cadres of social scientists. The maturity and external liaison of letters and arts were achieved by Argentine and Chilean vanguardism, Brazilian modernism, and Mexican painting, soon followed by renewal of the novel. Literature was now no longer subject to constraints of the political milieu or tied to the example of the solitary 'genius' (Martí, Machado de Assis, Darío). A generation after the modernist impact came the new lease of university education and its force-fed social science programs ('applied' and 'theoretical'). Pioneer experiments in the late 1930s at the University of São Paulo and the Colegio de México led to the training of social scientists en masse in the late 1950s. The intellectual dialectic that Lepenies documents for the Europe of more than a century earlier was now loosely replicated in Latin America.

By the 1960s the paths of science and literature became distinct. Social scientists, despite their domestic quarrels, drew energies from new or modernized universities; from unprecendented salaries and fellowships; from a common project to demystify colonialism, positivism, and belletrism; and from an ambition to blaze paths for national development. Although social science set off a more sudden and compact explosion than did the literature of the period, the event was not seen as a 'boom', given its rationality of purpose and its matter-of-fact management by governmental and philanthropic agencies. In contrast the literary 'boom' was so called because of factors external to literature itself, such as the availability of elegant translations and editorial campaigns to enrich the lackluster metropolitan literary menu of the period with exotic narratives. Two citations make the deeper point. In 1864 Dostoevsky's anti-Benthamite underground man had discovered that two times two makes five is 'a charming little thing'. A century later Brazil's poet-musician Caetano Veloso rediscovered in his poem 'Like two and two' that 'everything's certain like two and two are five'.

The appearance of establishments for science and literature did not create the explicit ideological warfare represented by the Bentham–Coleridge duel in England, for here the contenders were united by the camaraderie of a joint search for identity vis-à-vis the metropolis. They enjoyed relatively fluent communication. Yet the scientists (Celso Furtado, Fernando Henrique Cardoso, González Casanova), whatever the provisos and nuances of their analyses, rationally perceived Latin America as 'inserted into' explicable schemes of metropolitan domination, manipulation, and desacralization. On the other hand the 'marvelous realists' of the literary boom (Carpentier, Guimarães Rosa, Lezama Lima), whatever their political sympathies, *instinctively* 'marveled at' the intransigence of Latin American societies toward the imperatives of Western rationalism, capitalism, and political management.

The purpose of this terminal digression is to call attention to the historical role of the identity essay, placed as it was between modernism (1920s) and the advent of social science (1950s). The fusion of expressive and instrumental orientations was still possible and may be recoverable now that the 'booms' of the 1960s have receded, to give the long-standing holism of the regional culture a new lease.

Notes

1. See Mariátegui (1971); Chavarría (1979); Aricó (1980); Price-Mars (1983); Antoine (1981); *Témoignages* (1956).
2. The point made here is that these two writers represented important facets of Latin American thought, not that they were exclusive national spokesmen. The Peruvian Luis Valcárcel's early *indigenismo* approximated Price-Mars's position, while Jacques Roumain's adaptation of Marxism for Haiti was in the spirit of Mariátegui. Each pair moreover – the Peruvians and the Haitians – were mutually influential (Valcárcel, 1981:234-56; Fowler, 1980:139-73).
3. Gobineau served as French minister to Brazil in 1869–70. He was friendly with Emperor Pedro II but scorned his multiracial subjects (Raeders, 1988).
4. Mário's *Macunaíma* was published in 1928, the year of the three books under discussion. The first utterance of the hero as a child appears on the first page as 'Ai! que preguiça!' – 'Ay, what laziness!' or 'Aw, what a drag!' (M. de Andrade, 1984).
5. See Ortiz (1947); Pérez Firmat (1989:16–66); Benítez-Rojo (1992:150–76).
6. See J. and V. Martínez Alier (1972:108). In fairness to the authors it should be said that as a young man Ortiz saw blacks as primitives whose bizarre sexual practices and ritual killings deserved careful study in the positivist manner. During the 1920s, however, he became a vanguardist with increasing understanding and affection for Afro-Cubans and their culture (González Echevarriá, 1977:46–50).
7. The Puerto Rican identity controversy was shaped for a generation by Antonio S. Pedreira's *Insularismo* of 1934 (Pedreira, 1946), who cast the antagonism of Hispanophiles and Americanizers in Spenglerian and Orteguian terms of culture versus civilization. In lieu of their insular oscillation between Madrid and Washington he urged his countrymen to set out to fish in deep waters even though, as in the faraway past, a Dutch pirate might lurk there. Flores (1979) offers a 'new reading'.
8. See Paz (1974:78–164). For implicit and explicit critiques of Paz see Candido (1964, II:23–4) and González Echevarría (1985:35–9).

References

Andrade, M. de, 1972[1918], 'A divina preguiça', in Batista, M.R. *et al.* (eds), *Brasil: 1° tempo modernista – 1917–29*. São Paulo: Instituto Estudos Brasileiros, pp. 181–3.
────── 1984[1928], *Macunaíma*, translated by E.A. Goodland. New York: Random House.
Andrade, O. de, 1972[1924 ff.], *Do Pau-Brasil à antropofagia e às utopias*, Rio de Janeiro: Civilização Brasileira.
Antoine, J.C., 1981, *Jean Price-Mars and Haiti*, Washington: Three Continents Press.
Aricó, J. (ed.), 1980, *Mariátegui y los orígenes del marxismo latinoamericano*, 2nd edn, Mexico City: Pasado y Presente.
Benítez-Rojo, A., 1992, *The Repeating Island*, translated by J. Maraniss, Durham: Duke University Press.
Candido, A., 1964, *Formação da literatura brasileira*, 2nd edn, 2 vols, São Paulo: Livraria Martins.
Chavarría, J., 1979, *José Carlos Mariátegui and the Rise of Modern Peru, 1890–1930*, Albuquerque: University of New Mexico Press.
Earle, P. and Mead, R., 1973, *Historia del ensayo hispanoamericano*, Mexico City: Ediciones de Andrea.

Flores, J., 1984, 'The Puerto Rico that José Luis González Built', *Latin American Perspectives*, Vol. 42, No. 11, 3, pp. 173–84.

——— 1979, *Insularismo e ideología burguesa*, Río Piedras: Ediciones Huracán.

Fowler, C., 1980, *A Knot in the Thread, The Life and Work of Jacques Roumain*, Washington, Howard University Press.

González, J.L., 1993[1980], *Puerto Rico: The Four-Storeyed Country*, translated by G. Guinness, Princeton: Markus Wiener.

González Echevarría, R., 1977, *Alejo Carpentier: The Pilgrim at Home*, Ithaca: Cornell University Press.

——— 1985, *The Voice of the Masters*, Austin: University of Texas Press.

Haberly, D.T., 1983, *Three Sad Races: Racial Identity and National Consciousness in Brazilian Literature*, Cambridge: Cambridge University Press.

Hoetink, H., 1967, *The Two Variants in Caribbean Race Relations. A Contribution to the Sociology of Segmented Societies*, London: Oxford University Press.

Leite, D.M., 1983[1954], *O caráter nacional brasileiro*, 4th edn, São Paulo: Livraria Pioneira.

Lepenies, W., 1988, *Between Literature and Science: The Rise of Sociology*, translated by R.J. Hollingdale, Cambridge: Cambridge University Press.

Levi, D.E., 1987, *The Prados of São Paulo, Brazil*, Athens: University of Georgia Press.

Lezama Lima, J., 1957, *La expresión americana*, Havana: Instituto Nacional de Cultura.

Maldonado Denis, M., 1982, 'En torno a "El país de cuatro pisos": aproximación crítica a la obra sociológica de José Luis González', *Casa de las Américas*, Vol. 23, No. 135, 151–9.

Mariátegui, J.C., 1971[1928], *Seven Interpretive Essays on Peruvian Reality*, translated by M. Urquidi, Austin: University of Texas Press.

——— 1972[1949], *El alma matinal*, 4th edn, Lima: Editora Amauta.

Martínez Alier, J. and Martínez Alier, V., 1972, *Cuba: economía y sociedad*, Paris: Ruedo Ibérico.

Martínez Estrada, E., 1971[1933], *X-ray of the Pampa*, translated by A. Swietlicki, Austin: University of Texas Press.

Ortiz, F., 1947[1940], *Cuban Counterpoint: Tobacco and Sugar*, translated by H. de Onís, New York: Alfred A. Knopf.

Paz, O., 1974, *Children of the Mire*, translated by R. Phillips. Cambridge: Harvard University Press.

——— 1984, 'José Ortega y Gasset: el cómo y el para qué', in Paz, O., *Hombres en su siglo*, Barcelona: Seix Barral, pp. 97–110.

——— 1985[1950], *The Labyrinth of Solitude*, translated by L. Kemp *et al*, Exp. edn, New York: Grove Press.

Pedreira, A.S., 1946[1934], *Insularismo*, 3rd edn, San Juan: Biblioteca de Autores Puertorriqueños.

Pérez Firmat, G., 1989, *The Cuban Condition: Translation and Identity in Modern Cuban Literature*, Cambridge: Cambridge University Press.

Prado, P., 1944[1928], *Retrato do Brasil, ensaio sobre a tristeza brasileira*, 5th edn, São Paulo: Editora Brasiliense.

Price-Mars, J., 1983[1928], *So Spoke the Uncle*, translated by M.W. Shannon, Washington: Three Continents Press.

Raeders, G., 1988[1934], *O inimigo cordial do Brasil, o Conde de Gobineau no Brasil*, translated by R. Freire d'Aguiar, São Paulo: Paz e Terra.

Ruiz, J., [Archpriest of Hita], 1978[1343], *The Book of True Love*, translated by S.R. Dalyu (bilingual edn), University Park: Pennsylvania State University Press.

Stabb, M.S., 1967, *In Quest of Identity: Patterns in the Spanish American Essay of Ideas, 1890–1960*, Chapel Hill: University of North Carolina Press.

Témoignages sur la vie et l'oeuvre du Dr. Jean Price Mars 1876–1956, 1956, Port-au-Prince: Imprimerie de l'Etat.

Valcárcel, L.E., 1981, *Memorias*, Lima: Instituto de Estudios Peruanos.
Wenzel, S., 1967, *The Sin of Sloth: Acedia in Medieval Thought and Literature,* Chapel Hill: University of North Carolina Press.

CHAPTER 3 | Ethnic difference, plantation sameness

Sidney W. Mintz

Anyone who has read *The Two Variants in Caribbean Race Relations* (1967) recognizes that Harry Hoetink's work is marked, perhaps above all else, by an interest in the subtleties of socially relevant distinctions. His concept of the 'somatic norm image', for example, is based largely on inferences about the subjective dispositions of individuals: how they perceive each other's appearance and how they idealize appearance, even if there is no clear recognition on their part that such perceptions are 'pre-classified' by culture. Though the concept turns ultimately on individual perceptions (for only individuals have eyes), the concept of somatic norm image is tied to normative – that is, shared and judgmental – ideas about how people look. In culturally conventionalized terms, it is also tied to how they should look. Hoetink effectively introduces the concept as a 'way of looking' (the *double-entendre* here is intended) that is at once historically determined and historically determining. It is a subtle idea; and though it may be hard to prove, it has proved eminently persuasive. Indeed, more than thirty years after the concept was first adumbrated, no one seriously interested in understanding Caribbean 'race' relations can really afford to ignore it. How people are perceived, to put it crudely, is in part a matter of how they are *supposed* to look. If I understand him, Hoetink thinks such suppositions are historically (culturally) determined; I infer that he suspects they are not entirely conscious.

There are objections to such a formulation, particularly since social science has not yet provided a sure means by which to establish the existence of such images.[1] But the concept remains persistently convincing to those of us who have done fieldwork, perhaps particularly in the Hispanic Caribbean. The concept of somatic norm image itself, and the ways in which Hoetink employs it, exemplify his long-standing recourse to the broad movement of historical forces in interpreting social behavior, and his healthy readiness to tolerate uncertainty in the development of theory.

Though Hoetink did not carry out work of a comparable scale on the subject of language, his views on the genesis of Caribbean creole lan-

guages, based as they are on estimates of the effects on systems of communication of differing socioracial structures, also rely heavily on factors
that appear to be historically created yet socially creative. Implicit yet again
are subtle differences of a sort that can affect the ways that social behavior
proceeds. Hoetink writes:

> The best illustration of this [social] homogenization [in the
> Hispanic Caribbean] is probably provided by the fact that in all
> Latin Caribbean societies the language of the Iberian mother
> country became the commonly spoken and written language,
> while in virtually none of the societies of the North-West Euro-
> pean variant is one language the official as well as the common
> language. In Haiti, French is the official language, Creole the
> common one; in the British West Indies English is the official
> language and Anglo-Creole or French Créole the common one; in
> the French islands, English and French-Créole, respectively; in
> the Dutch Windward Islands, English or Dutch and Anglo-Créole;
> in Surinam, Dutch and Sranang (apart from the Asian languages);
> in the Dutch Leeward Islands, Dutch and Papiamentu. The lin-
> guistic situation in the North-West European variant reflects the
> cleavage that has always existed between the original dominant
> segment and the great majority of non-whites, while in the Iberian
> variant the linguistic situation reflects the linking function of the
> coloured group (1967:178).

This astute insight – which has received far too little attention, I think –
demonstrates both the enhanced value of a comparative approach to Caribbean problems (in contrast to analyses resting on data from one country or
island, or from one language group, such as the anglophone West Indies),
and Hoetink's long-term adherence to the view that a fundamental social
difference sets the Hispanic Caribbean apart from the rest of the Antilles.[2]

Race and ethnicity

Hoetink has spent less time in studying Caribbean ethnicity, strictly conceived, though the subject has certainly not been ignored by him.[3] In a piece
on Caribbean race and color (1985), he does discuss Caribbean migrations
and their significance for race perceptions and relations, both in the Caribbean and elsewhere. In other work he has looked at so-called 'East' Indians,
at the Jews of the Dutch Antilles, and at other such groups. But valuable as
those discussions have been, we may carry this analysis even further,
turning to the role of ethnicity in Caribbean social formations.

Readers may wonder whether the present writer has any grounds for distinguishing race relations from ethnic relations, and so he had better explain. As noted earlier, so-called race relations have to do with perceptions of others which are based on physical differences; these differences are thought of as diagnostic features of membership in groups, called 'races'. Race is a socially-constructed category. But those who endow it with everyday meaning usually treat it as if it were biological bedrock, not as if it were socially constructed. Yet Hoetink himself showed us long ago that the same person can be perceived as being in different 'racial' categories, depending upon whether he/she is in Martinique, in the United States, in Haiti, or in Jamaica, for example. In each place, the assignment of such a person to a specific category is thought by the assigner to be based on solid biological, and not cultural, data. It is the assumptions about inheritable physical differences that underlie and support social behaviors having to do with what is called 'race'.

In contrast, ethnicity has to do with culturally-determined features, such as language, dress, cuisine, and like aspects of social behavior, which are not determined by physical differences. The two categories, biological and cultural, are frequently confused or, more commonly, are viewed as one, in everyday life. Assumptions are frequently made about the behavior of people who are thought both to look in a certain way and to share behavior, and this is a common aspect of contemporary social life. But this does not mean that the two categories, race and ethnicity, are readily reducible to one. As a practical definition of 'ethnic' I shall borrow from Eriksen:

> The systematic and enduring social reproduction of basic classificatory differences between categories of people who perceive each other as being culturally discrete (1992:3).

Eriksen himself recognizes that his definition is quite open-ended. Indeed, it could be applied to so-called racial categories as well. As it happens, the cases which most interest Eriksen are of people whose ancestors went from India to Mauritius and Trinidad. In both of those places, the descendants of those Indians are commonly viewed as being both culturally and racially different.[4] In my view, however, that does not justify collapsing 'ethnic' and 'racial' into a single label.

As with other bases of social assortment in the Caribbean region, the strength and character of ethnicity there is to a large extent the specific outcome of local conditions, though of course useful comparisons and contrasts may be drawn with other world areas. Today, as more and more of the world becomes enveloped in 'ethnic' struggles (and as these grow ever more violent and ugly), it may serve a purpose to return to some issues in

Caribbean ethnicity, even if we argue that ethnicity in this region is in certain ways *sui generis*. I would claim that since the early sixteenth century, Caribbean ethnicity has always taken on its character in the context of a larger social division, that between 'white' and 'other', no matter how these bigger categories are conceptualized.[5] In the Antilles, ethnicity is always an *added* distinction, whatever else may be the case.

Viewed over time, it is possible to see how specific Caribbean ethnicities arose as the products of particular events. We also observe that some ethnicities have mattered a very great deal in the shaping of Caribbean life, while others mattered hardly at all. But beyond these platitudes, there is another of greater importance. Ethnicity and race are intertwined in Caribbean social history, and it is useful to notice when ethnic terms there do, or do not, carry a complexional message. Thus, for instance, the use of labels such as 'Jew', 'Potogee' and 'coolie' in specific Antillean locales and eras may be contrasted with the use of '*moreno*', '*trigueño*', '*jaba(d)o*' or other such terms meant to be descriptive of physical appearance.

As soon as we list such terms, however, a question arises: are the former ('Jew', 'Potogee', 'coolie') really non-racial? In answer, I would claim that such terms cannot be, even if the specific Caribbean society in question has no people in it that are considered (or who consider themselves) to be nonwhite. Otherwise said I would argue that white/nonwhite is the global underlying distinction in Caribbean societies, even when it is not referred to. It may be useful to reflect on this polar contrast in the light of the now common assertion, first set forth by Joan Vincent, that there can be no ethnicity without the Other (Vincent, 1974). It apparently requires two, for one to be 'discovered'. That said, it may serve some purpose to discuss the emergence of ethnic groups in the Caribbean region over time, as a preliminary step in disentangling race and ethnicity there.

The peopling of the region

As with all grand American areas, Caribbean post-Columbian history was marked by the successive though intermittent arrival of Old World peoples, the destruction of indigenous groups and cultures, and the interpenetration of the Old World and the New, both cultural forms and population stocks. Typical of the Caribbean islands – in contrast to the mainland – was the near-total extirpation of aboriginal societies. Only on Dominica and St Vincent – and marginally so – can there be said to be any survivals of an indigenous (Cariban) people. The Windward Reserve in Dominica, which is populated by the descendants of the Island Carib, people who are in fact physically heterogeneous, most of them phenotypically more negroid than mongoloid, can be described as the only public acknowledgment of the aboriginal Caribbean past that is linked to the present, outside museums.[6] The genetic contribution of aboriginal peoples to contemporary Caribbean populations is certainly real; nowhere outside Dominica is it connected to anything other than archaeology.

The major source of in-migrating population to the Caribbean islands over the centuries, rather than being Europe, was Africa, beginning less than two decades after the Discovery. The first enslaved Africans arrived around 1505. Enslaved people were still being smuggled in during the second half of the nineteenth century; Caribbean slavery ended only with emancipation in Cuba in 1886. Almost a third of all enslaved Africans imported to the New World during those nearly four hundred years reached the Caribbean islands. British Jamaica (1655–1838) and French St Domingue (1697–1789) must have received nearly one million enslaved Africans each; of all Old World regions that supplied human beings to the Antilles, Africa was the most represented.[7]

European migration was predominantly Spanish, of course, until well into the seventeenth century. Around 1625–30, North Europeans – Dutch, English and French for the most part – began to colonize. Outside the hispanophone societies, these newcomers were mainly distinguished by their lack of interest in remaining permanently in the region. Cuba, Santo Domingo and Puerto Rico in contrast built up substantial populations of Spanish migrants who had come to stay (and did), even before the seventeenth century; the 'creolization' or 'indigenization' of the hispanophone islands started very early. In striking contrast, the non-Hispanic islands (which began to be colonized by other Europeans after 1625) were typically represented by people who came 'to make a killing' before returning home. This difference, which emerged in Cuba within decades of the Spanish colonization of the Greater Antilles, persisted. The descendants of the Spanish colonists of those islands never thought of themselves, not even at first, as exiles from Spain. This truly creole outlook was still typical for the hispanophone peoples when the North Americans invaded the region in 1898–99. Otherwise said, the Hispanic Caribbean is truly home to the people who call themselves Dominican, Cuban and Puerto Rican. This has always seemed to be much less the case for most people in, say, Jamaica or Martinique. The major non-Hispanic case of a comparably rootedness of identity may well be Haiti, which became a sovereign state in 1804, and therefore differs markedly from the British, Dutch and French areas, which either secured political autonomy up to 150 or more years later, or are still dependent today.

Near the middle of the nineteenth century, Asian migrants, predominantly from India but also from China, and later from Indonesia and old French Indo-China, began to people the region. Most Asian people arrived under contract, as plantation laborers; their numbers were substantial.[8]

People of Indian origin remain important economically, culturally and politically in Guyana, Suriname and Trinidad, and are present (though less noticeably so) in Martinique, Guadeloupe, and a few other places. These Asian peoples were the last important building block in Caribbean social structure, adding to the European and African blocks, and sharing with them in some societies an awareness, usually little demonstrated, that the first Caribbean peoples were American Indians.

Plantations and the layering of ethnic communities

The preceding paragraphs describe the main roots of regional population in terms of the aboriginal past, and the three major population sources: Europe, Africa and Asia. Over time, there occurred a kind of 'layering' of migrants, marked by certain sorts of cultural (and physical) intermixture, and by the differential emergence of new 'identities' in different Caribbean societies. To a considerable extent, the patterning of newcomer ethnicity had to do with the waxing and waning of imperial economic intentions in the region, and the labor demands embodied in their expression (Mintz, 1984, 1988). Since that interest was usually expressed in the form of large-scale overseas agriculture, many observers have dwelled on the great importance of the plantation system in shaping this aspect of Caribbean society. Thus the movement of Africans, Indians and Chinese, and even of many Europeans, had to do primarily with plantation labor needs.

But of course the plantation system did not eliminate historically determined cultural differences, by any means. In the hispanophone islands, where the plantation appeared very early but soon declined to minor importance, only receiving a new stimulus much later, Asian migration was to be of no significance until the mid-nineteenth century, when Cuba received more than 150,000 Chinese contract laborers (Look Lai, 1993, Cuba Commission, 1993). Neither in Puerto Rico nor in Santo Domingo did Asian labor matter, because the plantation remained weak in Santo Domingo, while Puerto Rico already had a labor force that could be coerced into working (Mintz, 1951). The Santo Domingo case is of some additional interest, since it only began to become dominated by plantation development in the twentieth century, sustained by regional migration from the anglophone Caribbean and Haiti. Thus the plantation histories of these three societies differed widely, but they shared important cultural features, of which language was only one. Something quite other than the plantation system made and kept them similar.

Many other Caribbean societies had no plantation past at all – islands too small, too dry or too mountainous to have become plantation locales – but seem to share a sort of 'rurality' or 'backwardness'. Yet places such as

Saba, Grand Cayman, Les Saintes, Carriacou and San Andrés are so different from each other sociologically that their only common features beyond
their smallness of size and rural ambience seems to be the fact that they
were plantationless. There are, then, substantial reservations about the
sociological consequences of the plantation system. Still, I think it can be
claimed that plantation history was a major source of explanation of Caribbean ethnicity, and it is certainly worth attempting to demonstrate in what
ways this may have been so.

To begin, we note the formation of one kind of group that can be said
to have taken shape over time, and to have crystallized out of the plantation
presence. The people who are called 'Redlegs' in Barbados are perhaps the
best example.[9] Following L. Chavis (1994), I shall refer to them here as
Barbadian poorer whites. The people called *blancs matignons* in Guadeloupe
may be another example of an ethnic category largely created by the
plantation presence. In effect, small-farm societies which are swamped by
plantation expansion can end up with ethnic 'islands', such as the Barbadian
poorer whites, in their midst. But the contrast between the poorer whites and
other Barbadians is not primarily one of phenotype: it is one of social
integration. These poorer people are not part of the larger Barbadian white
community; and their exclusion is not 'racial'. Whenever we look at the
integration of culturally or physically different populations into larger
polities, relative numbers are important, and it must have mattered in the
Barbadian case. The social fate of Barbadian poorer whites would have
undoubtedly been far different, had the total proportion of whites in that
society been much larger. A contrast may help to explain that assertion.

In Puerto Rico, European settlement had been early, and its plantation
development remained quite feeble until the late eighteenth century. During
that time a substantial population of mixed ancestry, but tending toward the
'lighter' end of the continuum, developed in the interior highlands, before
the expansion of the plantation system. Had the settlement of Puerto Rico
by Europeans been more meager and their reproduction slower, and had
plantation development there been greater, phenotypically Caucasoid highland *jíbaros* of the mid-nineteenth century might have become an 'ethnic
group', in terms of both class *and* color, encased within a more solidly
nonwhite Puerto Rico – rather like what happened with the Barbadian
poorer whites. Though less convincing, a parallel imaginary case might
even be made for the *guajiros* of Cuba.[10] In both of these cases, however,
we deal with societies both large and environmentally differentiated enough
to have accommodated varying economic adaptations in different subregions,
with early European populations that multiplied during an era of little
plantation activity. This is the background for both Puerto Rican *jíbaros* and
Cuban *guajiros*; analogous social processes probably explain the 'hill-
billies' and 'rednecks' who emerged as highland populations in the moun-

tainous US South, driven off the lowlands by the expanding slave planta-tions. In Puerto Rico, the highlanders forced onto the plantations alongside the slaves by the workbook legislation of the nineteenth century produced an unusual cultural situation (Mintz, 1951), while the evolving code of race relations in both Cuba and Puerto Rico eventuated in cultural changes different from those in the non-Hispanic islands such as Barbados.

A radically divergent such crystallization marked the emergence of Maroon communities. In those rare but important cases, the plantation system was rejected with sufficient force and in sufficient strength to lead to the emergence of 'tribes' in the case of the Guianas, and of something analogous in the case of Jamaica, and possibly elsewhere (as in the Hispanic portion of Santo Domingo, before the Haitian Revolution). Of course plantations did not 'produce' ethnic communities, or Maroons. But Maroon communities arose for the most part because slaves were escaping conditions of plantation labor, as in Suriname and French St Domingue. Maroon ethnicity arose out of the collective struggle of people escaping oppression, and pooling their resources, cultural and individual, to create new life conditions. Of course many factors, including local environment, played a role in making this possible. Caribbean societies were frequently typified by internal frontiers, when the colonial state lacked sufficient police power or even population to dominate its own interiors. Dense forest, mountains and large rivers, together with unfamiliar flora and fauna, played a part. At the same time, variable forms of social organization and of settlement may have facilitated – or obstructed – the growth of Maroon communities. It seems to me at least possible that the paucity of Maroon activity in the US South – though Aptheker (1939) thinks otherwise – may have been owing in part to differences in the organization of agri-cultural labor there.

Yet another plantation-based process had to do with the new labor needs of the nineteenth century: the stabilization of Indian ethnic groups in Suriname, Guyana and Trinidad; of a Javanese ethnic group in Suriname; and of Chinese ethnic groups in Trinidad, in Jamaica and (in far greater numbers, but on balance less successfully) in Cuba. Such groups varied in size and coherence; many others were too small to matter, though their arrival suggests how desperately the planters searched for labor.[11] Until the twentieth century in the case of the Indian groups in Guyana and Trinidad, they were too small ever to be viewed as politically significant to the majority. In all cases, however, they were perceived as culturally and physically different. Being neither 'white' nor 'black', their status might be compared on some grounds to that of now-growing Asian migrant com-munities in North American life today.

But not all of these newly-emerging 'communities' were nonwhite. The Portuguese who arrived in British Guiana are commonly labeled in a way to set them apart from other 'whites' locally, as are the Jews in Jamaica – at times even by social scientists.[12] Of these groups it appears as if one might almost say 'They're white, but . . . ' Again, the central issue of white and nonwhite as primary categories imposes itself on other classifications, but 'white' is not always enough. It seems likely that ethnic labels such as 'Potogee' may serve two classificatory purposes: it not only says members of the group are not simply white; it also seems to imply on social grounds that they are something less than white.

The Jews in Jamaica, the Lebanese in Jamaica, Haiti and the Dominican Republic, and a few other small ethnic clusters are also linked historically to the plantation, but quite differently from (say) the people of Javanese and Indian ancestry, who were introduced primarily as plantation laborers. Though the plantation was not the cause for the emergence of these other ethnic communities, it was people's needs for services that plantation society could not provide that helped to make it possible for such groups to become stabilized. In the case of both Indians and Chinese, there are small groups of fellow ethnics who did not come as plantation labor, but appeared later, as service providers. In the case of the Chinese of Cuba, for instance, or the Indians of Trinidad, small 'follow-up' groups of higher class position appeared, long after their ethnic predecessors had become relatively stable elements in local society. Hence trading communities of the same cultural background may overlap ethnically with these others; but only slightly.

An ordinal presentation of this kind detracts from the idea of the layering of ethnic communities, as suggested earlier. But there is a point to it. The writer has long contended (Mintz, 1958, 1979) that convincing historical interpretation of any Caribbean social phenomenon will have to be systadial ('same stage'), rather than synchronic ('same time'), in charac ter.[13] Granting the crucial differences that mark each historical epoch and the past of every society, it is nonetheless the case that events that take place in different places and at different times may share significant structural-processual features. Thus this writer sought to demonstrate, for instance, that Jamaican society was escaping from a period of frantic plantation expansion at the start of the nineteenth century, just as Puerto Rico was entering into such a period (Mintz, 1958). The differences had to do, *inter alia*, with the economic courses of the imperial societies in question, Britain and Spain. The structurally conjoint comparison would have been Jamaica around 1730 and Puerto Rico in 1815, or perhaps Jamaica in 1838 and Puerto Rico in 1876: the systadial dates of entry and departure from the region's second plantation phase. The development of Caribbean plantations, after all, was spread over nearly five centuries, from the early Spanish experiments in Santo Domingo almost until the present time; and the center of expansion kept shifting. As that center moved – as different imperial powers raised or lowered the stakes – the social and human consequences could be seen in the ways that people adapted to changing local conditions, and by the economic and social niches which groups of newcomers dug out for themselves over time in each locale. Hence the layering of ethnic communities can best be seen as sequential (chronological, diachronic) in terms of the region as a whole, but consisting in substantial measure of long-term, *local* group responses to the changing character of the plantation, and its fit within competing imperial systems. That the lengthy history of the plantation in the Caribbean marked that region's ascent to a status of dizzying importance in Europe's imperial economies, only then to descend more slowly (but just as drastically) to a level of derisory importance, marks the differing fates of Caribbean ethnic groups, as it did all else. It must not be forgotten that these processes of ethnic building and maturation were not so much *created by* the plantation system as an integral part of *resistance to* its regimen.

Ethnicity in the contemporary Caribbean

The contemporary ethnic picture in the Caribbean region reveals that there is much work still to be done. The startling success of Puerto Rican businessmen in the US Virgin Islands during the last forty years parallels the equally impressive success of Cuban businessmen in Puerto Rico; but no one has explained why each group has done so well on foreign soil. The fates of the francophone 'Cha-chas' or 'Gorots' who have gradually drifted northward into anglophone communities in the Leeward chain are not wholly understood, particularly since these are 'white ethnics' in black host communities. The destiny of the Dominican Republic's Japanese migrants has received little serious attention as yet, and the same is true for what appears to be a growing Chinese migrant community. The anglophone people of Samaná in the Dominican Republic, of whom Hoetink has written, have not been studied further, to my knowledge. The newly-emerging Bush Negro populations in French Guiana who once lived in Suriname, so sensitively studied by Kenneth Bilby (1990), deserve additional attention. The Vietnamese of French Guiana, descendants of Vietnamese political prisoners of the French, originating in an earlier era of resistance and struggle, are almost unknown to the social sciences. The Puerto Rican community of Hawaii, now a century old and still sturdily Puerto Rican in outlook and self-identity, richly deserves attention, and has received none, for about forty years. For Trinidad, Viranjini Munasinghe (1993) has opened a new chapter in the study of ethnicity and politics. Recent books on Trinidad by Miller (1994; on consumption and modernity) and Eriksen (1992; on ethnicity and nationalism), following on Ching's thesis (1985)

and contemporary with Yelvington's (1993) excellent collection on ethnicity, suggest that Trinidad may be receiving special attention. But Olwig's
(1993) work on Nevis, and Virginia Young's (1993) on St Vincent, show
that the smaller islands are not being neglected. The complex ethnicity of
some of those lesser islands is revealed in a thoughtful and nuanced dissertation on St Martin/Sint Maarten by Joanna Rummens (1993).

But there is more to this than simply filling in those places on the map
too little known or understood. The world has entered a new, unexpected
and awful epoch of political violence linked (at times in somewhat mys-
terious ways) to the issue of group identity. In Europe, ethnic group
membership seems to have served recently as a kind of ultimate refuge for
people oppressed by impersonal, unheeding state bureaucracies. But that
reason for falling back on ethnic identity would hardly seem to apply in a
country such as Rwanda, where unspeakable recent violence, which capital-
ized on ancient – but, it had seemed, declining – ethnic categories served
to underline events in Middle Europe.

In the Caribbean region, however, where terrible political violence still
occurs (as in Haiti), interethnic hostility pales to insignificance when ranged
alongside events in Africa and Europe. In the islands and on their surrounding shores, almost everyone feels him/herself in some way to be a newcomer, and political energies were for long absorbed in winning a living
wage, and in shaking off the colonial overlords. That no serious ethnic
violence has occurred there in more than half a century may be related to
that distinctive past; and understanding it better might also help us grasp the
frightening added significance of ethnic feelings when they are associated
with a *specific* locale. In the New World generally, group identity happily
seems to lack – at least for the most part – the *Blut und Boden* mystique of
the Old. Whether the lack of a system of stratification tied to the land, the
absence of a nobility, the fact that everybody except Amerindians harks
back to elsewhere, or some other such missing factor lies at the basis of this
difference, is by no means clear. Yet if we were able to understand it,
perhaps contemporary events in places such as Bosnia and Rwanda would
seem less horrifyingly enigmatic.

Notes

1. The author offered such a criticism in Mintz, 1971.
2. In a paper on 'race' and color in the Caribbean, Hoetink (1985) extends this contrast to
   other spheres, such as religion.
3. In nearly all of his work, concerned as so much of it is with distinctions between and
   among social groups, Hoetink has dealt with ethnic categories of one kind or another. See,
   for example, Hoetink, 1963.

4. Generally speaking, it is usually felt by *outsiders* that races are bigger than ethnic groups, such that all Africans, regardless of their countries of origin, languages or other differences, are 'Negroes'; and people from China, Japan, Korea, etc. are all 'Asians'. Not surprisingly, people who are *inside* such 'racial' categories are entirely aware of the numerous divisions that make the wider category quite irrelevant, *except to outsiders.*

5. Of course there is no consensus on this basic 'division' at all. Many students of 'race' in Latin America and the Caribbean believe that in Luso-Hispanic societies the continuum is seen as more important than the division, while in non-Hispanic societies the division itself (the two categories, ideally conceived) is seen as more important. Since we are talking in practice about mental images, which are almost impossible to evoke without calling attention to them, the methodological problem this poses for the student is immense.

6. The subject lies too far outside the central concern of this paper to be given the attention it really deserves. Interested readers can refer to Boucher (1992), which provides the most recent account of the history of European and Island Carib contact.

   No reference is made here to the Arawakan-speaking (Taino) peoples who inhabited the Greater Antilles at the moment of the European arrival. Like the Island Carib, though a century or more earlier, they were destroyed by the Europeans, and little of their original cultures survives in any form. Of course many Caribbean populations carry the genes of aboriginal New World peoples, and individuals may refer to their origins as being partly 'Indian'. But no functioning aboriginal communities remained in the Antilles after the seventeenth century.

7. We cannot here address the tormenting problem of 'tribal' affiliation among African peoples enslaved and transported to the Caribbean region. It is clear on the one hand that such people came from particular ethnic groups or 'tribes', and some experts have employed what is partially known in imaginative and interesting ways (see, for example, Mullin, 1992). But on the other, it is equally clear that the details are mostly incomplete and sometimes may be highly inaccurate.

8. There is a substantial literature on migrants to the Caribbean (and now, on emigration from the Caribbean as well). In this regard, ethnic difference has certainly been remarked by the specialists. Works on this phase of Caribbean history include Laurence (1971), Lowenthal (1972), Look Lai (1993), and Cuba Commission (1993). One scholar, geographer David Lowenthal (1972), has tried to inventory what he thought to be the major minority categories: Amerindians, Bush Negroes, Jews, Javanese, Syrians, Chinese.

9. Sheppard's book (1977) deals with the history of these people. A good case can be made for comparing their experience to what happened to white farmers in those regions of the South overtaken by rapid plantation expansion. I accept Larry Chavis's view that the term 'Redleg' is pejorative; he refers to the people as 'poorer whites', which is the term I use here.

10. The Germans of Seaford Town, Jamaica, and the whites of Cazales (and supposedly, Fonds des Blancs) in Haiti, are thought to be the outcome of different processes – the Jamaican Germans the descendants of German migrant farmers of the nineteenth century, and the people of Cazales of Polish mercenaries who went over to the enemy during the Revolution.

11. R.T. Smith (1962:42–3) nicely characterizes that desperate quality in the case of the planters in British Guiana: 'In 1835, one planter imported some Germans on a four-year contract; English ploughmen with their ploughs and horses were also introduced; in the same year 429 Portuguese arrived from Madeira; in 1836 44 Irish and 47 English labourers were imported; in 1837 43 labourers from Glasgow; in 1838 396 persons arrived from India; in 1839 208 Maltese and 121 Germans were landed.'

12. In his 1985 paper Hoetink points out, somewhat puzzled, that R.T. Smith's analysis

(1982) of race and class distinguishes in Jamaica 'Creole whites' and 'Jews', as if Jews were neither white nor creole. Perhaps this is additional evidence that separating ethnicity and race in the Caribbean region is not easy.

13. In the same vein, Knight, on the last page of his study of Cuban slavery, has written: 'Both the nature of the slave society, therefore, as well as the fact of the sugar revolution, must be vital considerations in the comparative study of the slave systems of the Americas. *These comparative studies should be concerned less with concurrent time spans and metropolitan institutional differences than with equivalent stages of economic and social growth*' (1970:194; italics added).

References

Aptheker, H., 1939, 'Maroons within the Present Limits of the United States', *Journal of Negro History*, No. 24, pp. 167–84.

Bilby, K., 1990, 'The Remaking of the Aluku: Culture, Politics and Maroon Ethnicity in French South America', Ph.D. dissertation, Johns Hopkins University, Baltimore.

Boucher, P., 1992, *Cannibal Encounters*, Baltimore: Johns Hopkins University Press.

Chavis, L., 1994, 'The "Redlegs" of Barbados: An Identity Without a People', Paper presented to the Department of Anthropology/Institute for Global Studies Seminar, Johns Hopkins University, Baltimore.

Ching, A.M.T., 1985, 'Ethnicity Reconsidered, with Reference to Sugar and Society in Trinidad', Ph.D. dissertation, University of Sussex.

The Cuba Commission Report, 1993, Baltimore: Johns Hopkins University Press.

Eriksen, T.H., 1992, *Us and Them in Modern Societies*, Oxford: Oxford University Press.

Furnivall, J.C., 1948, *Colonial Policy and Practice*, Cambridge: Cambridge University Press.

Hoetink, H., 1963, 'Change in Prejudice. Some Notes on the Minority Problem, with References to the West Indies and Latin America', *Bijdragen tot de Taal,- Land- en Volkenkunde*, No. 119, pp. 56–75.

——— 1967, *The Two Variants in Caribbean Race Relations*, London: Oxford University Press.

——— 1985, ' "Race" and Color in the Caribbean', in Mintz, S.W. and Price, S. (eds), *Caribbean Contours*, Baltimore: Johns Hopkins University Press, pp. 55–84.

Knight, F.W., 1970, *Slave Society in Cuba during the Nineteenth Century*, Madison: University of Wisconsin Press.

Laurence, K.O., 1971, *Immigrants into the West Indies in the Nineteenth Century*, St Lawrence, Barbados: Caribbean Universities Press.

Look Lai, W., 1993, *Indentured Labor, Caribbean Sugar: Chinese and Indian Migrants to the British West Indies, 1838–1918*, Baltimore: Johns Hopkins University Press.

Lowenthal, D., 1972, *West Indian Societies*, New York: Oxford University Press.

Miller, D., 1994, *Modernity. An Ethnographic Approach. Dualism and Mass Consumption in Trinidad*, Oxford: Berg.

Mintz, S.W., 1951, 'The Role of Forced Labour in Nineteenth-Century Puerto Rico', *Caribbean Historical Review*, No. 2, pp. 134–41.

——— 1958, 'Labor and Sugar in Puerto Rico and Jamaica', *Comparative Studies in Society and History*, Vol. 1, No. 3, pp. 273–83.

——— 1971, 'Groups, Group Boundaries and the Perception of Race', *Comparative Studies in Society and History*, Vol. 13, No. 4, pp. 437–43.

——— 1979, 'Slavery and the Rise of Peasantry', *Historical Reflections*, No. 6, pp. 215–42.

———1984, 'Labor Needs and Ethnic Ripening in the Caribbean Region', *Woodrow Wilson Center, Latin American Program Working Papers* No. 137.

_____ 1988, 'Labor and Ethnicity: the Caribbean Conjuncture', in Tardanico, R. (ed.), *Crises in the Caribbean Basin. Political Economy of the World System Annuals*, No. 9, pp. 47–57.

Mullin, M., 1992, *Africa in America*, Urbana: University of Illinois Press.

Munasinghe, V., 1993, 'Calaloo or Tossed Salad: Renovating National Identity and Culture in Trinidad', Ph.D. dissertation, Johns Hopkins University.

Olwig, K.F., 1993, *Global Culture, Island Identity. Continuity and Change in the Afro-Caribbean Community of Nevis*, Chur: Harwood.

Rummens, J., 1993, 'Personal Identity and Social Structure in Sint Maarten/Saint Martin: a Plural Identities Approach', Ph.D. dissertation, York University.

Sheppard, J., 1977, *The 'Redlegs' of Barbados*, Millwood: KTO Press.

Smith, R.T, 1962, *British Guiana*, London: Oxford University Press.

_____ 1982, 'Race and Class in the Post-Emancipation Caribbean', in Ross, R., (ed.), *Racism and Colonialism: Essays on Ideology and Social Structure*, pp. 93–113.

Vincent, J., 1974. 'The Structuring of Ethnicity', *Human Organization*, Vol. 33, No. 4, pp. 375–9.

Yelvington, K. (ed.), 1993, *Trinidad Ethnicity*, Knoxville: University of Tennessee Press.

Young, V.H., 1993. *Becoming West Indian. Culture, Self and Nation in St Vincent*, Washington: Smithsonian Institution Press.

CHAPTER 4

Haiti and the terrified consciousness of the Caribbean

Anthony P. Maingot

Harry Hoetink has always taken the phenomenon of racial fear into account. In *El pueblo dominicano*, he analyzes the deep fear of Saint Domingue whites in terms of the sheer difference in numbers between them and the black slaves (1971:296–7). Driven by this fear, the whites unleash a 'regimen of terror' which, as might be sociologically predicted, generates not only a self-fulfilling prophecy but a grotesque inversion of logic: you justify the terror against the black on the grounds that what you perceive to be his intrinsic and natural barbarity terrorizes you. In other words, whites construct their own terrified consciousness of blacks. This explains the child who sits opposite a black man and tells his mother: 'Maman, un nègre, j'ai peur!' Hoetink calls this an 'archtypical fear and . . . repugnance' (1967: 78–9). While he once stated that such fears are directed mostly at the black male, it is clear from his broader sociological work that it also operates at a much larger group level.

According to Hoetink, relative racial numerical strength is only one of the factors which affects the majority group's image of what a minority is. Another important element is the degree to which the majority perceives the minority as being integrated into the societal whole (1963:65–6). Since it is the majority which sets and maintains the norms, it is their perceptions which create the minority. There are then two fundamental types of minorities: a 'real' minority which the majority perceives as a competitor because it is integrated into the existing normative structure, and the 'exotic' minority which the majority perceives as being outside that structure and, thereby, noncompetitive.

This paper has three purposes. First, to explore the process through which 'real' minorities come about and, specifically, the nature of the fear and menace which Hoetink believes they inspire in the majority group. What provokes and then sustains this panic, this 'terrified consciousness'? Secondly, it attempts to unravel the nature of changes in majority group perceptions (prejudices), a process which Hoetink hypothesizes can convert real minorities into exotic groups. Finally, through a series of comparative, albeit short, case-studies I hope to establish the generalizability – and therefore policy relevance – of Hoetink's concepts. The latter is of especial importance because of the increasing concern that the twenty-first century will be a period of racial and ethnic strife. In many a multiracial society, it is said, numerical minorities will live in terror of the majoritarian rule of groups of different race.

Theoretical focus

It is a widely held postulate of social conflict theory that the intensity of strife will vary with the weight of two factors: the acuteness of the competition for power and the depth of the ideological divide. I pick no fight with this position. What this paper probes, however, are the peculiar dynamics of a special form of social conflict, one which generates not just fear but indeed panic, a terrified consciousness. It is my contention that while certainly generating fear, neither the competition for power nor ideological differences *per se* tend to produce panic. In addition to perceptions about imbalances in numerical strength which Hoetink correctly emphasizes, two additional conditions are necessary to engender such a terrified consciousness. First, there has to exist a fissure within the majority group which leads to ideological challenges to a previously hermetically sealed normative order. This normative order governs behavior at three levels: the personal, group and international. Deviance at any of these three levels can generate fear. When the challenge occurs – or is perceived to occur – at all three levels simultaneously, the response is panic.

Secondly, the original fears generated by the ideological challenge to norms have to be confirmed, sustained and reinforced by a 'living example'. There has to exist a case of 'actual' behavior which is perceived as so deviant that it challenges the existing norms at all three levels. In other words, the panic is not purely ideological; historical and material factors contribute to the sense that the challengers operate outside any acceptable civilized order. For instance, the use of force by those who enforce the norms is regarded as legitimate and termed 'establishing order'. Those who are not defined as within the existing normative structure and who use force, even if in self-defense, are seen as engaging in 'violence'. And violence, according to Chalmers Johnson, is not just threatening, it is by definition disorienting since it is action that deliberately or unintentionally disorients the behavior of others. Violence is either behavior which is impossible for others to orient themselves to or behavior which is deliberately intended to prevent orientation and the development of stable expectations with regard to it. In short, violence is 'antisocial' action (Johnson, 1966:8).

Where the anti-social violence is carried out by individuals who themselves are regarded as ipso facto outside the normative order, the likelihood is that panic will outlive the end of actual hostilities over power and ideology. This certainly was the case with blacks in the nineteenth century. Because race, at least over the shorter term, is an involuntary point of identity and identification, it did not easily lend itself to the political bargaining and social exchanges which normally brought conflicts to an end. Involuntary social traits contribute to the irrationality of the fears and, as such, block the path to social and political reconciliation.

In the nineteenth-century Caribbean, the conflict was over slavery and its abolition, and the dominant ideology was a combination of racism and paternalism. That ideology was challenged everywhere by small groups of whites. But that challenge in itself would not have created the terrified consciousness which characterized the nineteenth century had not the Haitian revolution provided a example of actual behavior. Haiti was the living 'proof' that the gate-keepers of the dominant ideology had interpreted correctly the threat to its existing norms at all three levels.

The panic about Haiti: the international context

Nowhere in the Caribbean did the emancipation of the slaves fundamentally change the racial stratification system. If anything, it was reinforced by two quite powerful forces: the racism of most of the metropolitan ideologues, and the specter of another Haiti, which scared metropolitan and white settler alike.

Local whites used metropolitan whites, who held ultimate power over the fates of these minute colonies, as reference groups. Colonial ideologies everywhere were racist. The majority of English scholars, for instance, steadfastly held to two fundamental tenets: first, that Teutonic, and especially Anglo-Saxon, races were superior in all regards; and secondly, that the other races' inferiority could only be ameliorated through tutelage by the former. But this was not limited to British ideology; French, Dutch, Belgians, Italians, and Germans all shared this racial vision. So did the United States; US Manifest Destiny expansionism as well as the imperialism of the 1890s was driven by racist ideas (Horsman, 1981).

The 'white man's burden' thus combined racism with paternalism. The latter was deemed essential to avoiding another Haiti. As Thomas Carlyle warned after observing the results of emancipation in the mid-nineteenth century, 'Let him, by his ugliness, idleness, rebellion, banish all white men from the West Indies, and make it all one Haiti . . . a tropical dog-kennel and pestiferous jungle . . . '[1] Similarly, Oxford historian James Anthony Froude, having toured the Caribbean's British colonies in the mid-1880s, was convinced that the white population was gradually disappearing everywhere in the region. Emancipation had finally ruined an already weak planter class, and black majority rule was in the future. 'Were it worthwhile', wrote Froude, 'one might draw a picture of the position of an English governor, with a black parliament and a black ministry. . . . No Englishman, not even a bankrupt peer, would consent to occupy such a position.' Indeed, he wrote a friend in 1887, the islands were already 'becoming nigger warrens and were in danger of lapsing into barbarism, of turning into Haitis'.

Douglas Hall has noted the terror of nineteenth-century British official views on the Caribbean (1959). What they boiled down to was the opinion that if European overlordship were removed, these islands would be thrown 'into the primitive savagery of forest darkness'. It is precisely such a view which led to the terrible retributions which followed such incidents as Jamaica's Morant Bay rebellion in 1865. Not only did it lead to the execution of some 500 blacks, it led to the suspension of self-government and the implementation of dictatorial Crown Colony rule.

US policy towards Haiti was similarly tinged with fear of its terrible example. According to Senator Thomas Hart Barton of Missouri, America does not recognize Haiti because, 'It will not permit the fact to be seen, and told, that for the murder of their masters and mistresses, they are to find friends among the white people of these United States' (cited in Montague, 1940:53).

It is an interesting point that some Haitian leaders were quite aware of the nature of the 'terrified consciousness' and went to extraordinary pains to minimize the fear. Thus, Haitian President Jean-Pierre Boyer, seeking US recognition in 1825, made two offers to ameliorate American opposition: he would prohibit any Haitian from traveling to the slave-holding states south of the Potomac, and secondly, he would send a diplomatic agent 'such in color as not to offend the prejudices of the country'. All in vain, however, for as a US Senator stated in 1825, the Haitian threat was so enormous that there would 'never' be recognition, indeed, the issue would 'not even be discussed'.[2]

The point is that the Europeans, Americans and white *criollo* groups, were governed by what Fanon called a '*manichean* delirium': beautiful versus ugly; intelligent versus ignorant; civilized versus savage; white versus black; order (force) versus violence; white paternalism versus future Haitis.

Had it been purely a matter of the ideology which invariably accompanied slavery and the plantation system, it might not have been so vehement. After all, even the slaves had their friends in courts throughout Europe. Haiti in the nineteenth century seemed to have none. Haiti represented the living proof of the consequences of not just black freedom but, indeed, black rule. It was the latter which was feared; therefore, the former had to be curtailed if not totally prohibited.

The central point is that precisely because the Haitian revolution and the subsequent rule by blacks fit no established norms, it really did not matter what efforts the Haitians made. The fear of 'Haitianization' had survived the events in Haiti to become the dominant metaphor behind the terrified consciousness of the whites. Indeed, even those who rejected European paternalism and found exile, friendship and material help in Haiti could not escape the generalized metaphor. Nothing illustrates better the depth of the fear that Haiti inspired than the behavior of Venezuela's Simón Bolívar, his precursor Francisco de Miranda, and their social class, the *mantuanos*.

The group context: mantuano perceptions

Like most other Spanish American liberators, Miranda aimed at political independence, not social revolution. And so, finding himself in 1806 in Haiti – the one country which had already proven itself disposed and willing to assist any anti-colonial venture – Miranda was able to accept Haitian assistance without even a slight amelioration in attitude towards the Haitian case. Miranda's fear of the Haitian experience, a deep and pervasive apprehension, was already widespread among the area's whites. That Miranda shared this view of blacks was evident even before he visited Haiti. Contact with reality is never a prerequisite for the shaping of stereotypes. Note, for instance, his appeals for British assistance to his liberation project: it reflected his own views as he also cleverly tried to appeal to the Great Powers' fears of Haitian expansion in the area. 'I have to liberate Venezuela rapidly,' he wrote Lord Melville on 27 September 1804, 'or it will be prey to Haitian blacks and mulattoes who already have their emissaries in the Province of Caracas.'[3]

The fact is, there was nothing in either his upbringing or in the international arena which formed the context of his work, which would have made Miranda think differently. His disposition and world view were those of the New World aristocrat, polished in Europe. The fact that they themselves were disdained *criollos* often rejected by the metropolis, was no reason to expect them to change their views about those they perceived to be socially below them. In fact, the opposite was true: their own personal insecurity as *criollos* whose *limpieza de sangre* was always suspect in Spain, contributed to their anxieties. They dreaded being identified with the Haitian mulattoes who, to the outsider, did not look much different.

Miranda's outlook was shared by Libertador Simón Bolívar. Not surprisingly, the image of Haiti would be central to it. In 1795, when Simón Bolívar was twelve years old, the slaves in Coro on the Northern coast of Venezuela rebelled. The French Revolution and the incipient struggles in Haiti had already reached their ears, probably through Curaçao which lay only miles off-shore. Marauding Jacobin corsairs, including Victor Hughes, operated freely throughout the waters around Trinidad, inciting slaves and freemen to rebel.[4] Thus, by 1805, at the very time that Bolívar was swearing on the Monte Sacro in Rome not to rest until Hispanic America was liberated, the Haitians had declared themselves free and accorded citizenship to any escaped slave who reached Haitian shores. Haiti's ports were open to rebels and corsairs of all ilks who then spread the word about the révolution to the farthest corners of the hemisphere.[5] In many cases, it was the very character of the messenger as much as the message itself which generated fear.

It was the failure of the early attempts at liberation which had literally forced Bolívar to turn to Haiti and its President Alexandre Petion. Twice he sought refuge there. He got to know southern Haiti well, traveling often from Jacmel or Les Cayes to Port-au-Prince. It should not be believed, however, that this meant an acceptance, indeed, even a recognition of the Haitian contribution. It merely meant that the precursors of Spanish American independence had no other options. As Bolívar himself recognized, it was a strategy based on the law of necessity. He revealed precisely this motivation when he signed off a letter to the *Royal Gazette* of Jamaica saying: 'when men are desperate, they are not fastidious in choosing the means to extricate themselves from danger'.[6] Expediency and necessity motivated the recruitment of blacks. In addition, there was the question of a future racial balance, as Bolívar wrote Santander on 20 April 1820. Noting that in Venezuela whites had died and black slaves survived, he pointed to one of the dominant questions of the nineteenth century when he asked: 'Is it fair that only free men die to emancipate the slaves? Would it not be useful that the latter earn their rights on the battlefield, and that their elevated number be diminished by a powerful and legitimate means?'[7] Indeed, a change in strategy in no way meant changing a set of attitudes and perceptions on matters of race and class which were held by the individual, by the group and reinforced by the international community.

The recruitment of foot soldiers was not the only problem Bolívar faced as he began this new phase of his war of liberation. Recruitment of officers presented him with a tremendous challenge. The pool of potential recruits had completely changed. He now had to draw from a group of men little prone to accepting Bolívar's *mantuano* conception of the world and of the wars of independence. He had to struggle and fight for their respect at a conclave of rebels in Les Cayes, Haiti in February 1816. Now no longer surrounded by his *mantuano* social equals, Bolívar's leadership was not at all assured given the opposition of men like Bermudez, Mariño, Aury and Manuel Carlos Piar. Bolívar would later reveal his great anguish and fear of these very men. In a letter dated 24 May 1821, to Dr Pedro Gual, Bolívar explained:

> You have no idea of the spirit which animates our military leaders. They are not the same men you know. They are men you do not know, men who have fought for a long time . . . who believe that they have great merit and who are now humiliated, miserable and hopeless of ever gathering in the fruits of their labors. They are *llaneros*, determined and ignorant, men who have never considered themselves the equals of others who know more and make a better appearance than they . . . I treat them with the greatest consideration, yet even this consideration is not enough to give them the confidence and frankness which should exist among comrades and compatriots. We find ourselves at the top of an abyss, or rather on top of a volcano that may soon erupt. I fear peace more than war.

Bolívar was describing, and the facts indicated, an inconsistency between the official position – political and military responsibilities – of the nonwhite military officer and the social compensations and recognitions awarded him. One of these officers, for instance, complained that the white civilian lawyers 'flatter the military when they are possessed with fear, and insult them in the prosperity of peace'.[8] They were resentful and bitter of what they perceived to be ingratitude and injustice.

The cases of Admiral José Padilla and General Manuel Piar, both mulattoes, is especially important since Bolívar was later to have them executed for insubordination and rebellion.[9] Piar was born on the island of Curaçao of a mulatto mother and a Canary Islander seafaring father. Expelled from the island in 1807 by the Dutch authorities, he ended up where so many of his likes did, in Haiti. There he joined Miranda's expedition out of Jacmel and when the Second Republic fell he again returned to the island which gave him his first exile and whose revolution is said to have deeply influenced him.[10] But fortunately for Bolívar, Haiti had also given exile to men like Luis Brión, known as 'the jew', also from Curaçao. This swarthy, merchant-mariner embodied a fundamental fact of the new stage: the raising of monies within the Caribbean since no outside allies had been forthcoming.

Despite the fact that moral support, money and fighting men all came from the Caribbean,[11] Bolívar continued to seek legitimation from Europe and especially England. 'What immense expectations this small part of the New World holds for British industry', he wrote Maxwell Hyslop, a British merchant in Jamaica in 1815. In return for 'the most insignificant' means of war, Bolívar promised the English 'extensive benefits' including the provinces of Panamá and Nicaragua which the British could turn into centers of commerce and where they could build canals to 'permanently establish British commercial supremacy'. The English made no moves on his behalf.

Despite the fact that Bolívar did make a sincere effort to come to grips with slavery he tended to be passive and reconciled with its political inevitability even if it meant corrupting the kind of society he visualized. 'The soul of a serf', he noted, 'can seldom really appreciate true freedom', and turned to Montesquieu's notion that it is harder to release a nation from servitude than to enslave a free nation.

In one of his September 1815 letters to the *Royal Gazette* of Jamaica, Bolívar showed that his mind was still very much that of a *mantuano*. He still refused to believe that domestic disputes stemmed from differences of race; they were, he insisted, a result rather of the personal ambitions of a few men and of divergent political opinions encouraged by outsiders. He still wanted to believe that 'the most perfect harmony has reigned among those who were born on this soil'. Not surprisingly his view of the Indian was that he was 'sweet' (*dulce*) and wished only to be left alone. The slave? He 'vegetates in complacent inertia . . . he feels that he is leading a natural life, as a member of his master's family, whom he loves and respects'. His analysis of the behavior of 'the colored people' was that they were forced to follow leaders such as Boves, Morales, Rosete, Calzada . . . all royalist leaders whose troops were drawn largely from the *castas*, the colored classes. All were motivated by a hatred of the white *criollo* class from which Bolívar came.[12]

Whatever the local causes of the conflict, the Haitian example was never far removed. In a letter to *The Gazette*, the dark image of Haiti makes its appearance when Bolívar notes that the colored people followed the example of Saint Domingue (Haiti), 'but without understanding the real causes of the revolution'. The question remains, did Bolívar himself at that stage understand the causes of the Haitian revolution?

Despite his friendship with the Haitian leader Petion, Bolívar shared the generalized dim view of the isolated island.[13] Haiti was Africa, the dark continent, the great unknown with all the preconceptions which conjured up images of social revolution and disorder. This is evident in his warning to Vice-President Santander, on 23 December 1822 that the coasts of Colombia are threatened not only by the neighboring European colonies but also by 'the Africans of Haiti, whose power is greater than the primitive fire'. Haiti, he says in the same letter, is 'so complex and so horrible that no matter how you consider it, it doesn't present other than horrors and misfortunes'. Again, on 11 March 1825 Bolívar writes Santander that the Haitian Revolution could serve as a model in certain respects, 'but not in the horrible area of destruction which they adopted . . . ' Bolívar's fear was ultimately the fear of *pardocracia*, rule or, better said, anarchy, led by the nonwhites. This would appear repeatedly in Bolívar's writings and had its roots in his social class origins and in his ceaseless efforts to find legitimation in European eyes. It is crucial to understand, therefore, that Bolívar, like Miranda, not only perceived that the Great Powers shared his social values and views on Haiti and on nonwhites generally, but they also believed that they would somehow reward him and his cause for adhering to those commonly held prejudices.

History records an example of these expectations when, on the verge of seeing the second Republic collapse through the victories of the *pardos* and freed slaves led by the Royalist leaders Boves and Morales, Bolívar appeals to the English authorities in Barbados. His petition of 19 June 1814 states specifically that the British troops requested were not to fight the Spaniards but rather to destroy the 'bandits' and return the fugitive slaves to 'their duty'. It recalls similar appeals of Miranda to the British in which he cited the Haitian menace to all civilized interests. Contact with Haiti, far from reducing Bolívar's fear of *pardocracia*, appeared to have inflamed it. Like his social group, he feared Haiti's influence on internal conflicts which could challenge their authority; because they understood that the international community also feared Haiti, they feared being associated with that island.[14] Two events demonstrate both dimensions of this collective fear.

Chafing under the total isolation which the world had imposed on his island, Haitian President Boyer decided in 1824 to take the initiative. He sent his emissary Chanlatte to Colombia to propose an Alliance of Defense, Commerce and Friendship.[15] The reaction was one of panic. First Vice-President Santander writes Bolívar (busy in Perú) saying that he understands that a Haitian emissary is coming and 'we'll see what he brings and how we shall get out of the mess (*embrollo*) of Englishmen, Americans, Frenchmen, Haitians'. Received by the Minister of External Relations, the Venezuelan Pedro Gual, Chanlatte is given an evasive first response: Gual had to consult his government. This was done in July, 1824. The Gran Colombia government discussed the matter on 8 July and declared it to be an 'extremely delicate' issue. Not that the decision was in doubt, only the manner and form of the response. Finally the government instructed Foreign Minister Gual to respond 'skillfully' (*con habilidades*). By 15 July the final version of Gual's response was approved and it was a masterpiece of international relations double talk. The response had its share of political 'realism': why generate the enmity of old, strong states through friendship with new, weak ones? The response also had its share of legalistic sophisms: Haitian help to Venezuelan liberation was a *personal* act of Haitian President Petion, not a commitment of the Haitian State, thus no reciprocal State obligation was incurred. There was also a good deal of historical distortion: had not the Haitians themselves more than once obstructed Venezuelan shipping in an effort to ingratiate Spain? Finally, Gual's response contained this critical piece of straightforward candidness: all the countries of the 'old world' (*mundo antiguo*) he noted, had their eyes on the New Spanish American States. Under those circumstances, 'el más ligero desvío de las formas, usos y costumbres establecidas'[16] would delay the acceptance by those 'civilized nations' of these new states. Clearly, Gual felt that the Europeans considered any recognition of Haiti to be outside the established norms and, thus, too great a risk to the reputation of the new republic he represented.

Similar sentiments and perceptions contributed to Bolívar's decision not to invite Haiti to the Panamá Congress. The letter of instructions of 24 September 1825 given to Gran Colombia's two delegates to the Panamá Congress of that year, ordered them to encourage commercial exchanges with Haiti but to make sure they discouraged all other types of contact. The very language of these instructions point to the depth of fear of dealing with Haiti, to an incipient terrified consciousness:

> . . . que el gobierno de Colombia siente mucha repugnancia a guardar con Haiti aquellas consideraciones de etiqueta generalmente recibidas entre naciones civilizadas . . . De ésta manera están Uds. autorizados para evadir toda cuestión que tenga por objeto reconocer la independencia de Haití, enviar y recibir ministros diplomáticos . . . [17]

It is not a trivial fact that both the writer of the memo, José Rafael Ravenga, and the chief recipient and chief delegate to the Panamá Congress, Dr Pedro Gual, had once found refuge in Haiti. Like Miranda and Bolívar, these gentlemen held opinions which were not even faintly generous to the Haitians. The antagonism of the Great Powers towards Haiti, thus, while a powerful enough reason for prudence, also provided a convenient and comfortable support for the existing anti-Haitian attitudes of the Latin American elites. The decision not to invite the Haitians to the Panamá Congress, thus, cannot be attributed solely to opposition by the Great Powers, or indeed by the North Americans: one has to reckon also with the attitudes of those who composed the government at the time, Bolívar and his class. First of all, the invitation to the Congress came directly from Bolívar, he dictated it personally on 7 December 1824: Haiti was not on the list. Nor was North America. When Vice-President Santander, supported by Mexico and Central America, extended an invitation to the United States, Bolívar was not happy. 'Haiti, Buenos Aires y los Estados Unidos', he wrote Santander on 20 May 1825, 'tienen cada uno de ellos sus grandes inconvenientes' (each have their own major inconveniences). On 30 May he wrote Santander again emphasizing that the North Americans and the

Haitians have the character of strangers. 'Por lo mismo, jamás seré de opinión de que los convidemos para nuestros arreglos americanos' (Therefore, I will never feel that we should invite them to partake in our [Latin] American agreements).

Antonio Gómez Robledo correctly points to Bolívar's 'psychology' as an explanation of his exclusions of North America and Haiti from the Panamá Congress (1958:56–66). Bolívar's plan, he maintains, was 'racial' (meant in the Spanish term of *raza* as culture) but not racist (in the biological sense). Whatever truth there might be to this interpretation, history records that the United States was eventually invited to Panamá, but Haiti was not. This island and its government fell outside the parameters of the norms which defined civilization and acceptability.

While necessity forced Bolívar to recruit nonwhites as officers, the white elite of Colombia felt no necessity to agree with these choices. Their fear of *pardocracia* was even more intense than Bolívar's. In fact, this was a major reason for their opposition to his rule. As an important spokesman for this group explained:

> In his last years, when he became a dictator, Bolívar represented these three things: the arbitrariness of the sword, the insolence of the Venezuelans who were regarded as intruders, and the rebellion of the mixed bloods.[18]

Similarly, José María Samper, an influential contemporary, in referring to the high status civilian group to which he himself belonged, revealed their value system when he noted that 'it is they who guide the revolution and are the source of its philosophy. The other races or castes . . . do nothing more than obey the impulses of those who have the prestige and intelligence, the audacity and even the superiority of the white race' (Caballero Calderón, 1960:67).

The fear and disdain for Haiti was part of the broader fear and disdain of nonwhites. Existing social norms had been relaxed in the military area because of the necessity and exigencies of war. Traditional social norms, however, had not disappeared. This was made evident in the arrest on a murder charge, and subsequent execution, in 1824 of a black colonel, Leonardo Infante. This case had enormous consequences for Bolívar in that it destroyed the loyalty of Infante's fellow mixed-blood officers towards the Gran Colombian government.[19] But the language surrounding the Colonel Infante case bears witness to the fears which a weakening of norms elicit. Colombian historian José Manuel Groot's description of Infante's situation is highly relevant to the analysis:

> [His neighbors] were afraid of him because he was a complete plainsman (*era todo un llanero*) and plainsmen have obnoxious

games (*chanzas pezadas*): to which was added his imposing presence. He was a Negro of the purest type, a plainsman from Maturin [Venezuela], a fierce cavalryman (*de lanza brava*), robust, well shaped . . . He always wore his uniform with its silver epaulets and high ribboned hat [although he was not a drunkard nor did he ever misbehave with anyone]. Even so, with these manners of a plainsman he bothered those of the neighborhood, and even those whom he knew regarded him with hostility, because a plainsman in a society of educated people (*gentes cultas*) is like a bulldog which enters a hall wagging its tail and even though its owner says that it does not bite, they all look with hostility and want it thrown out (1941:327).

In short, even without misbehaving, this black officer instilled terror. The inoffensive but feared bulldog is an appropriate metaphor to describe the clashing styles and their racial components. Even one as sympathetic to Infante as the priest who heard his last confession and accompanied him to the gallows could not help describing him in terms other than those of the dominant group:

Although Colonel Infante was a pure Negro and was not known to have any political education, *even so* he was a Roman and Apostolic Catholic: and *even though* he could not express himself except in harsh and barbaric terms, one cannot deny that he had great talent (Ley, 1941:331–6, my emphasis).

Infante, on his way to the gallows, is reported to have looked up at several civilian representatives standing near the Congress building and exclaimed, 'I am the one who put you in those positions!' Again, before dying he shouted to the assembled troops, 'This is the payment I am given . . . I am the first, but others will follow me.'[20]

This resentment and anger, according to Vallenilla Lanz, explains a great deal about the rise of the nonwhite *caudillo* in the nineteenth century (1961:4lff).[21] Beyond that historical interpretation there are the sociological ones. War did cause fissures in the traditional colonial social structure. Necessity forced leaders such as Bolívar to recruit nonwhites into positions of leadership. Their behavior did offend the sensibilities of the white elite.[22] But any inclination to be more liberal with Haiti or with local blacks were kept in check by international as well as social group pressures. At the individual level, as Colombian historian Liévano Aguirre points out, the fear was of being *descastado* (outcast) (1964, III:36). This had its equivalent at the international level: being considered an international outcast.

The Cuban case

The Cuban case too is an apt demonstration of the universality of this fear of Haiti. Charles Chapman cites three reasons why Cubans did not follow the rest of Latin America into independence: they did not want to abolish slavery (as Bolívar had promised); being an island, they felt that Spain would have an overwhelming military advantage; third, ' . . . the Cubans had almost before their eyes the gruesome scenes that had attended the winning of independence in the black republic of Haiti . . . there the whites had been killed off by the negroes or forced to flee . . . There were too many negroes in Cuba for the people to be willing to risk emancipation' (1927:31).

Chapman noted that throughout the nineteenth century Cubans were obsessed with the issue of the racial balance. The whites, he said, were 'in terror lest Cuba become "another Haiti" '. There certainly were some grounds for apprehension. In 1812, José Antonio Aponte led a black rebellion which had Haiti as a model and, according to Levi Marrero, entertained contacts with a Haitian general (1972–1987, IX:34). Between 1841 and 1843, there were several minor slave rebellions; however, the 1844 rebellion of 'La Escalera' provoked '*el gran susto*'. Again, it was said that Haiti was the model for the Cuban blacks. As the Castellanos note, it was the fear that the Cuban blacks would make contact with blacks in Jamaica and Haiti which gave rise to a 'collective hysteria' (1988–1992, I:165, 175). What followed were years which Cuban history knows as those of the '*Gran Terror*' and the '*Gran Miedo*'. Haiti was central to these fears. Virtually every major Cuban thinker in the nineteenth century favored a reduction of the black population citing the Haitian example as the reason. The Castellanos put it succinctly: 'The great preoccupation could be summed up in one simple question: Will what happened in Haiti repeat itself in Cuba?' (1988–1992, I:250). Otherwise enlightened thinkers such as José Antonio Saco looked at the Caribbean islands and said: 'Who does not tremble upon realizing that the population of African origin which surrounds Cuba amounts to more than five million?' (Castellanos and Castellanos, 1988–1992, I:251).

Leopoldo Zea, who has put this Cuban fear in a broader Latin American context of Darwinist and Spencerian views of biology in social affairs, cites the Cuban scholar Medardo Vitier who maintains that were it not for the large black presence in Cuba, Saco and many of his contemporaries would have favored annexation to the United States. 'Oh', wrote Saco, 'if Cuba had today two or more million whites, how gladly would I see her pass into the hands of our neighbors! Then, however great the immigration of North Americans, we would absorb them and increasing and prospering to the astonishment of nations, Cuba would always be Cuban.'[23] Whether it was Father Félix Varela, Domingo Delmonte, José de la Luz y Caballero, Francisco Arango y Parreño or Saco, they all perceived the black slave as irreconcilable enemies and Haiti as the place from which the leadership would come. Their abolitionist fervor was, as Leonardo Griñan Peralta put it, 'hijo del temor, no del amor' (child of fear, not of love) (Zea 1963:260).

It is this fact which has led more radical Cuban students of race relations to categorize these nineteenth-century celebrities as racists. Raúl Cepero Bonilla believes that they all shared an 'exclusivist' concept of Cuba: a white Cuba which meant that 'había que *limpiar* el país de los otros colores que lo *ensuciaban*' (it was necessary to cleanse the country of the other colors which stained her).[24] Virtually all thinking about Cuba's political future was somehow impacted by this race issue. Spain rightly believed that fear of the blacks was the best weapon it possessed to keep white Cubans loyal; annexationists and their American allies operated under the same assumptions.

The fear of 'Haitianization' thus hung over Cuban life like a sword of Damocles. It came into play again in the early twentieth century as Cuba began its independent life. At this point, as Nancy Leys Stepan has documented, US racist views on eugenics and racial purity fell on receptive ears (1991:174–7). Racial fears even permeated the debate around the introduction of universal suffrage, for as *The New York Times* on 7 August 1899 headlined: 'Cuba may be another Haiti; results of universal suffrage would be a black republic' (cited in Fermoselle 1974:30). Similarly, when Cuban blacks rebelled in 1912 to protest blatant discrimination in job placements, *The New York Times* (22 May 1912) headlined: 'Haitian negroes aid Cuban rebels'. The possibility, as Rafael Fermoselle theorizes, that the many Haitian (and Jamaican) blacks working in the Cuban sugar industry had merely gotten caught in the middle of the Cuban warfare, never occured to these observers obsessed with fears of Haiti. The retribution meted out in 1912 to the 4,000 black rebels was ferocious. Chapman relates how President Gómez took note of the 'feeling of panic' which the 'ferocious savagery' of the blacks had caused among the whites in Havana and vowed to 'make short work of them' (1927:311–13). Over 3,000 blacks were killed.

The 'terrified consciousness' of white Cubans led to the perversion of Cuban democracy and the poisoning of their race relations. Cuban constitutionalist Manuel Marques Sterling commented in 1925 that emancipation freed the slaves but not the blacks, 'and this miserable slavery . . . weighs down the spirit of the country' (Beals, 1933:34). Indeed, as Carlton Beals commented sixty years ago, the race question 'runs submerged in all Cuban politics' but Cubans had not faced this fact head-on (1933:69).

Massive Spanish immigration in the first decades of independence turned the numerical balance considerably towards the whites. Blacks in Cuba tended to become a minority. However, since the Cuban revolution, whites have sought exile in large numbers, with the result that the black proportion has proportionally increased. Today, opponents of the Castro regime are once more starting to speak of the 'Haitianization' of Cuba.[25] Despite their disclaimers about it not being a racial concept, there is too much history behind this metaphor for the informed to see it in any other terms. Ominously but perhaps predictably, there are those who are again arguing that not only was Republican Cuba negrophobic but so is the exile community in Miami and the Castro Revolution (Moore, 1988).

The non-Hispanic Caribbean

Given the history of racism in the nineteenth century, not only should one expect the 'terrified consciousness' to have survived into the twentieth century but to be strongest where the whites are much fewer in numbers than they are in Venezuela and Cuba. The issue, then, is how much, if any, of this terrified consciousness survives today in the non-Hispanic Caribbean? Let us start with a *literary* search. Assume that you come upon this passage in an evidently autobiographical novel, published in 1969:

> I loved the house. My father had built it four years before . . . In it I was safe against the insecurity and embarrassment which continually plague a young boy. I wasn't really comfortable anywhere else. In my heart I jealously guarded this fortress against aliens. Sometimes I imagined a thousand men besieging it, and I the hero repulsed them every time . . .

The passage is by white Trinidadian Ian McDonald, in *The Humming-Bird Tree* (1969:29), one of the most lyrically written accounts of growing up white in the tropics.

Although he does not include McDonald in his analysis, Kenneth Ramchand does analyze many such passages in novels written by white West Indians (1972). The plots and styles of those novels, he maintains reveal a 'natural stance . . . a terrified consciousness'. More often than not, Ramchand's analysis turns to Dominica-born Jean Rhys' *Wide Sargasso Sea*. In this autobiographical novel, Rhys describes the terrifying experience of the *downwardly* mobile white, a 'poor white' to the *grand blancs* and a 'white cockroach' to the middle-class, upwardly mobile blacks. Critics have alluded to Rhys' 'dispossession and alienation', her 'passion for stating the case of the underdog' (Angier, 1985) as a function of her being 'a product of an inbred, decadent, expatriate society . . . alienated, menaced, at odds with life' (Wyndham, 1986:12). What was the source of what virtually all critics call Rhys' 'nightmare'? It is a telling fact that Caribbean critics see Rhys' terror resulting from her being a white minority in a black society, while American and European feminists believe that her terrified consciousness resulted from her being another type of minority, a woman, vulnerable in a male-dominated world.

What, beyond literature, might reveal this terrified consciousness hypothesized by Ramchand? In a rare study of the phenomenon of collective fear in Jamaica, James Mau compares the Jamaican government's April 1963 response to an uprising of six Rastafarians with the exaggerated response of the British in 1865 to the Morant Bay Rebellion. If that latter incident led to the execution of over 500 rebels and the flogging of 600 more, the 1963 response was hardly as horrific, even though it did stem from the same syndrome of perceptions, as Mau notes:

> The reaction was probably intended to intimidate any others who might be a threat to order and stability, and to put to rest the easily aroused fear of many Jamaicans who viewed the lower social orders as malevolent and barbaric (1968:99).

Mau was not ignorant of the history behind these fears: 'Jamaica's confrontation with the experience of Haiti and the republics in and around the Caribbean basin lends credibility to their fears of lower class antagonism' (1968:101). Interestingly enough, while 61 per cent of Mau's political elite sample believed that the lower classes were actually hostile, only 20 per cent of these lower classes expressed any hostility towards the elites. In fact, fully 56 per cent indicated that they wished to emulate the elites (1968:103).[26] But Mau's study is even more interesting in that it shows an inverse relationship between degrees of power and knowledge about the society and perceptions of popular hostility: Mau's 'most powerful' and 'most knowledgeable' were the least prone to perceive popular hostility.

Confirmation of the absence of a terrified consciousness among Jamaica's upper class is provided by Lisa Douglass (1992). She is well aware of the fact that 'whites apparently feared a Haitian style revolution and they always felt outnumbered on an island where 90% of the population was black' (1992:104). She is aware that the white population has been declining but notes that this has been occurring since the early nineteenth century. However, she rejects the notion that whites have been 'fleeing' in larger numbers since independence. In fact, Douglass believes that the elites have carved a 'niche' for themselves in Jamaican life, based on a love of family and hierarchy which they share with Jamaicans as a whole. Douglass notices the fact that whites still 'hedge their bets' by securing foreign passports, US green cards and maintaining homes and businesses abroad. 'But on this account, upper class Jamaicans show no less patriotism than people of other classes who probably have higher rates of emigration overall and many of whom also fled to safer shores in the 1970s' (1992:14). In short, the powerful persistence of traditional patterns of family, says

Douglass, result from the fact that 'they feel right' in the Jamaican context . (1992:24). In other words, that they share important norms with the rest of the society. In this sense, the Jamaican case shows great similarities to what exists elsewhere in the Caribbean where white minorities have become fully creolized.

In the 1970s, the white creole elite of Martinique was composed of 150 patronymic names, the so-called *békés*, who could trace their roots as follows: 39 per cent arrived before 1713; 22 per cent arrived between 1713 and 1784; another 35 per cent arrived in the nineteenth century; while only 4 per cent were first-or-second generation Martinicans (Kovats-Beaudoux, 1973). To the *békés*, race, class, and ideology (shaped by a sense of their historical role on the island) formed the pillars of their ethnocentrism. Each *béké* child was first socialized into 'the cult of the family name' and then into the 'sacred duty' of maintaining the *béké* group's social characteristics. The mechanism of this group's hierarchical stability has always been endogamy: any marriage outside the group's strict norms was regarded as a 'stain'. The mere length of their residence and continued social status, however, reveals that despite their social exclusiveness, they, like the Jamaican upper class, have a niche which is, if not accepted, at least tolerated by the black majority. Here, again, there must exist a sense of 'fit', an absence of any terrified consciousness among this elite. A similar white creole group is found in Trinidad, an island which, as distinct from Martinique, was led into independence by a black nationalist party whose theme was 'Massa Day Done' (Oxaal, 1968; Williams, 1961). Some of the island's foremost intellectuals had already put race at the center of gravity of their scholarship and politics. In the late 1930s, George Padmore had advanced the theory that the black revolution should precede the socialist one while C.L.R. James popularized the Haitian revolution through his *Black Jacobins*. It was Eric Williams, however, who would become the grand master of historical interpretations serving as hand-maidens to the political leader (Maingot, 1992).

To what extent is there evidence that the 0.5 per cent who are French creoles suffer from a terrified consciousness? Let us analyze the data of the first major survey of youthful aspirations among Trinidad students, done in 1958, four years before independence. Vera Rubin and Marisa Savalloni found that, compared to many of the black, colored and Indian responses which reflected extraordinary ambition and aspirations, the white students seemed spiritless and timid. The authors found the whites to have the least 'striving orientation'. Examples of a white response:

> Look around. All the other boys must be writing about their ambitions to be famous. I want to live a moderate life . . . I don't want to be chief justice of the Federation or anything like that . . . (1969:230)

The difference between the understated white responses and the others were never significantly highlighted by Rubin and Zavalloni, both American. Trinidadian Vidia S. Naipaul, on the other hand, did pick up on this. In an essay entitled 'Power?' this irreverent and irascible novelist wrote: 'Without the calm of the white responses, the society might appear remote, fantastic and backward.'[27] To Naipaul, local whites showed themselves to be realistically adjusted to their environment. Had he studied the autobiographical literature by creole whites which began to appear just years after he wrote this, Naipaul would certainly have found confirmation of his conclusion: there is not one iota of terrified consciousness evident in that literature.[28]

And yet, a counterintuitive question is called for: might not this 'calm' on the part of the whites, this evident lack of great ambitions, reflect a fear of the future? Could it explain Ian McDonald's befuddlement every time his mother would say, 'If things [on the island] continue like this we shall have to raise you in England'? Or, is this last response the reaction of McDonald's expatriate parents who, being Irish, had the option of returning to the original ethnic group? What ethnic group do local whites who have been on the island for seven or more generations 'return' to? Fifteen years after Rubin and Zavalloni did their survey, their study was replicated among students in the three top secondary schools in Trinidad (Maingot and Bender, 1974). The same understatement of local ambitions among whites was evident but this time also evident among blacks, coloreds and Indians. The pre-independence surge of political idealism had already been moderated. In fact, there was a striking similarity between the answers of all groups; only in the open-ended self-description part were white students more prone to mention family ties. They were still talking like the student who said that he would stay on the island 'and try to live up to the traditions that my father built up'.

Is this 'tradition' the functional equivalent of McDonald's house, that 'fortress' perpetually perceived as under siege by the 'aliens', the rest of society? Or was it perhaps the calm resignation typical of economically comfortable minority groups who look inward making up for their small numbers by finding strength in their group identity but also setting strict limits to their mental parameters and ambitions? As Jean Rhys points out in *Wide Sargasso Sea*: 'They say when the trouble comes close ranks, and so the white people did.' Is this the explanation for the survival of these groups: the very existence of a sense of threat which forces each group to close ranks? It certainly is Georg Simmel's emphasis on the group binding functions of conflict. In fact, Simmel maintained that mutual group 'repulsions' help sustain total social systems (1955). Might this help us understand Lisa Douglass' conclusion that the survival of the white Jamaican elite cannot be distinguished from the nature of Jamaican society as a whole? 'The history of Jamaica', she says, 'is one of intimacy along with distance, of similarity and distinction, and of love and hierarchy' (1992:15).

It appears that once numerical balance is no longer an issue, then rootedness in the local normative structure rather than race becomes the fundamental explanation of social 'fit'. The data from the 1974 survey of Trinidad youth indicated that they expected to fit in even better in the future:

Table 1   Expectations of greater racial equality

	Nonwhite N=283		White N=56	
	N	%	N	%
Yes	175	61.8	35	62.5
No	108	38.2	21	37.5

There is little evidence, therefore, to support Ramchand's assumption of the persistence of a terrified consciousness among white minorities in the Caribbean. But just studying the question might tell us something very important about the nature of majoritarian black governance in these newly independent islands. Why? For the simple reason that the racism and oppression which characterized white colonial behavior would lead us to believe that the black majority would, upon decolonization, engage in *apocalyptic* retribution, but it has not. Specifically, a review of the 'terrified consciousness' caused by the dominant racist ideology of the colonizers and the elevation of Haiti to a grand metaphor – what the Cubans called 'el gran incendio' – would lead us to expect not only the presence of such a terror but its intensification in an age of black governance. One would expect to find confirmed Frantz Fanon's thesis that the decolonization process necessarily meant a complete change of the social structure, driven by the 'impetuous and compelling' nature of the consciousness of the colonized, by definition 'always a violent phenomenon'. These twentieth-century expectations and formulations deserve further analysis.

The twentieth-century concept of 'terrified consciousness'

The word *terror* is not new to the history of political and social conflict. Whole periods of history have been labelled with the word or with phrases such as 'a reign of terror', 'white terror', and 'red terror'. Certainly the Jacobean menace terrorized many, in France and elswhere, in the late eighteenth and early nineteenth centuries.

As it is used in the literature of the postwar decolonization process, however, 'terror' has very specific origins, meanings and applications. These meanings can be encapsulated in three concepts:

- *Georges Sorel's* concept of proletarian *millenarian* (or Messianic) violence: According to Sorel, this was 'sublime work': 'terrifying to the bourgeoisie but *psychologically liberating to the oppressed*' (1961). To the extent that the proletariat could create a generalized myth of inevitable violence in the minds of the bourgeoisie, *liberation* was possible.
- *Jean-Paul Sartre's* concept of the ultimate *manicheism* of the colonial situation. According to Sartre, if you are not a direct *victim* of the situation, you are irreparably an 'executioner' of 'race murder'. Because every European is an exploiter, Sartre says, they are 'bound hand and foot, humiliated and sick with fear . . . ' (1968).
- *Frantz Fanon*'s general sociology of colonial violence. This violence, says Fanon, *is manichean*, has *millenarian* dimensions and its fundamental purpose is to have an *apocalyptic* outcome, that is, the 'psychological cleansing' of the black, oppressed by the terror and violence he inspires in the white oppressor (1968a:94).

To Fanon, this race violence is different from Marxian (or even Sorelian) proletarian violence because in the latter there were still plausible, structured expectations (*norms)* between the adversaries. The whole purpose of liberation in the colonies is to eliminate all existing norms, all commonly held legitimating structures, by eliminating those who created and controlled them: the whites. Racial hatred thus does not permit proportionality of means or ends or other traditional methods of defining conflict.

According to elite theorists such as Gaetano Mosca, since the time of the Romans the traditional way of defusing conflict and avoiding violence was by circulating elites. Racism, because it does not accept the black's behavior as legitimate (it is, after all, violence), made such concessions within the normative structure impossible. Circulation of elites would be equally impossible under Fanon's manichean approach to liberation. They are both in their own way manichean strategies. To Fanon, the intellectual task was to show why violence was the only legitimate revolutionary stance in colonial situations. Apocalyptic violence against the white oppressor was the only way of redirecting the violence colonial blacks executed on themselves in the form of self-hatred, self-doubt and psychological self-mutilation.[29] The essence of Fanon's concept of the 'terrified consciousness' of the colonial white is contained in the manichean principle that 'It is them or us.'

The look that the native turns on the settler's town is a look of lust, a look of envy; it expresses his dreams of possession – all manner of possession: to sit at the settler's bed, with his wife if possible. The colonized man is an envious man (1968a:39).

The white settler, says Fanon, knows this and is terrified. It was Frantz Fanon's teacher in Martinique, the Frenchman O. Manoni, who first called his, and our, attention to the syndrome of circumstances and relationships he called the colonial situation. Manoni emphasized the fact that it involved first of all economic exploitation; but he did not stop there, noting that it was also 'embodied in struggles for prestige, in alienation, in bargaining positions and debts of gratitude, and in the invention of new myths and the creation of new personality types' (1965:8).

To both Manoni and Fanon, the most powerful of these myths has been that of racial superiority. It is race more than virtually any other factor which molds and creates the particular human dimension of the colonial situation. 'When you examine at close quarters the colonial context', Fanon wrote, 'it is evident that what parcels out the world is to begin with the fact of belonging to or not belonging to a given race, a given species.' (Manoni, 1965:17; Fanon 1968a:40). This being the case, the liberation movement (which is more than a revolutionary one) cannot allow the retention of any of the old norms and mores; it cannot admit any except those who fit the mold of the new myth and its racial embodiment. Not surprisingly, the new Algerian myth allowed only 'Algerians', thus recognizing no minorities, no pluralism.[30]

If Marxian revolution involved replacing one system of production with another, the violence of colonial liberation requires replacing one race with another. This explains the 'terrified consciousness' of those who perceive themselves as targets for replacement. The interesting aspect of all this is that this twentieth-century advocacy of violence and the existence of a terrified consciousness is precisely what existed among whites in the Caribbean in the nineteenth century. The fact that such racial antagonisms did not contribute to black liberation in that century, and that liberation came in the twentieth century without it, is an important lesson.

Conclusion

If past experience suggests that ultimately such racial manicheism did not prevail in the Caribbean, there is value in the counterfactual question: why did it not happen that way and what lessons for the twenty-first century might this contain? The fact is that black dominated parliaments did emerge peacefully and democratically everywhere in the non-Hispanic Caribbean after World War II, and that the small white elites remained. They survived the decolonization process, though the exact nature of their influence and status varies from island to island.

How, then, to explain the persistence of white social elites, even as political, and often economic power (in terms of state control of the heights of the economy) shifted toward new black sectors? The fundamental answer is that through the long decolonization process, a set of national norms were successfully established. While certainly political and social conflict are a fundamental part of this new order, these collective norms were both engendered and sustained by a set of attitudes and behaviors accepted by most Caribbean peoples. The absence of a 'terrified consciousness' among post-independence white minorities stems from the fact that racial threats, while certainly present, were not the sole and definitely not the most important weapon used by the new black elites in the struggle for power. This tells us that violence is not the only path to liberation, the sole 'cleansing' or cathartic act. This is the central lesson of the West Indian case. The very act of resistance, of self-assertion, of challenging injustices is also liberating.[31] More often than not in the West Indies this has taken the path that James Scott calls using the 'weapons of the weak': contesting symbolic authority, asserting the very citizenship rights promulgated by the powerful (1985). Although Scott does acknowledge the role of the threat of violence, the primary option in the non-Hispanic Caribbean has been to mobilize around certain customary and shared values.

It is evident that a truly liberated leader is one who can exercise many options and strategies. Those caught in a manichean, dualistic and apocalyptic process have no such flexibility; theirs is the non-productive zero-sum game which usually leaves the whole system poorer. Describing the accomodating strategy chosen by black post-independence leaders leaves open the question of explanation: what enables them to opt for non-violent policies?

A first explanation has to address the material basis of competition. The fact is that in the Caribbean there has been very little competition or conflict over land.[32] Where the economies were 'open' ones, the ex-slaves simply squatted on public land (or abandoned estates) just as their forefathers had fled to create maroon settlements. Where the economies were 'closed' ones, the ex-slaves moved to the urban areas or to other islands. In the twentieth century, the conflicts have been over labor and its wages, and there the rich history of trade-unionism and its evolution into political power everywhere except Trinidad, is a critical example of the development of a normative system within which social conflict could be managed.

This gradual process allowed the new black leadership to seize much of the symbolic capital which contributes to the legitimacy of new elites.[33] The new black leadership gained the high ground in terms of both local and international moral standards. If the nineteenth century had utilized Haiti as the metaphor through which to resist change, the dominant ideology of the twentieth century has promoted the exact opposite: liberal pluralism. Even if the local white elite would have wanted to deny political change, they would have been condemned by the very international community they depend on for their economic capital. The South African case is living proof of that. Values, and international enforcement of them, do play important roles. 'So long as men and women continue to justify their conduct by reference to values', Scott rightly observes, 'the struggle for the symbolic high ground between groups and classes will remain an integral part of any conflict over power' (1985:235).

One form of political capital is control over the interpretation of the past. Certainly, there is much there to be bitter about. 'History' has indeed been widely used by the new elite; equally true, it has not been used as a sort of 'avenging angel'. One has heeded Derek Walcott's call for a Caribbean without 'a literature of revenge written by the descendants of slaves or a literature of remorse written by the descendants of masters' (1974:1–27). Walcott's own poetry reflects the struggle to avoid ethnocentrism and find the core of humanity in Caribbean existence. There is of course more than idealism in this posture, there is a pragmatic adjustment to political realities. As R.T. Smith notes, there is a realization among Caribbean leaders that 'recriminations about the past – no matter how justified – have failed to mobilize and direct the energies of the population' (1992:xii).

Black Caribbean leaders have proven themselves to be strategically astute. They have taken to heart Lord Acton's dictum that governments can be judged in terms of how they treat their minorities. An Eric Williams or Aimé Césaire may have used racial identifications to boost their political careers: they never used them to oppress others. Race and ethnicity in the Caribbean has held strategic, not inherent or absolute, value. To be otherwise would be to replicate the white racism they so abhorred and combatted.

The other choice the majority of the West Indian leaders made was to retain the parliamentary pluralist systems inherited from the colonial powers. And, on this score, West Indian history teaches us that political institutions do matter. At a macrosociological and political level we note that open, pluralistic political systems might well generate heightened racial or ethnic sentiments, but they also channel conflict into realistic directions, forcing negotiations and cross-cutting alliances. One consequence of such political pluralism is the intellectual pluralism evident in the brio and vivacity of studies in Caribbean race relations. Contrast, for instance, with the Cuban case, where the study of race relations has remained what Jorge Domínguez calls a 'classic "non topic" ' (1988:ix). How, for instance, to evaluate Carlos Moore's (1988) assertion that the discrimination of blacks in Cuba today owes as much to the nature of Cuban authoritarianism generally as it does to traditional white Cuban racism? Only serious and open research can answer such a question, and this in turn requires an open political system.

The great majority of the political leaders in the non-Hispanic Caribbean chose the more conservative path to liberation, and in so doing they assured the development of a normative context all groups could participate in (Maingot, 1984:362–80). It was a wise choice, freely supported by Caribbean majorities, and an example for those – in the Caribbean and elsewhere – who aspire to decolonization and liberation, however they define those processes. Decolonization without terrified consciousness should be the metaphor for the twenty-first century.

Notes

1. These and other negrophobic statements by English scholars are collected in Williams (1964).
2. Senator Y. Hanes of South Carolina, quoted in Schmidt (1971:28).
3. All correspondence regarding Haiti is taken from Verna (1970:Appendices).
4. On Victor Hughes we have to resort to *belles lettres*. See Alejo Carpentier's historical novel, *Explosion in the Cathedral*. On the assortment of rebels and corsairs who gathered in Trinidad to join the Venezuelan fray see Paul Verna, *Monsieur Bideau.*
5. On this see the excellent work of Paul Verna, *Bolívar y los emigrados patriotas en el Caribe* (1983).
6. Bolívar wrote two letters to the *Royal Gazette* during the month of September, 1815, one dated the 28th and the other undated. Reference here is to the undated one. Both are in the UNESCO compilation done by J.L. Salcedo-Bastardo (1983).
7. Henceforth, Bolívar's letters are only cited by their date. The source of these letters is the compilation of Vicente Lecuna (1951).
8. José Antonio Paez cited in Fortoul (1907:397). That material benefits were not enough to satisfy these officers' sense of their own worth is indicated by the fact that Paez had received an estate worth $200,000 as a bonus, as had other high-ranking officers in Venezuela (Bushnell, 1954:227). Personal and social esteem (status) was a strong determinant of behavior or at least of attitude. To what extent this attitude, which Bushnell claims Bolívar identified as a 'sort of inferiority complex' (1954:297), was shared by the rest of the military sector is an important question.
9. Charles C. Griffin maintains that had Padilla and Piar been white they would not have been executed (1949:178–9).
10. A Venezuelan historian would claim that Piar was 'el único procer de nuestra independencia que podrá hablar con autoridad de lo que es una verdadera revolución' (González, 1979:30).
11. Colombian historian Liévano Aguirre states it with the drama it deserves when he notes that 'extraordinary events – truly extraordinary – would occur. Liberty would not come from the South but from the Caribbean islands' (1983:152).
12. Here I am indebted to the excellent analysis of the historical role of Boves by German Carrera Damas (1964).
13. Paul Verna's excellent book (1970) corroborates the view of a Bolívar loyal to his friend Petion but not to Haiti as a nation.

14. Juan Bosch claims that the most important influence of Haiti was to make Bolívar more determined than ever *not* to allow a Haitian-like outcome to take place in Venezuela (1979:152).

15. A full discussion of this mission, complete with textual reprints of all important documents, is contained in Verna (1970).

16. 'Even the slightest departure from established forms, ways and customs' (Cited in Verna, 1970:Appendices.)

17. ' . . . that the Government of Colombia regards with repugnance the idea of treating Haiti with the same considerations of etiquette generally maintained between civilized nations . . . On this score you are authorized to evade any topic which has as object recognizing the independence of Haiti, the exchange of diplomats . . . ' (Cited in Verna, 1970:Appendices.)

18. Samper n.d:183–4. The Spanish historian Salvador de Madariaga quite correctly points to Bolívar's marginality: 'In fundamentals he was not at one with himself.' He only reveals his own racial biases, however, when he attributes Bolívar's change of policy towards recruiting nonwhites and new emphasis on race mixing to his own mixed racial heritage. If we did not know of his mixed heritage, or if Bolívar were 'a pure white', says De Madariaga, his utterances would be 'the ravings of an irresponsible demagogue' (1969:71–80).

19. On the importance of this case see Ibañez (1905, 1906), Bushnell (1954:278) and Fortoul (1907:363–4).

20. These incidents were reported by both Groot and Fray Ley (Groot, 1941:335).

21. This controversial work presents one of the best interpretations of the role of race in the development of Latin American political culture generally and *caudillismo* specifically.

22. For a *llanero*'s own later admission of the numerous insults and affronts to Bogotá civilians, especially against the civilian intellectuals, and the violent reaction of these through the press, see Paez (1869, II:14).

23. Medardo Vitier (1938) cited in Zea (1963:108).

24. Cepero Bonilla (1971:106); emphasis in original.

25. This author has counted many uses of the term in just one newspaper since October, 1992. See also Franqui (1993).

26. Mau compares this to the finding of Jalioda (1961) who discovered that just before independence, 66 per cent of Ghanians were well disposed towards Europeans.

27. *The New York Review of Books*, 3 September 1970.

28. In the 1970s and 1980s there appeared a series of memoires by white Trinidadian upper class white creoles. There is not a hint of a terrified consciousness in the lot (Mavrogordato, 1977; De Lima, 1981; Bridges, 1988; O'Conner, 1978; De Vertenil, 1973).

29. Fanon had analyzed this self-hatred and self-mutilation in his doctoral thesis (1952).

30. This explains why the liberation movement in Algeria could not recognize publicly those whites who contributed to their cause (Fanon, 1968b:36–54).

31. I adopt here the position of Gunnemann (1979).

32. I am grateful to my colleague Ralph Clem for bringing to my attention the difference between conflict generated by competition over labor as distinct from competition over land.

33. The reader will notice the influence of Pierre Bourdieu's notion of various forms of capital (1984).

References

Angier, C., 1985, *Jean Rhys*, London: Penguin Books.
Beals, C., 1933, *The Crime of Cuba*, Philadelphia: J.B. Lippencott Co.

Bosch, J., 1979, *Bolívar y la guerra social*, Santo Domingo: Editora Alfa y Omega.
Bourdieu, P., 1984, *Distinctions*, Cambridge: Harvard University Press.
Bridges, Y., 1988, *Child of the Tropics*, Port-of-Spain: Aquarela Galleries.
Bushnell, D., 1954, *The Santander Regime*, Newark: University of Delaware Press.
Caballero Calderón, E., 1960, *Historia privada de los colombianos*, Bogotá: Antares.
Carpentier, A., 1963, *Explosion in the Cathedral*, Boston: Little, Brown.
Carrera Damas, G., 1964, *Sobre el significado socioeconómico de la Acción Histórica de Boves*, Caracas: Universidad Central de Venezuela.
Castellanos, J. and Castellanos I., 1988–1992, *Cultura Afrocubana*, Miami: Ediciones Universal. 2 vols.
Cepero Bonilla, R., 1971, *Azúcar y abolición*, Habana: Editorial de Ciencias Sociales.
Chapman, C.E., 1927, *A History of the Cuban Republic*, New York: The MacMillan Co.
De Lima, A., 1981, *The De Limas of Frederick Street*, Port-of-Spain: Inprint.
De Madariaga, S., 1969, *Bolívar*, New York: Schocken Books.
De Vertenil, A., 1973, *Sir Louis de Vertenil*, Port-of-Spain: Columbus Publishers.
Domínguez, J., 1988, Foreword to Carlos Moore, *Castro, the Blacks and Africa*, Los Angeles: Center for Afro-American Studies, pp. ix–xvi.
Douglass, L., 1992, *The Power of Sentiment: Love, Hierarchy and the Jamaican Family Elite*, Boulder: Westview Press.
Fanon, F., 1952, *Masque blanc, peau noir*, Paris: Editions de Seuil.
_____ 1968a, *The Wretched of the Earth*, New York: Grove Press.
_____ 1968b, *Sociologie d' une revolution*, Paris: Maspero.
Fermoselle, R., 1974, *Política y color en Cuba*, Montevideo: Ediciones Geminis.
Fortoul, J. G., 1907, *Historia Constitucional de Venezuela*, Berlin: s.n.
Franqui, C., 1993, 'Cuba 93: haitianización o libertad', *El Nuevo Herald*, 3 January.
Gómez Robledo, A., 1958, *Idea de la experiencia de América*, Mexico: Fondo de Cultura Americana.
González, A., 1979, *Manuel Piar*, Valencia: Vadell.
Griffin, C.C., 1949, 'Economic and Social Aspects of the Era of the Spanish-American Independence', *Hispanic American Historical Review*, No. 29, pp. 170–87.
Groot, J.M., 1941, *Historia de la Gran Colombia*, Caracas: Academia de la Historia.
Gunnemann, J.P., 1979, *The Moral Meaning of Revolution*, New Haven: Yale University Press.
Hall, D., 1959, *Free Jamaica*, New Haven: Yale University Press.
Hoetink, H., 1963 'Change in Prejudice. Some Notes on the Minority Problem, with References to the West Indies and Latin America'. *Bijdragen tot de Taal-, Land-, en Volkenkunde*, No. 119, pp. 56–75.
_____ 1967, *The Two Variants in Caribbean Race Relations*, London: Oxford University Press.
_____ 1971, *El pueblo dominicano 1850–1900. Apuntes para su sociología histórica*, Santiago: Universidad Católica Madre y Maestra.
Horsman, R., 1981, *Race and Manifest Destiny*, Cambridge: Harvard University Press.
Ibañez, P.M., 1905[1906], 'El coronel Pedro Infante', *Boletín de Historia y Antiguedades*, Vol. 2, No. 32, pp. 449–66, Vol. 3, No. 33, pp. 513–32.
Jalioda, G., 1961, *White Man*, London: Oxford University Press.
Johnson, C., 1966, *Revolutionary Change*, Boston: Little, Brown.
Kovats-Beaudoux, E., 1973, 'A Dominant Minority: The White Creoles of Martinique', in Comitas, L. and Lowenthal, D., (eds), *Slaves, Free Men, Citizens. West Indian Perspectives*, Garden City: Anchor Press/Doubleday, pp. 241–75.
Lecuna, V., 1951, *Selected Writings of Bolívar*, Bierck, Jr. H.A. (ed.), New York: The Colonial Press. 2 vols.

Ley, F.A., 1941, *Capilla y suplicio del Coronel de la República de Colombia Leonardo Infante*, Reprinted in Groot, J.M., *Historia de la Gran Colombia*, Caracas: Academia de la Historia, pp. 331–6.

Leys Stepan, N., 1991, *'The Hour of Eugenics': Race, Gender, and Nation in Latin America*, Ithaca: Cornell University Press.

Liévano Aguirre, I., 1964, *Los grandes conflictos, sociales económicos de nuestra historia*, Bogotá: Ediciones Tercer Mundo, 4 vols.

––––––– 1983, *Bolívar*, Bogotá: Editorial Liberal.

MacDonald, I., 1969, *The Hummingbird Tree*, London: Heinemann.

Maingot, A.P., 1984, 'The Structure of Modern-Conservative Societies', in Black, J.K. (ed.), *Latin America: Its Problems and its Promise*, Boulder: Westview, pp. 407–23.

––––––– 1992, 'Politics and Populist Historiography in the Caribbean', in Hennessy, A. (ed.), *Intellectuals in the Twentieth-Century Caribbean*, London: Macmillan, pp. 145–74.

Maingot, A.P., and Bender J., 1974, 'Youthful Aspirations in Post-Independence Trinidad', Port-of-Spain: s.n. unpublished manuscript.

Manoni, O., 1965[1950], *Próspero and Caliban: the Psychology of Colonization*, translated by P. Powesland. New York: Frederick A. Praeger.

Marrero, L., 1972–1987, *Cuba: Economía y sociedad*, Rio Piedras: Editorial San Juan, 13 vols.

Mau, J.A., 1968, *Social Change and Images of the Future*, Cambridge: Schenkman Publishing Co., Inc.

Mavrogordato, O.J., 1977, *Voices in the Street*, Port-of-Spain: Inprint.

Montague, L.L., 1940, *Haiti and the United States, 1714–1938*, Durham: Duke University Press.

Moore, C., 1988, *Castro, the Blacks and Africa*, Los Angeles: University of California Press.

O'Conner, P.E.T., 1978, *Some Trinidad Yesterdays*, Port-of-Spain: Inprint.

Oxaal, I., 1968, *Black Intellectuals Come to Power*, Cambridge: Schenkman Publishing Co., Inc.

Paez, J.A., 1869, *Autobiografía del General José Antonio Paez*, New York: Hallet & Breen, 2 vols.

Ramchand, K., 1972, *The West Indian Novel and Its Background*, London: Faber & Faber.

Rhys, J., 1986, *The Wide Sargasso Sea*, New York: WW Norton, Co.

Rubin, V. and Zavallone, M., 1969, *We Wish to be Looked Upon*, New York: Teachers College Press.

Salcedo-Bastardo, J.L., 1983, *Simón Bolívar: The Hope of the Universe*, Paris: UNESCO

Samper, J.M., n.d., *Ensayo sobre las revoluciones políticas y la condición social de las Repúblicas Colombianas Hispanoamericanos*, Bogotá: Biblioteca Popular de Cultura Colombiana.

Sartre, J.-P., 1968, Preface to Frantz Fanon, The *Wretched of the Earth*, New York: Grove Press, pp. 1–26.

Schmidt, H., 1971, *The United States Occupation of Haiti, 1915–1934*, New Brunswick, Rutgers University Press.

Scott, J.C., 1985, *Weapons of the Weak: Everyday Forms of Peasant Resistance*, New Haven: Yale University Press.

Simmel, G., 1955, *Conflict and the Web of Group Affiliations*, New York: The Free Press.

Smith, R.T., 1992, Foreword to Douglass, *The Power of Sentiment: Love, Hierarchy and the Jamaican Family Elite*, Boulder: Westview Press, pp. xi–xv.

Sorel, G., 1961, *Reflections on Violence*, New York: Collier Books.

Vallenilla Lanz, L., 1961[1950], *Césarismo Democrático*, Caracas: Tipográfica Garrido.

Verna, P., 1970, *Petion y Bolívar*, Caracas: Ministerio de Educación.

––––––– 1983, *Bolívar y los emigrados patriotas en el Caribe*, Caracas: Gráficas la Bodoniana.

––––––– n.d., *Monsieur Bideau.* Caracas: Ministerio de Educación.

Walcott, D., 1974, 'The Muse of History', in Coombs, O. (ed.), *Is Massa Day Dead? Black Moods in the Caribbean*, New York: Doubleday & Anchor, pp. 1–28.

Williams, E.E., 1961, *Massa Day Done*, Port-of-Spain: PNM Publishing Co.

_____ 1964, *British Historians and the West Indies*, Port-of-Spain: PNM Publishing Co.

Wyndham, F., 1986, Introduction to Jean Rhys, *Wide Sargasso Sea*, New York: WW Norton, Co.

Zea, L., 1963, *The Latin American Mind*, Norman: University of Oklahoma Press.

CHAPTER 5

Museums, ethnicity and nation-building: reflections from the French Caribbean

Richard and Sally Price

Just off the north-south road that skirts the Atlantic coast of Martinique, 'a mini-village made up of rural huts from the 1950s . . . permits the new generation to discover the scenes their ancestors knew, the way of life of their parents and grandparents. . . . Four years in the making, this open-air museum is a gem of tradition. On Sunday afternoons . . . members of the folkloric troupe Madinina install themselves there to recreate a living portrait of that bygone era' (Staszewski, 1993:48–50). A few kilometers to the south, in the cove of Anse Figuier, another privately-run museum, the island's first '*éco musée*', also targets the 1950s – 'the traditional society we have forgotten in our rush to modernity . . . *la Martinique profonde*' (E. H-H., 1992:44–5).[1]

Nostalgia for the 'ancestral' way of life is big in 1990s Martinique. Celebration of the '*patrimoine*' permeates the local press, radio, and T.V., animated by artists, musicians, dancers, tale-tellers, writers, theater groups, and cultural associations. Commercialized folklore is available at every village fête and large hotel, and it floods the airwaves. One might well ask, why this surge of interest in the everyday life of only a generation ago?[2]

The early 1960s marked a watershed in Martinique and its sister department of Guadeloupe. France began an aggressive program of development and integration that transformed these island neo-colonies into modern consumer societies with the highest standards of living in the region. Infrastructure boomed: roads, electricity, telephones, and piped water arrived in the most remote communities, and airports and hotels were dramatically expanded. Social programs (a panoply of welfare benefits, pensions, unemployment insurance) pumped cash into family budgets. The standard size of houses tripled even as family size began to plummet. Agriculture was encouraged to atrophy as service industries (and the civil service) burgeoned. The number of cars per family quickly came to rival that in the US. Supermarkets, as well as megastores for building products, appliances, and other consumer goods, sprang up across the landscape; in the context of both France and the wider world, Guadeloupe and Martinique became the largest per capita consumers of champagne anywhere. The media were modernized and contributed to making the French language a part of everyone's daily life. The two urban centers, Fort-de-France and Pointe-à-Pitre, mushroomed to represent half the islands' populations, as people abandoned the countryside in droves. And large numbers of Antilleans were lured to the metropole in the 1960s and 1970s by official French programs designed to fill particular employment niches, creating the present situation which finds some 40 per cent of the 'Antillean' population settled in the hexagon.

This unusually rapid modernization, imposed from the metropole, is profoundly assimilationist in spirit. And it demands the explicit rejection of much of Martiniquan culture as it had developed during the previous three centuries. Television advertisements ridicule old ways in favor of new (grating fruit to make juice rather than buying it readymade in a carton at the supermarket, gardening with a machete rather than with a gasoline-powered brushwacker) and constantly promote new 'needs' (electronic front gates, home security systems, canned dog food). And, in terms of values and self-perception, Martiniquans are encouraged to situate them-selves as thoroughly modern, bourgeois members of the First World (and Europe) and to look with pity upon, say, Haitians, Saint Lucians, or Brazil-ians as their disadvantaged and backward Third World neighbors.[3]

Yet Martiniquans (most Martiniquans) do not feel fully French. Nor, of course, do most Frenchmen consider them to be. At best, they are Frenchmen-with-a-difference, because of the racial discrimination they confront at every turn. In Paris, Antilleans are routinely confounded with, for example, illegal Malian immigrants in police sweeps of the subway. And at home, where white immigrants from metropolitan France now constitute more than 10 per cent of the island's residents, the battle for who 'owns' Martinique is played out through hundreds of minor confrontations each day: a retired metropolitan gendarme complains to the police about the loud music at a Martiniquan restaurant next door and a highly-politicized court case centered on charges of racism ensues; a Martiniquan protests that a tourist has blocked the entrance to his house with his rented car and a fist fight breaks out; and disputes flair up with regularity over the hiring of metropolitan workers for local construction projects or in civil service positions. For Martiniquans, these kinds of incidents are tremendously charged, and leave unresolved the personal tension inherent in being simul-taneously Martiniquan and French.

Two decades ago Édouard Glissant argued that cultural symbols of Martiniquan identity – music and dance, the creole language, local cuisine, carnival – take on remarkable power in such contexts by fostering in people the illusion that they are representing themselves, that they are choosing the terms of their 'difference', while at the same time obscuring the rapidity and completeness of the assimilationist project. This focus on '*le culturel*' and '*le folklore*', he wrote, serves both the assimilators and the assimilating, by lulling the latter into complacency and helping mask the crushing force of the *mission civilisatrice* (1981:213).

If in Martinique (or Guadeloupe) identity politics is structured by a polarity (how to be at once Antillean and French), in the sister Overseas Department of Guyane it is multiplex. And if Martinique is, relatively speaking (and leaving aside the 1 per cent white planter families and 10 per cent white metropolitans) ethnically/racially/culturally homogeneous,[4] Guyane is anything but, and new immigrants (largely illegal) continue to pour in. As Kenneth Bilby has written,

> There are probably few areas of the world where one finds a more problematic fit between 'ethnic identity' and 'nationality'. . . . To say that one is 'French' often amounts to little more than a statement of legal status and economic rights in this overseas department, where a portion of the French citizenry speaks no French and has not the slightest idea where metropolitan France is (1990:93–4).

Guyane's population jumped from about 25,000 in 1945 to 55,000 in 1975 to 100,000 in 1985 and to at least 125,000 today; more than half of Guyane's population was born somewhere else. No 'ethnic group' constitutes a majority; the population is divided among Creoles of various origins (with roots in Guyane, the French Antilles, the anglophone Caribbean, Suriname, or Guyana), Haitians, metropolitan French, Maroons and Amerindians from various groups, Brazilians, Hmong, Chinese, and Levantines.[5] In this demographic context, it is not surprising that Guyane has 'become a society thoroughly preoccupied with the question of identity' (Bilby, 1990:94).

But in contrast to Martiniquans, most residents of Guyane do not pose the 'who-are-we?' question in terms of a French-Antillean dichotomy, since they have an 'ethnic' identity that is stronger than either of these – Kaliña, Brazilian, Aluku, Haitian, Hmong, and so on. Only the Creole segment of the population (about a third of the whole) finds itself in a situation at all comparable to that of Martiniquans, but because of their simultaneous monopoly of local power and less-than-majority status, their identity politics is in significant ways different.

In the late 1980s, the local legislatures of both Martinique and Guyane committed themselves to museum projects designed to represent regional identity: Martinique's Musée d'Histoire et d'Ethnographie, in a colonial building on the Boulevard du Général de Gaulle, was to feature 'furniture from Martinique and other Caribbean islands, traditional costumes, and historic paintings', and Guyane's Musée Régional, an ultra-modern ethnography museum in a suburb of Cayenne, was to portray the full cultural patrimony of that *département*. Both were scheduled to open in 1992 but because of financial crises have been put on hold. Although we are not privy to detailed information about the projected Martiniquan installations, we are – as members of the Comité Scientifique of the Guyane museum – in a position to analyze the unrealized exhibitions of that institution, in the hope of shedding light on some of the broader political and social realities that operate in the former colony that de Gaulle hoped would become 'France's show-window in America'.⁶

From the first, Guyane's Musée Régional was intimately linked to the Conseil Régional's more general project of modernization. In the local context this meant, at one and the same time, the contradictory projects of defining a true Guyanais identity (always under the French umbrella), engineering the rapid *francisation* of the more 'primitive' segments of the population (Amerindians and Maroons), and dealing with the more dispossessed groups (including recent immigrants such as Haitians, Brazilians, Hmong, and Surinamers), either by 'assimilating' them fully or expelling them outright. In other words, several simultaneous, linked, and often contradictory processes were at work in late 1980s Guyane: the ongoing steamroller of French (neo)colonialism, with its destructive bending of consciousness and identity; the attempts by the recently 'decentralized' regional government, controlled by the highly 'assimilated' Creole elite, to forge a dignified Guyanais identity within France and Europe; the joint projects of France and the local government to 'modernize' the whole of Guyane and to bring to all its citizens the full privileges of French nationality; and numerous forms of resistance, individual and collective, to these various state initiatives on the parts of targeted segments of the population. The creation of the new, modern museum – which seemed only natural in a land trying to replace its notoriety as a penal colony with an image as Europe's Space Center and home of the Ariane rocket – must be firmly situated within this complex political field.

The origins of the Musée Régional trace back to another political context as well. Its patron body, the Conseil Régional, is one of Guyane's two, roughly equal and competitive, elected assemblies, the other being the Conseil Général, which oversees the operation of Guyane's only already-functioning museum, the venerable Musée Franconie. The ambiance of this colonial institution was captured by a visiting journalist:

> A giant black caiman, varnished. A sloth with open mouth, hanging from a branch by its long nails, belly up. A howler monkey that seems to be suffering from a stomach ulcer. In a fish-bowl case, the kepi and epaulets of Governor General Felix Eboué. The fieldglass of General Pichegru. Several romantic pictures, including: *Victor Schoelcher, liberator of the slaves, on his death bed,*

by E. Decostier, gift of M. Léon Soret, Magistrate; *Rouget de Lisle singing the Marseillaise* by L. Pils, etching by Rajou; *Washington crossing the Delaware among the ice floes (winter 1776)* by Leutze. A clay caiman fashioned by the Indians. A Boni Grand Man's wooden throne, incised with the chief's insignia. The rosary that had belonged to the reverend mother Javouhey. A vertebra from a whale beached at Mana about 1876. And photographic views of the ceremonies that took place in Cayenne on the occasion of the inauguration of the statue of Governor General Felix Eboué on the first of December 1957 on the famous Place des Palmistes . . . (Doucet, 1981:102–3).

It was against the backdrop of this veritable cabinet of Guyanais curiosities that the idea first arose, among the forward-looking, development oriented, modernizing elite of Cayenne, to build a true state-of-the-art museum.

In 1988, the first 'Detailed Technical Plan' for the Musée Régional was circulated. There were outlines, diagrams, schedules, financial projections, sketches of the building and parking areas, texts of ordinances, decrees, and other fixtures of the legal armature upon which it rested, xeroxes of brochures from kindred projects already in place elsewhere on French soil, and letters from officials in the Departments of Education and Culture. Its statement of purpose was filled with italics, bold print, and capital letters, and it expressed a tone of alarm:

At the present time Guyane is a land of profound economic, social, and cultural change. For this reason, traditional ways of life are threatened . . . with . . . outright oblivion and disappearance. The transformation of ways of life . . . is taking place before our very eyes. What saves us from disaster is the . . . management of this evolution. In this sense, the knowledge and understanding of traditional cultures is not a backward-looking endeavor. On the contrary, it allows modern man to situate himself in his historical context, in his geographical region, in the context of his origins and his roots. It thus allows him to participate actively in evolution without cultural impoverishment, expanding his range of possibilities and thus his freedom. Modern man has, for example, much to learn from the way in which Amerindians or [Maroons] have intimate knowledge of the forest . . .

In Guyane, however, the situation is URGENT. The cultural goal of the museum demands rapid attention. The traditional cultures are in peril. Lifestyles, ways of speaking, languages, everyday technology, musical instruments etc., etc. . . . are on the road to oblivion. To meet the challenge, it is therefore necessary to *go fast* and *do everything at once* (SEMAGU, 1988:5–7).

The Conseil Régional moved quickly to get the project underway, appointing a director (a dynamic Creole woman with a recent doctorate from a French university), an official counsellor (a leading French museum anthropologist), and an international advisory board of scientists. Activists and other representatives of various ethnic groups from the Guyanais hinterlands were also included in the ongoing dialogues. At the same time, generous funds were appropriated for temporary offices, administrative staff, photography, data-processing, and conservation, as well as for museological collecting. By the summer of 1989, anthropologists were fanning out through the Guyanais interior to collect from various Amerindian groups, and they were joined, in 1990, by additional specialists (including ourselves) for the Maroon collecting. In 1991, a French firm was chosen, in an architectural competition, to design the new museum building.

The future museum was envisioned by its political supporters as a celebration of modern Guyanais identity. But Guyane's anomalous geo-political situation renders problematic the process of defining a 'national' identity – such as has been occurring among many of its Caribbean neighbors. After all, Guyane is not officially a 'nation', but rather a distant, strikingly multi-ethnic appendage of France, in which a small Creole elite holds nearly all the local reins of power, and in which even the awesome force of the French state (including a sizeable Foreign Legion presence) appears increasingly impotent against the massive incoming tide of illegal immigrants. Is it a possible task to celebrate, while cradled in the bosom of the Jacobin state, both multi-ethnicity *and* Guyanité?

It was not long before political leaders of each of the non-Creole groups to be included in the museum harnessed the project to their ongoing campaigns for the recognition of their group's cultural legitimacy within the Guyanais whole. The various Amerindian groups, who had formed an activist 'association' to protect their interests, stressed that *they* had no doubts about *their* identity – they'd been there from the first. Aluku Maroons, now represented in the regional government, insisted vigorously on their proud heritage as freedom-fighters and underscored their uniqueness among Maroons as longstanding *permanent* residents of Guyane. And Saramaka leaders living in Cayenne took whatever opportunities they could find to remind Guyane that their people had been productive (usually migrant) workers there for more than a century.

To cite a couple of Saramaka examples: in 1991, Ronald Pansa, a Saramaka long resident in Cayenne, helped organize a several-day visit by the mayors of Cayenne, St Laurent, and Kourou to the Saramaka heartland in central Suriname, in order to show them, he said, that 'Saramakas are neither Alukus nor Ndjukas but have a separate culture of their own', and that 'Maroon youths are not necessarily delinquents'. And more recently, as a delegate to a meeting in Kourou, he protested the government announcement that Saramakas would have to pay rent for the public housing being built to replace the shantytown 'Village Saramaka' at Kourou on the grounds of the long-standing contribution of Saramakas to Guyane's development:

> If we're to start paying rent, it *must* be applied toward the house's purchase. In 1962, when I came to Kourou, I myself shot howler monkeys out of the tree that was standing right where they've made the big BNP [Banque Nationale de Paris]! It was Saramakas who built this whole town – the bridges, the roads, the houses. Whatever plans the state makes for us now, that contribution ought to be recognized.[7]

In the game of 'clientelism' which the Creole elite plays with subordinate groups, there is considerable inter-group competition for scarce resources. And in this political context where ethnicity looms so large, is so frequently manipulated, and carries such tangible consequences, the leaders of the non-Creole groups saw the new museum as holding promise as a tool for their efforts to gain more recognition.

This promise was balanced by fears. At the initial planning meetings, various participants candidly expressed concern that the Creole bourgeoisie would dominate the enterprise; after all, they were the ones who controlled appointments, budgets, and the entire decision-making process, and they were the ones (in contrast, say, to Amerindians, Maroons, or Hmong) expressing anxieties about their cultural identity. There were discussions about how to assure fair representation of the Amerindian, Maroon, and other 'minority groups', and the acquisition of artifacts from these non-Creole populations was made an initial priority.

However, as the provisional storerooms began to fill with world-class collections of basketry, pottery, woodcarvings, and textiles from every settlement in the hinterlands, the Creole artifacts were slow to arrive. The counterparts of the *missions scientifiques* being undertaken to Indian and Maroon populations, carefully planned out to the last metal trunk, barrel of gasoline, and roll of toilet paper, were not conducted among the Creoles.[8] Instead, the director of the museum, herself a member of the urban Creole bourgeoisie, informally contacted potential donors, attended auctions of antique furniture, and thought about the collection in the rare free moments that her full-time administrative duties allowed. Among the objects she did acquire for the Creole exhibition area, few were witnesses to contemporary realities; instead, there was a strong tendency to locate Creole culture in the historic past, a culture of nostalgia located somewhere in the girlhood days of the grandmothers of present-day adults. And the objects seen as the star acquisitions for this section, the remarkable 'late eighteenth- or early nineteenth-century Creole Orchestra', carried a Suriname provenance.[9]

Yet despite the relative weakness of the Creole artifactual collections, we believe that the Creole elite was building a museum very much in their own image, one that privileged their own distinctive vision of Guyane and themselves. A visit to this *musée imaginaire* will allow some elaboration; in the following paragraphs, we write as if the latest of the numerous planning documents and architectural blueprints (dated 1991) had been realized – quoted passages are from the 1991 plans.[10]

Visitors to the Musée Régional arrive by car, passing the mammoth new high school on coastal Route D-1 and turning into a landscaped expanse, in the suburb of Remire, dominated by three modernistic buildings: the new gendarmerie, the new mairie, and the museum. Within a five-kilometer radius (as the museum prospectus points out), one can visit the historic Fort Diamant, pre-Columbian petroglyphs, the ruins of a nineteenth-century plantation, an abandoned distillery, and what remains of a wind-driven sugar mill. The museum's glass-walled structure spreads itself up the hillside on three levels, connected by interior ramps. Just outside there are full-scale examples of 'the principal types of traditional houses' of Guyane, each surrounded by its appropriate garden of medicinal and other useful plants. These gardens are complemented by another botanical space, a 'systematic' collection of plants used for pharmacological and other scientific research. And in a 'crafts village', artisans of various groups make and sell their wares. 'These various zones, well-tended and clearly marked by tasteful signs, will be connected by paths and complemented by relaxation areas.'

Through the main entrance into the spacious reception area, with its attractive museum shop, we ascend the first ramp, lined with materials for the opening theme: 'The Myth, . . . ' Guyane as the land of gold and the search for El Dorado, with antique maps of Lake Parima; Guyane as Green Hell, with travelers' engravings and texts and a pith helmet; Guyane as the land of scientific exploration illustrated by cartographic and ethnographic documents. Then comes the penal colony, 'a fertile theme for negative stereotypes of Guyane' (Devil's Island and all that). Finally, the ways in which all these themes contribute to the contemporary image of Guyane are summed up in 'adventure tourism' and 'the adventure of space'.

At the top of the ramp, we turn into a second introductory area: 'Europe "discovers" Guyane'. The master artifacts here are a polished stone axe and an eighteenth-century European trade axe. Stereotypes of 'the Indian' are evoked through early depictions and texts. Cultural exchange is represented by European trade goods, such as beads, and European borrowings from Amerindian material culture: pottery, crops, and techniques of food processing. And then, using the Jesuit relations and travel literature, there is an evocation of the destructive effects of the Europeans' arrival on Amerindian culture and society. Another theme of this 'Discovery' section is the slave trade and slavery, but the 1991 plans give no information on the objects, texts, or images that would evoke this phase of Guyanais history.

We now 'leave the introductory areas behind and are led into those that present the different cultures of Guyane, in terms of their own histories as well as their place in a shared history'.

First, 'Amerindian Cultures': this large exhibit space begins with an archeological section showing the main types of pottery and lithic materials made by the various groups through time. The master artifact is a cast of a massive rock with petroglyphs. Then, acknowledging both shared and unique cultural traits, aspects of contemporary life among the various Amerindian groups are featured. Material techniques and division of labor are illustrated by women's ceramics and men's basketry. 'Social organization' covers the family, rites of passage, the village space ('with models of a Wayampi or Wayana village in its forest environment'), and domestic spaces. A section on cosmology deals with shamanism, ethnomedicine, and myths. Amerindian esthetics are illustrated by Wayana feather arts, by various kinds of music (with audio-visuals), and the application of Kaliña esthetic ideas in various media.

We next enter a small room exploring relations between 'People and the Forest', with principal focus on Amerindians: hunting and fishing along the rivers (eighteenth-century zoological engravings and various types of bows, arrows, and traps) and swidden agriculture (focusing on manioc and including a video on horticultural techniques).

Then into the 'Maroon Cultures' area where a slide show introduces the history of the various groups. Texts and images evoke their diverse African origins and the brutality of slavery on the Suriname plantations from which their ancestors escaped. Maroon economic life and material culture are viewed historically, with stress on the combination of African and Amerindian influences and the early westernization of Maroons in the New World. Photos and objects present social, political, and spiritual life, and explore African influences. The largest section covers Maroon art history, using objects made by men and women in different media to illustrate stylistic changes since the eighteenth century, and the role of artistic production in social life. A final area clarifies both shared and divergent aspects of culture among the various Maroon groups: diet, dress, dance, tale-telling, art, religious practices, and the gender-based division of labor.[11]

Along another ramp to the museum's upper level, we arrive at 'La Guyane Créole'. The master artifact for this four-room area is a stringed instrument from the museum's late eighteenth- or early nineteenth-century 'Creole orchestra'. This object is said to 'embody the various aspects of the culture under formation during the plantation era, which was marked by a double, ambiguous dynamic that characterizes the process of creolization: an affirmation on the part of the slaves of a cultural identity of their own and the full weight of the colonial system, which together lead to the quest for the kind of cultural assimilation that can open the door to upward social mobility'. The first section is devoted to life on the *habitation*, showing – through documents, pottery, and other archeological remains – three plantations of different scale, character, and crops. Here, emphasis is on contesting traditional historiographic images of a rigid hierarchical order; we are told, for example, that some of 'the earliest colonists, often poor, lived under conditions that were scarcely better than those of their slaves'.

For an evocation of life in Cayenne at the end of the eighteenth century, we move into a small enclosed space housing a relief map of the city and an audio-visual show 'stressing the African and European, and to a lesser extent the Amerindian, sources of Creole culture'. The final and largest part of the Creole exhibit covers the 1880s to the 1920s, 'the crucible in which today's Creole culture took shape'. First comes the nineteenth-century gold rush, 'evoked by photographs, press clippings, novels, and film posters, leading into the present-day Brazilian *garimperos*' dreams of venturing to Guyane, the new Eldorado', plus a brief sketch of the 'micro-culture of prospectors'. Next, 'Le Bagne' – 'a light evocation of the penal colony by means of the convicts' crafts production: painted plates, decorated objects, drawings, etc.'

And finally, 'Creole Culture', showing everyday life in Cayenne and the rural towns at the beginning of the twentieth century by means of '1/20 scale models of the principal types of Creole architecture'. Costumes illustrate social hierarchies within the Creole population. Creole furniture and musical instruments complete this area, demonstrating 'the formation of an original culture out of an initial African base, the integration of various historical influences, and a movement toward assimilation to a dominant European model in a colonial context'.

The penultimate exhibition room is devoted to 'Transplanted Cultures: the Hmong Example'. To exemplify that part of the present-day Guyanais population 'who are bearers of cultures radically different from those long established on this soil, and who face the double challenge of socio-economic integration into a for-them foreign milieu and the maintenance of their cultural identity', there are displays centering on Hmong ironwork and costume.

Finally, what is billed by the museum planners as a 'surprise-filled conclusion': 'The Guyane of Today'. The recent history of Guyane is evoked by 'a genuine piece of an Ariane rocket, supplied by the Space Center'. And then, in an attempt to balance the dual cultural processes of ongoing metissage and ethnic resistance to creolization, the museum presents exhibits of Cayenne's famous Carnival (featuring recent Brazilian costumes) and 'arts with foreign cultural influence: locally made Haitian paintings, Saramaka woodcarvings, and Brazilian crafts', and an evocation (whose details had not yet been developed in the latest plan) of Amerindian resistance to the 'cultural metissage that will mark the Guyane of tomorrow'.

The abstract statements-of-intent by the organizers of this museum (which, they stress, was 'born of the collective will of a people and its elected representatives' [Collomb and Jean-Louis, 1989:2]) are thorough, intellectually sophisticated, and politically aware. Conscientiously striving to 'go beyond folklore', they declare that

> The Musée Régional will not be a mere repository for nostalgic but sterile dreams about Guyane's past. It can become a veritable tool with which a population can understand and reappropriate its history and identity, encompassing its diverse ethnic components and considered in all its historical depth, including even the most contemporary developments (1989:3, 11).

But between the formulation of these intellectual goals and the concrete plans for exhibition spaces, a certain amount of slippage seems to have taken place. Let's retrace our walk-through to see how this has happened.

The museum site lies outside of the city in a comfortable suburb reachable only by car. When we raised the problem of its accessibility to people without private transportation, we were told flatly that 'everyone in Cayenne has a car'. Considering that the Maroons and Amerindians who are contributing their art and material culture to the enterprise are more likely to own a dugout canoe than a car, this aspect of the museum plan suggests the wisdom of Pierre Bourdieu's remark that 'the true function of museums is to reinforce for some the feeling of belonging and for others the feeling of being excluded' (Bourdieu and Darbel, 1969:165). The entire edifice of the Musée Régional – from its location, architectural splendor, and land-scaping to its crafts village, auditorium, and cloakroom – seems to have been designed as a monument to the cultural identity that its organizers really care about projecting to the world, a show-window for France in the Americas.

Despite the museum organizers' programmatic disclaimers, the actual exhibits are permeated with a celebratory tone: evocations of a memory-culture that effectively masks current change and turmoil; the relegation of contemporary immigrant groups to folkloric manifestations; the white-washing of violence and terror in slavery and the penal colony; and a near-total silence about the phenomenon of colonialism. Glissant's per-spective, already mentioned, helps explain how a museum thus conceived so perfectly serves the interests of the Creoles: in the French Caribbean, he reminds us, official 'cultural activity . . . comes to carry political stakes. . . . The provisions of Plan VIII for the Overseas Departments and Territories (1980) underscore "the importance of cultural politics for law and order" ', and '*le culturel*' (including museums, 'folklore' and the search for 'authenticity') may easily become a veiled means of oppression, even when it remains 'totally alienating and alienated' (1981:168–70).

From the museum's two introductory areas through to the final Ariane rocket chunk, power relations between colonizers and colonized are soft-pedaled. The master artifacts for the 'Discovery' area are axes of stone and steel, objects chosen to emphasize 'the distance separating the two cultures'. But with a different political sensibility mightn't they rather have been an Amerindian bow-and-arrow and a European musket? Most remarkably, there is not a single reference to the fact that colonization was carried out by the French; instead, responsibility for everything from the introduction of new diseases among Amerindians to the establishment of slavery is attributed to genericized 'Europeans'. Social and economic programs undertaken by the French state, most recently the aggressive *francisation*, which has effectively transformed the lives of Alukus and Amerindians, are never mentioned.

In a similar vein, the brutality of slavery is relegated wholesale to the neighboring colony of Suriname. Slavery in Guyane is presented in distinctly gentler terms, with emphasis on the significant presence of free blacks and mulattos, and of small-scale 'European' cultivators who were valiantly struggling to build a new life and to make ends meet in a harsh new environment. The objects highlighted in the plantation section are pottery and a Creole stringed instrument allegedly made by an eighteenth-century slave; there is no mention of chains, iron collars, or other instruments of discipline and control.

For comparison, it may be useful to evoke a recent museological parallel in Germany, a country with almost no involvement in the Atlantic slave trade or in colonial America. *Afrika in Amerika*, a temporary exhibit at the Hamburgisches Museum für Völkerkunde. Covering, in the curator's words 'the culture no one is fond of', the exhibition managed to balance a celebration of African contributions (from exhibits on Trinidad Carnival and Brazilian Umbanda to a photomontage of such US African Americans as Zora Neale Hurston, Arthur Ashe, Duke Ellington, Martin Luther King, Jr., Wilma Rudolph, James Baldwin, Michael Jackson, and Whoopi Goldberg) with a representation of the long history of oppression (via recreations of African slave factories and a New World slave market, exhibits on neck rings and whipping posts, and allusions to political turmoil in contemporary Haiti). Yet its relatively unblinking depiction of the hardships and horrors of New World slavery was conveyed largely through materials about Hamburg's Significant Other, Denmark, and focused on the moral crusade against slavery in the Danish colonies led by a prominent Hamburger, H.C. Schimmelmann (Raddatz, 1992).[12]

Back in the Musée Régional, the penal colony, until recently the uncontested symbol of Guyane to the outside world, is given only a bit part, which focuses delicately on 'the convicts' craft production'. There is no attempt to convey the institution's raison-d'être, its internal organization, or the lived experience of its inmates. A visitor's guide to Guyane, endorsed by the president of the Conseil Régional, states the perspective somewhat more bluntly than do the museum documents: the prison system is a shame to be exorcised.

> The emblem of the *bagne*, a man in prison stripes with manacled feet – that's what we would like to make our visitors forget. . . . Recently, the prison . . . has been taken over by local authorities, who plan to turn it into a recreation center and museum. What better way to exorcise a cursed past than to embrace it! (*Destination Guyane*, 1991:86–8; local rumor had it that the 'recreation center' was to be run by the Club Med.)

In the representation of Guyane's 'transplanted cultures', the decision to spotlight the Hmong is particularly revealing. This group was brought to Guyane 'benevolently' as part of an international resettlement program in the late 1970s, and it lives communally in two new rural settlements isolated from other populations. The Hmong carry on distinct, and from a Western perspective, picturesque cultural traditions; they dress in colorful ethnic costumes, and interact with Guyane's elite largely in the market, where they provide them with the finest in fresh fruits and vegetables. In short, the Hmong seem tailor-made for a museological vitrine.

But more important, the choice of the Hmong allows the museum to sidestep what may be the most pressing social problem facing Guyane today: massive illegal immigration, largely by Haitians, Brazilians, and Surinamers. During the past decade, as the wave of immigrants crested, Creoles have become increasingly apprehensive. Nearly all these immigrants are poor, barely literate, and non-French-speaking: the antithesis of everything most Creoles idealize. There is a strong sense, both in the capital and in outlying communes, of a loss of control. During a 1990 visit, Prime Minister Michel Rocard tried hard 'to calm the fears of the population, and especially of the local [Creole] politicians', pointing out that 'with 2,400 people escorted to the borders in 1988, Guyane was the leading *département* of France in this regard'. But in the same speech he had to admit that actual 'clandestine immigration is probably ten times this figure. Although Guyane is vast and underpopulated', he went on, 'it should not be made any more responsible than the rest of France for welcoming the flotsam and jetsam of its poor neighbors' (*Libération*, 9 April 1990). And he promised help. In mid-1992, the French military command in Guyane was strengthened, according to official explanations not only to better protect the European Space Center but in particular to fortify the borders with Brazil and Suriname.

Additional Foreign Legion and regular army troops were flown in to what was already a heavily militarized environment.

Today, the crime section of Guyane's major newspaper regularly highlights the activities of new immigrants. All four articles on 4 November 1992, for example, concerned people said to be *en situation irrégulière* ('illegals'): the knifing of one Brazilian by two others in Kourou; the arrest of two Brazilian canoemen for smuggling seventeen compatriots over the eastern border; the arrest of a Brazilian for stealing a motorcycle; and a complex story, recounted with dripping sarcasm, about a Haitian arrested for the triple crime of trying to build his house (in Remire, not far from the new museum site) without a building permit, using undocumented (illegal immigrant) laborers, and making use of materials stolen from the site of the new *lycée* under construction.[13]

Once again, despite the museum planners' programmatic intentions, an opportunity to engage the realities of contemporary Guyane has been declined in favor of a picturesque folkloric display. The final area of the exhibition space, 'The Guyane of Today', features, in addition to its chunk of rocket, Haitians, Brazilians, and Surinamers – the very populations that were left unmentioned in the 'Transplanted Cultures' area. But what are we shown? The enrichment of Guyane's cultural life through pretty Brazilian crafts and carnival costumes, colorful Haitian paintings, and decorative Maroon woodcarvings.

At the same moment, far across the southern Caribbean, in the new nation of Belize a similarly grandiose museum project was taking shape. The projected Museum of Belize, designed by Mexican and Cuban architects, is twice the size of Guyane's Musée Régional. We propose a brief detour to examine the politics of its exhibit strategies – particularly in regard to its handling of ethnic diversity – as a way of casting into relief the choices made in Guyane. A bit of background may be useful.[14]

Belize has much in common with Guyane: less than two hundred thousand people; one of the lowest population densities in the world; an extraordinarily rich ethnic and linguistic mix; a sizeable and diverse set of recent immigrant groups; abundant forest and marine resources; significant potential for eco-tourism; an important role as conduit in the international drug trade; and a strong colonial heritage.

But this young nation, independent from Great Britain since 1981, differs sharply from Guyane not only in its political status but in its relative poverty, its lack of 'development', and its strong cultural ties to both the Central America/Caribbean region and the United States. While Guyane's thick umbilical cord to France effectively precludes relations, whether economic or cultural, with its neighbors in the Americas (other than its sister Départements d'Outre-Mer of Martinique and Guadeloupe), Belize is proudly oriented toward the New World. Bombarded with North American mass culture, from satellite-dished television to all the consumer products (including cars and trucks) that can simply be driven down through Mexico, Belizeans have made the United States their primary destination abroad. Compared to the relative orderliness of Guyane, Belize has something of the air of a rough-and-ready frontier society.

Its projected national museum reflects these realities. 'Zap! Wham! Boom! As you go up the grand staircase, the whole chaos of Belize explodes in your face, Bam!' Artist Joan Duran, who has been described as 'a kind of transvanguardist of abstraction, setting alight the arsenal of modern forms and gestures' (Fox, 1991), is the indisputable creative force behind the museum project. 'Every tourist book', he goes on, 'says "Belize is a nation the size of Massachusetts, a land of perfect harmony among its ethnic groups – Mayans, Creoles, Mestizos, British, Hindus, Garifunas ['Black Caribs'], and Mennonites." I say, "Fuck the size of the state of Massachusetts!"' And he launches into an impassioned defense of why the notion of ethnicity will have no place in the MOB's exhibits: 'It's fine to know that people have different ways of doing things', he argues – 'some people shoot each other from the back and others do it from the front' – but, he affirms, it's counterproductive to constantly label people by ethnic identity. That kind of 'tribalism' works against the national good, he insists, and the MOB is being put together in the interests of tolerance and nation-building.[15]

The MOB plans are profoundly informed by Duran's artistic and political vision. When he described his dream to us in 1993, veering from movie, video and comic-book metaphors (panning, zooming, fast-forwarding, zapping) to the re-creation of the social warmth of the 'casinos' of his native Cataluña (where, in his youth, he'd go to relax, play dominos, or drink a coke with friends), the idea of 'collections' rarely came up. The MOB is unblinkingly non-elitist: just like the Mexico City subway, Duran explained, where many people are not literate, the museum will use symbols more than labels to help visitors find their way. Indeed, in their more radical moments, planners contemplated banishing all texts from the museum, leaving only images; textual information would in any case be available in a CD-ROM archive accessible to those visitors who sought it out. And when visitors left the MOB they would be able to take home with them a personalized video cassette of their visit which they'd put together themselves, using devices Duran was installing with the financial and technical help of his friend, Francis Ford Coppola.

The idea for the MOB was first broached to the Minister of Education only a week after Independence. With encouragement from the government, led by the People's United Party, Duran took the helm and began exploring museological ideas with colleagues in Mexico and Cuba. There were ups and downs during the mid-1980s as the opposition came to power, but when the PUP returned in 1989, Duran was named Ambassador Extraordinaire and began raising funds and support for the MOB through his international contacts.

There were strong ideological tie-ins between the creation of the MOB and the revamping of the new nation's schoolbooks and curriculum, which had been British until Independence, then Jamaican, and were now being made proudly Belizean. There were to be practical tie-ins as well: Duran told us that a law would require every school to bring its pupils to the MOB twice a year. 'To pass their exams', he added, 'they'll have to visit even more frequently, and each time they'll bring along a parent or other adult who's never been before'.

In contrast to the pristine orderliness of the Guyane museum plans, with each ethnic group in its assigned space, the MOB deliberately projects a vision of chaos. As visitors enter the exhibition space, they find themselves surrounded by light, sound, and images, as Duran describes: 'busy streets, deforestation, Chinese immigrants, crack dealers, Belizeans abroad, contradictions between what politicians are saying and what they're doing, wanted posters for pot-hunters, some archeological fakes'. This postmodern montage assaults visitors with statistics, floods them with demographics (a giant fiber-optic map flashes population figures through time), and shakes up their certainties with a barrage of misconceptions. 'We love to believe our own lies,' says Duran's friend and fellow intellectual Assad Shoman, and the exhibit, in which communication and the production of knowledge are foregrounded (telephones from different decades, disorderly piles of theses and government reports), in part forces visitors to come to grips with this truth.

Again in contrast to Guyane, the MOB doesn't shy away from social criticism and controversy. One major exhibit is devoted to 'The Class of '79 at St Mary's School'. Beginning with yearbook pictures, it follows up on each person's life since graduation, painting a devastating picture of the ways the lack of productive opportunities in Belize have led to migration to the US, involvement with drugs and crime, and a shockingly low survival rate. Nation-building is envisioned as a process that needs both constructive and critical reflection.

The PUP's vision of the role of ethnicity in nation-building runs through the entire MOB. In various parts of the building, on grillwork above the visitor, there are some 25 black-and-white photoportraits showing different Belizean 'types' (Mayan, Garifuna, Creole, Mennonite . . .). But each time, they are juxtaposed differently. The cumulative effect is intended to be kaleidoscopic, with the varying arrangement of faces symbolizing the transcendent unity of the Belizean people.

The exhibit on migrations, which forms an important conceptual module, is designed to demonstrate that *all* Belizeans arrived as immigrants (whether walking across the Bering Straits, chained in the hold of a slaver, fleeing the Caste War in nineteenth-century Yucatan, carried on a ship bringing indentured laborers from India, or escaping from the ongoing civil war in El Salvador) and that all, therefore, should be treated with tolerance and respect. The idea, for example, that Garifuna or Maya are 'indigenous' is explicitly rejected. 'My Belizean passport is as old as any in the world', Duran remarks with feeling. As in the repeated kaleidoscopic mélanges of faces, the migrations area combines physical/ethnic diversity and universal moral values: this exhibit space is topped with angled mirrors reflecting yet another photo-montage of Belizean physical types, which incorporates the reflected image of the upward-gazing visitor.

In the MOB, Belize's nation-building is envisioned as an active process involving all citizens. The focus is on the present and future, on people working together to forge a nation from diverse parts, in a cooperative, democratic effort. PUP ideologists choose to promote national unity through a strategy that soft-pedals the attribution of meaning to ethnic, linguistic, and phenotypic diacritics, which they view as a legacy of colonialism. The balance is delicate: Minister of Education Said Musa has written that 'We seek to promote a culture of freedom . . . a culture that stresses national community,' and that 'our cultural diversity should serve as a strength, not a recipe for racial stereotypes.' But his associate Assad Shoman, Chairperson of the Belize Arts Council, has cautioned that 'The quest for "unity" can be misleading, can lead to the imposition of uniformity, of conformity . . . Let freedom ring, let diversity reign, let creation flourish' (both cited in *Prospect*, 1992:4–5). A new Belizean schoolbook sums up the central message, under the banner of 'Culture and Sovereignty':

> Culture gives a nation its identity . . . [and] culture is also constantly being created by the people. Belize has its own rich culture which includes the heritage of the different ethnic groups of Belize. . . . For much of our history, the natural interaction of cultures which co-exist within one community was inhibited by the colonial policy of divide and rule, which ensured that our various cultures remained largely isolated from, and suspicious of, each other, and that the colonizer's culture remained dominant. An essential part of the decolonization process must therefore be the elimination of all colonially inherited prejudices about each other's cultures.
>
> The historical origins of our people and the more recent influences upon our culture have produced diversity. Out of this diversity we must seek unity, while recognizing the value of our different customs and traditions. . . . The Belizean culture will

develop out of this struggle. . . . Only when the people determine
and create their own culture is sovereignty assured (*History*,
1987:73).

On the same day that Duran explained how the MOB would avoid any
mention of ethnicity, we asked one of his employees how to find a route-
taxi for the several-mile return to our hotel. 'You need a Benque-based
taxi,' he told us. We asked how we could recognize a Benque taxi. 'There's
only one way,' he said. 'Look for a driver who's a Mestizo, not a Creole.
Otherwise you'll pay three times the price.' The next day we told the story
to Duran, suggesting that ethnic labeling might be more important in his
home town of Benque Viejo, a Mestizo community near the Guatemalan
border, than he liked to admit. He looked pensive and then thought of a way
to put our remark to the test. Calling over his long-time cook, Toñita, he
asked whether she had felt discriminated against when she first arrived
from Guatemala. 'Not just then,' she replied with feeling, 'I still am –
especially by the *negritos*.' And she recounted a recent incident in which
she and her children had been made to disembark from a bus by some
aggressive Creoles.

But for Duran and his peers, the emergence from colonialism and the
challenge of Belizean nation-building require transcending the phenotypical,
linguistic, and ethnic divisions that continue to operate in everyday life. The
MOB, at every turn, supports this soft-pedaling of difference, by constantly
mixing, scrambling, and recombining images in a Benetton-like aesthetic.

The elections of June 1993 brought an abrupt end to the MOB, just as
ground was about to be broken for the massive building. With the PUP now
in the opposition, Duran has returned to his canvases with the faint hope
that some day the project will be revived. Today, the grassy site in Belmopan
lies as empty and forlorn as its counterpart outside Cayenne. For the
moment, both the MOB and Musée Régional remain *musées imaginaires*.

Problems of nation-building in the Caribbean may be seen in another recent
museum space – *Sranan, Cultuur in Suriname*, a temporary exhibit at the
Rotterdam Museum voor Volkenkunde (van Binnendijk and Faber, 1992).
Officially opened by Suriname's First Lady, it represented the first
museological attempt at a cultural overview of Suriname since that nation's
independence in 1975. Adopting a deliberately celebratory tone, its explicit
intent was to counterbalance mass media reports in the Netherlands that
linked immigrant Surinamers with drugs and poverty, and Surinamers at
home with civil war and violence. Like the Musée Régional and the MOB,
its most challenging dilemma was how to portray at once ethnic difference
and national identity. Rotterdam's solution was to divide the exhibit in two:
first the cultural traditions of Suriname's various population segments and
then the national (shared) culture.

The exhibit-makers were able, in the large first section, to present each of five 'traditional' cultures through a major life-cycle rite – a Wayana initiation ceremony, a Maroon funeral, a Hindu wedding, a Javanese circumcision ritual, and a Creole birthday party – using mannequins, audio/ visual devices, objects, and graphics. But they found themselves stymied, according to curator Paul Faber, when they tried to figure out the national culture (modern, non-ethnically specific) part of the exhibition. First, they thought about the 'modern' equivalents of the rituals they'd chosen for the 'ethnic' exhibits, but soon realized that even among urban Surinamers, marriages, funerals, and so on continue to be carried out according to 'ethnic traditions'. And much of what they initially seized on as national culture turned out upon closer examination to be ethnically Creole. Unable to locate shared Suriname culture satisfactorily, they finally settled on a small exhibit area centered on a film about street life – scenes of the market, public transportation, Paramaribo stores and houses, all with a bustling mix of ethnicities, languages, and dress. The camera scans piles of vegetables in the market, majorettes cavorting, people at a dance – cheery nostalgia-making for Surinamers in the Netherlands but something of a colorful sideshow when set next to the rather grim realities of present-day Suriname. This exhibition, like the Republic of Suriname itself, was not quite able to come up with a museum representation that matched the words of the late Suriname poet Dobru: 'one tree, so many leaves . . . *wan pipel.*'[16]

Still focusing on museums, how might developments in Caribbean nation-states, such as Belize, shed light on cultural representations in France's overseas *départements*? The nationalist impulse stresses the present and future, the ongoing process of creating a new, shared culture – and this implies an ideological muting of various kinds of difference. Unlike Guyane (where the French model reigns supreme, and *assimilation* or exclusion are the only real-life options for people living within its borders), and in contrast as well to a plural society, multi-ethnic, or multi-cultural federation model (where tolerance is supposed to be based on appreciation of difference [perhaps like Suriname in the early 1970s?]), Belize actively encourages its citizens to focus on collective efforts to create a national culture. Along the hypothetical continuum that runs from erasing diversity to celebrating it (and where Guyane chooses the former 'on the ground' and the latter in its museum cases), the makers of the MOB take a middle path – recognizing its existence as a historical artifact but at the same time trying to contain its divisive potential. If in Guyane, France is imposing a cultural conformity that reduces ethnic difference to folklore, Belize is attempting, with some delicacy, to create national unity while treading on as few ethnic toes as possible. A gradual and 'natural' diminution of difference, as the new nation creates itself through time, seems more in line with the MOB ideology than the aggressive uniformization being engineered in Guyane.

The assimilationist thrust of the French state relegates difference to a historical past; and within the broader process of modernization and development in contemporary Guyane, 'residual' ethnic difference is most conveniently treated in ballet-folklorico fashion. In the Creoles' quest for an articulated identity, there are strong incentives, provided by their former colonizers and current cultural mentors, to emulate a European-authored model; their access to local power, recognition, and success has to a great extent been built on their mastery of skills and values defined and legitimized in Paris – life style, dress, ways of speaking, and leisure activities. If, as many people have suggested, Africans visiting displays of their cultural life at the American Museum of Natural History feel discomfort at being located somewhere between the bugs and the dinosaur bones, urban Creoles in Guyane surely could have ambivalent feelings about having their everyday lives represented alongside barebreasted Indians and 'Bush Negroes' of the tropical rain forest.

The conception of the Musée Régional perfectly satisfies these concerns. Conceived in the tradition of the venerable Musée de l'Homme in Paris, this project was in some ways custom-made to receive the stuff of exotic lifeways and to present it to worldly, French-educated museum visitors. Wayana fish traps, Aluku manioc spatulas, Kaliña feathered headdresses, and Saramaka pubic aprons all fit comfortably within traditional museum spaces; there is no question of whose culture is in and whose is out. Even after the fast-paced changes of the 1980s, the material cultures of Maroon and Amerindian populations could still be considered relatively adaptable to a view of anthropology museums as environments that delineate and display distinct cultural identities, with glass cases that keep the exotic and historical inside and the familiar and contemporary outside – lower-cased cultures in and upper-cased Culture out. Modern Creole visitors to such a museum would have no reason to feel uncomfortable ambiguities about their identity.

Another venue in Cayenne may help highlight the selectivity of the vision behind the Musée Régional – the '*Foire des Foires*', an extensive Trade and Crafts Fair we visited in 1992. Billed in the press as a celebration of local artisans, it featured boxes of precious woods turned on lathes, dolls in madras costume, jewelry made from Amazonian gold and gems, Saramaka woodcarvings, antique bottles, Amerindian baskets, Brazilian flower pots, souvenir rum bottles (which the artisan/salesman offered to personalize with our names, but which were already embellished with photos of tropical flowers, river rapids, a Creole woman, and an Ariane), 'Galibi' (Amerindian) clothing (sold by Creoles), scale-models of the entrance to the penal colony's *Camp de la Transportation*, iron driveway gates, jars of local honey, Creole-style furniture, framed butterflies and hairy spiders, as well as displays of Nissan and Renault pickup trucks and solar power panels. Two booths in particular captured our attention: the *Centre d'Esthétique Corporelle* and a locally-crafted four-poster bed. The purpose of the Body Esthetics Center was announced by a placard promising a technique that went 'well beyond mere slimming techniques' by means of 'full body architecture', and illustrating its claim by a large photo of a happy young white woman whose nude body was bound at several points by rubberized bands and whose hands were holding the controls of an electronic computer-like machine. The canopied four-poster was decorated in an antique nautical theme. Ship's wheels were carved into headboard and footboard, the latter with a clock inset in the middle. The draw-string curtains, in a polyester colonial print, were operated by cords ending in carved wooden handles. A double tape deck and AM-FM stereo were built into the headboard and a remote-control color television into the footboard. The top of the canopy was acoustically padded, with the TV antenna perched on top and the wiring discreetly set into grooves in the woodwork. Wings on the two sides of the headboard held swiveling bedside tables with lampshaded fixtures. The TV was set to a channel offering parimutuel tips on French horses seven thousand kilometers away.

If, as at least one tourist brochure claims, Guyane is best understood as 'a fascinating mixture of tradition and modernity, a painful past and a sparkling future' (*Destination Guyane*, 1991:56), who is to say that the relatively unfiltered selection of objects in the *Foire des Foires* doesn't represent Guyane's realities more fully than the meticulously programmed Musée Régional?

In this broader context, we would suggest that the projected Musée Régional might best be seen as a politically progressive stage (or cage or cemetery) for the celebration of colorful ethnic difference just at the moment when the state is bringing its full force to bear on the elimination of such difference through the militantly assimilationist program of *francisation*.[17] It offers Creoles who are uncomfortable with the idea of Maroons, Brazilians, or Haitians living next door (or entering their living rooms except as servants) a way to promote the cultural contributions of these people to Guyane's multi-ethnicity. And it provides a supremely elegant resting place for ethnic and cultural difference.

Notes

1. An earlier version of this chapter was presented at the conference 'Ethnicity, ideology, and colonial legacy in the Caribbean', organized by John Hawkins in December 1992, at Brigham Young University. This chapter forms part of a larger project funded by the National Endowment for the Humanities, the John Simon Guggenheim Foundation, and

the Wenner-Gren Foundation for Anthropological Research, to all of which we express our gratitude. Parts of this chapter are reprinted by permission from the *American Anthropologist* 97(1) 1995, and *Museum Anthropology* 18(2) 1994:3–15 (not for further reproduction).

2. Alongside these idealized recreations of the good old days of not so long ago, generally depicted as a timeless and ahistorical moment, one finds in Martinique another mode of institutionalized historical nostalgia – restorations of elegant eighteenth-century planta-tion houses, filled with period furniture. It may be worth noting that there is very little information provided, in either the '1950s' or the eighteenth-century exhibits, about the social relations of production – the fact that most work in both periods was agricultural gang labor (whether by slaves or waged men and women). Nor is colonialism more than a discreet backdrop in either context. The 1950s exhibits, ostensibly depicting the domes-tic economy, focus on such activities as household food processing and artisanal produc-tion. And the eighteenth-century restorations portray leisured life in the great house. Both stress contentment and provide privileged sites for collective nostalgia.

3. For discussion both of changes in Martiniquan ideas about 'race' during this period and the denial by people today that there ever was a time when Fanon's (1967) descriptions held true, see R. Price (1995b).

4. We are stressing *relative* homogeneity. Partisans of '*créolité*', such as Raphaël Confiant and Patrick Chamoiseau, would rather insist (against Afro-centrists or -centrists of what-ever stripe) on the diversity of the Martiniquan population's historical roots (see Bernabé, Chamoiseau and Confiant 1989, whose first epigraph reads '*C'est par la différence et dans le divers que s'exalte l'Existence*'). And for them this translates into an insistence on diversity in the present. During a debate broadcast in part on TV (25 September 1993), Confiant claimed proudly to have grown up among '*békés, chabins, milats*, and *koulis*'. But anyone with comparative experience in the Americas (and especially in such places as Guyane, Belize, or Suriname, which we have in mind in this paper) would be hard pressed to see the Martinique in which Confiant grew up as very differentiated ethnically, racially, or culturally. Indeed, in that same TV program, Chamoiseau argued forcefully (and more to the point, in our view) that what makes Martiniquans a people is what they share: their '*imaginaire*', the world of their collective imagination.

5. Accurate population breakdowns for Guyane are hard to come by – in part because the metropolitan French, whose presence is rapidly increasing, are not separately classified in the census, much of the recent immigration from neighboring countries is clandestine, and little effort is made to count the numerous Maroons along the Maroni. The rough 'ethnic' breakdown would now be something like the following: 'true' Guyanais Creoles 35 per cent, Haitians 19 per cent, metropolitan French 10 per cent, Maroons (Saramakas, Ndjukas, Alukus, Paramakas) 10 per cent, Brazilians 10 per cent, Creoles with roots in the French Antilles 4 per cent, Amerindians 3 per cent, Hmong 3 per cent, Creoles with roots in the Anglophone Caribbean 2 per cent, Chinese 2 per cent, Suriname Creoles 1 per cent, Levantines 1 per cent, and Guyanese (from Guyana) 1 per cent.

6. Readers interested in further background about the state of culture and society in Guyane, as well as the Musée Régional, are referred to R. and S. Price, 1992.

7. Pansa told us that at this same meeting at Kourou, an Amerindian leader said his people categorically refused to pay any rent at all for the new houses. They were willing to pay for electricity, which was supplied by the French, but not for the land. The land had been theirs long before the French came along, and God (not the French) put it there for them to build houses. (For an analogous discourse among Alukus in St Laurent, see Bilby, 1990:640.)

8. A 1989 planning document excuses the difference in collecting strategies among Creoles and other groups by invoking the 'demographic vastness and sociocultural complexity of

the multiple Creole communities, in contrast to the relatively homogeneous, small-scale' character of the other groups (Collomb and Jean-Louis, 1989:9). And the museum planners have insisted, in various of their documents, on the 'complex and shifting sociopolitical cleavages' within Creole society (see 'Faire un musée', 1990:13).

9. On the origins of these instruments, see R. and S. Price, 1995a.

10. Our understanding of the modus operandi leading to these plans is that Gérard Collomb, the French museum ethnologist who served as advisor to the project, coordinated input from the Comité Scientifique, in close consultation with the director, Marie-Paule Jean-Louis. Members of the Committee, which never met as a body, included: Pierre and Françoise Grenand (French anthropological specialists on Guyane's Amerindians), Marie-José Jolivet (French sociological specialist on Creole society), Arthur Othily and Jean Michotte (local sociologist and economist, respectively), and ourselves.

11. For a discussion of our own involvement in the planning of the Musée Régional – our original art historically oriented plan for the Maroon section, our revised, more *engagé* version, and the less than enthusiastic response it received from other museum planners – see R. and S. Price, 1994.

12. Curator Corinna Raddatz explained this emphasis in terms of the close historical ties between Hamburg and its Baltic neighbor, also noting that today many Copenhagen women come over to Hamburg to shop (a half-hour by plane) and Germans frequently vacation in Denmark. But we would underline the political convenience of this exhibition strategy. In this regard, it may also be worth pointing out that in the Hamburg photomural depicting jazz greats, writers, movie stars, and a plethora of American athletes, from Wilma Rudolph to Mohammad Ali, the only two who hold special meaning for Germans are conspicuously absent: the meteor of the 1936 Berlin Olympics, Jesse Owens, and the vanquisher of that paragon of Aryan manhood, Max Schmeling, the Brown Bomber himself, Joe Louis.

13. The article failed to mention that the largest French construction companies in Guyane also employ undocumented laborers on a regular basis – for example, hiring a Saramaka who has a work permit at 310 F for a ten-hour day and asking him to bring along eight or ten undocumented compatriots, for each of whom he will be slipped 150 F per day in his pay envelope.

14. For more detailed discussion of the MOB project, including its abandonment following the elections of 30 June 1993, see R. and S. Price, 1995b.

15. Duran and other PUP ideologues chide their party leader George Price for the 'one of each' mentality that made him want each 'ethnic group' of Belize to have a room of its own in the museum. During the Duke of Kent's visit to Belize, Duran scoffs, the government actually had six bouquets of flowers presented by little girls who represented six ethnicities – a colorfully-bloused Mayan, a blond Mennonite, a dusky Garifuna, and so on. And for the same reason, Duran and his political allies are opposed to Garifuna or Maya efforts to introduce their languages into the school curriculum.

16. Museums are but one context for the playing out of this central tension. In answering charges of human rights violations against its ethnic minorities before the Inter-American Court for Human Rights in 1992, the Government of Suriname argued that considerations of national unity must take precedence over the protection of ethnic difference. For details, see R. Price, 1995a.

It is worth noting too that the *Sranan* exhibition went very far toward treating '*Bosnegers*' (Maroons) as a single ethnic group, equivalent to 'Javanese' or 'Hindustanis'. Although, in the 'Amerindian' portion of the exhibit, some care was taken to make clear that the featured Wayana were but one of several local Amerindian cultures, the label texts in the Maroon area presented the various Maroon peoples (Ndjukas, Saramakas, Paramakas, and so forth) as if they had a fully shared 'culture'. Needless to say, this conflation is also in the interests of the modern state.

17. Germain Bazin makes the point more generally: 'The museum is an institution which feeds on the used forms of life; the Musée des Souverains of Napoleon III and Emperor Franz Joseph's Schatzkammer were created to justify monarchy at the very moment it was about to perish. . . . With the draining of the Zuider Zee a whole regional culture dependent on fishing disappeared; to perpetuate its memory a museum was installed at Enkhuizen, a port on the Ysselmeer, in a former customs house; the open-air annex consists of various types of boats grouped in a canal at the end of the building. Thus museums feed on the death of a culture' (1979:230, 237; cited in Errington, 1989:57).

References

Bazin, G., 1979, *The Museum Age*, New York: Universe Books.

Bernabé, J., Chamoiseau, P. and Confiant, R., 1989, *Éloge de la Créolité*, Paris: Gallimard.

Bilby, K.M., 1990, 'The Remaking of the Aluku: Culture, Politics, and Maroon Ethnicity in French South America', Ph.D. dissertation, Johns Hopkins University, Baltimore.

Binnendijk, C. van and Faber, P. (eds), 1992, *Sranan: Cultuur in Suriname*, Amsterdam: Koninklijk Instituut voor de Tropen.

Bourdieu, P. and Darbel, A., 1969, *L'Amour de l'art: les musées d'art européens et leur publique*, Paris: Les Éditions de Minuit.

Collomb, G. and Jean-Louis, M.-P., 1989, 'Note sur le projet de Musée de l'Homme Guyanais', manuscript.

Destination Guyane: guide pratique, 1991, Cayenne: Outre-Mer Editions.

Doucet, L., 1981, *Vous avez dit Guyane?* Paris: Denoël.

E. H-H., 1992, 'Le premier éco-musée de Martinique', *France-Antilles Magazine*, 28 November–4 December, pp. 44–5.

Errington, S., 1989, 'Fragile Traditions and Contested Meanings', *Public Culture*, Vol. 1, No. 2, pp. 49–59.

' "Faire un musée . . .": le Musée Régional de la Guyane', 1990, manuscript.

Fanon, F., 1967[1952], *Black Skins, White Masks*, New York: Grove.

Fox, L.S., 1991, 'Attics of Life: A Space to Live In', in *Joan Duran: Meridian*, Mexico: Museo Universitario del Chopo.

Glissant, E., 1981, *Le discours antillais*, Paris: Éditions du Seuil.

A History of Belize: Nation in the Making, 1987, Belize City: Sunshine Books.

Price, R., 1995a, 'Executing Ethnicity: The Killings in Suriname', *Cultural Anthropology*, Vol. 10, No. 4, pp. 437–71.

—— 1995b, 'Two Variants in Caribbean Race Relations', in Hasenbalg, C. (ed.), *Racism and Race Relations in the African Diaspora. Estudos Afro-Asiáticos*, No. 2, (in press).

Price, R. and Price, S., 1992, *Equatoria*, New York: Routledge.

—— 1994, 'Ethnicity in a Museum Case: France's Show-Window in the Americas', *Museum Anthropology*, Vol. 18, No. 2, pp. 3–15.

—— 1995a, *Enigma Variations*, Cambridge: Harvard University Press.

—— 1995b, 'Executing Culture: Musée, Museo, Museum', *American Anthropologist*, Vol. 97, No. 1, pp. 97–109.

The Prospect Now, 1992, Benque Viejo del Carmen: Museum of Belize Project Coordination and General Planning Office.

Raddatz, C., 1992, *Afrika in Amerika*, Hamburg: Hamburgisches Museum für Völkerkunde.

SEMAGU, 1988, 'Programme technique détaillé', manuscript.

Staszewski, G., 1993, 'Images et couleurs d'un village d'antan', *France-Antilles Magazine*, 6–12 March, pp. 48–50.

CHAPTER 6

Ethnicity and social structure in contemporary Cuba

Franklin W. Knight

Few subjects have been as difficult to explore dispassionately in contemporary Cuba as the subject of racial or ethnic differences. On the one hand the revolutionary government of Fidel Castro insists officially that ethnic differences no longer play an important role in public or private decision-making. The official position is that race is irrelevant – or at least of minor significance – in the construction of the socialist state. After 1959 the revolution sought to establish a state that deliberately privileged the lower orders of society, most of whom were black. In the rhetoric of the revolutionary government all forms of discrimination are legally prohibited (Lopez Valdes, 1973:6–14). Indeed, when the revolutionary Cubans finally wrote a new constitution in 1975 they made discrimination a violation of one's constitutional rights. Article 41 of the new *Constitution of the Republic of Cuba* declares that 'discrimination because of race, color, sex, or national origin is forbidden and is punished by law' (1976:13). This section mandated equal rights for all citizens. Formal institutional barriers to equality for any group were therefore removed by law. In practice, however, this constitutional equality does not exactly work itself out clearly or consistently. But matters of public policy and private action have always been highly contested and constitute an extremely ambiguous sphere of operations. Within the private domain the state is powerless to change the deeply held attitudes of some of its citizens, and these attitudes are especially important for matters of race and ethnicity. The degree to which citizens uphold the law is based on perceptions of self interest. When conformity brings greater reward than nonconformity, then citizens conform. At the same time, intellectual traditions may not reflect daily conduct at the levels of public and private spheres (Helg, 1990).

While the government cannot regulate private racial and ethnic considerations in daily life, it subordinates these considerations to those of class and social justice. By promoting the goal of an egalitarian society, the government projected an ideal that its supporters were obliged to accept publicly. Elizabeth Sutherland observed in the 1960s after spending a summer traveling and working with the Cubans that 'racism in the sense of the subordination of one racial group by another for the benefit of the oppressing group did not exist in Cuba' (1969:140). According to her, socialism fundamentally altered the social dynamics, liberating both black and white from their previously fixed positions of racial stereotyping. The revolution provided the new opportunities for decency and dignity for nonwhites and in a way 'whites began to be freed from whiteness'. Decency and dignity, however, did not fully correspond with equality, and by the late 1970s complaints about the handicaps of race were still being heard in Cuba. Jorge Domínguez (1978) described the complexity of the official attitude toward ethnic and racial diversity in Cuba in the late 1970s with considerable validity. While foreigners, especially from the United States, felt that the revolution failed to have reality match its rhetoric of a racially blind society, the government kept insisting that discrimination was a thing of the past. In some cases, the problem of race in Cuba was one of perception shaped by cultural experience. The revolution insulated Cuba to a great extent from the passionate civil rights movement that swept the United States in the 1960s. Most blacks and others who went to Cuba then were often ignorant of Cuban history and incapable of fully understanding the reality in which they found themselves. By putting the moral force of the government against racism Fidel Castro had altered the dynamics but not eliminated the problem. According to Elizabeth Sutherland, whites 'stopped using words like *niche* or *macri* (nigger) and *negrada* (a bunch of niggers). Even better, the phrase *gente de color* (colored people) gave way to *negros* (blacks) among most whites . . . But something was still wrong.' (1969: 140–1). In his study of the late 1970s Domínguez described the situation:

> Ethnic differences, in Cuba's present as in its past, are neither admitted nor discussed. Every Cuban government has acknowledged the existence of racial discrimination under previous administrations, but not under its own, and the revolutionary government is no exception. Although there are substantial differences in chances for success between Cuban blacks and whites in the 1970s, organizations on behalf of blacks and limited to blacks are illegal. Cubans, including blacks themselves, tend to denigrate blackness and frown on evidence of overt, collective political action by blacks. Blacks gained from the revolution because they were disproportionately poor and the poor benefited disproportionately from the change of political systems, but the problem of ethnicity in contemporary Cuba remains a mixture of substantial equality of opportunity, substantial inequality of result, illegal organized black politics, and social inferiority based on color in everyday life (1978:7–8).

These comments nevertheless require the inescapable qualifications imposed by time and the inherent idiosyncrasies of the Cuban revolution. The normal dynamics of a Caribbean society – the same as in many other places from Bosnia to Brazil – are such that consistency in racial and ethnic relations is impossible. This derives from two intrinsic forces. The first is that the terms themselves constantly undergo semantic and political changes. The second is that individual identity in Cuba and the wider Caribbean, as throughout much of the Americas, is bound inextricably with race and color. Already there is some evidence that Domínguez's observations of the late 1970s may no longer be quite as applicable as they once were – just as his description of the government and its attitude to the society is not what it was in the late 1970s. By 1994 the Cuban revolution had been overtaken by internal and external events over which it apparently has little or no control, and faces a new period of uncertainty politically, socially and economically. In the 1960s the revolution sought to create a 'new Cuban', but the degree to which it had succeeded by the mid-1990s was far from clear. If the revolution subsumed race and ethnicity in the quest for the socialist state, a retreat from that goal may reawaken their importance. A capitalist Cuban society may again return to the situation where the majority of the least competitive sector of that society are distinguished by race and color.

Race and ethnic identities were an important aspect of Cuban colonial society, a result of the corporate organization of the state. The republican government sought to eliminate the corporate organization, and made political parties based on color illegal. Many trade unions, religious cults, and self-help associations continued to exist based on an overt appeal to race and color. Initially the Castro government discouraged such groups, regarding them as redundant in a socialist state. Eventually the government relented, and aspects of ethnicity, color and race became important for the national ideology (Masferrer and Mesa Lago, 1974:348–84). During the past decade or so there has been an expanding literature on the subject of race and ethnicity in Cuba and a virtual resurgence in Afro-Cuban cultural manifestations such as the impact on language, music and dance.[1] In part this stems from the normal commodification of culture and cultural forms that has been a characteristic of the later twentieth century. *Santería* – a folk cult – and *rumba* – an exotic, suggestive dance – have moved from the poorer and formerly predominantly black masses to general and official acceptance. But the official mandate of equality has also brought the formerly marginal to the mainstream and thereby whetted the interest and curiosity of a wide range of scholars and artists. Moreover, with the weakening of the administrative and economic structure of the revolution the Cuban government appears increasingly less able to insist on general conformity among the population as it once did. All this has had incalculable impact on the general attitudes toward race and ethnicity, presenting a strange paradox: at the moment when the mutually reinforcing cleavages of race, ethnicity and color appear to be loosening in Cuba, the economic situation threatens to restore the status quo of prerevolutionary days.

Slavery, race and ethnicity

In a country where a consciousness of history still remains an integral part of the fabric of social and intellectual thought, it should not be surprising that attitudes toward race and ethnicity remain closely linked with the vicissitudes of the past. The major theoretical guideposts that have demarcated and channeled the wider Caribbean historiography also pertain to that of Cuba. Cuban scholars, as well as scholars writing about Cuba, therefore manifest a consciousness of the wider debate as the writers try to come to grips with their own complexity.[2]

If Eric Williams pointed out the importance of the economic and structural context to the understanding of the relationship between race and slavery in the American slave society in his *Capitalism and Slavery*, then Elsa Goveia made an equally important contribution in *Slave Society in the British Leeward Islands at the End of the Eighteenth Century*. In that work Goveia insisted that masters and slaves comprised an integrated community with a high degree of symbiosis between the social segments. Slavery as a social system certainly contributed to the genesis of general attitudes toward non-Europeans within the community, but it did not, by itself, act as a predictive determinant for race relations either within the slave society or after the emancipation of slaves.

Indeed, this is one of the perceptive observations that informed Harry Hoetink's enormously thoughtful inquiry, *The Two Variants in Caribbean Race Relations* (1967). Hoetink insisted that a common error in much of the historiography of American slave systems was the facile assumption that slavery and race relations were irrevocably linked. He further expanded and refined this aspect of his study in *Slavery and Race Relations in the Americas. Comparative Notes on their Nature and Nexus* (1973). In *The Two Variants in Caribbean Race Relations*, Hoetink persuasively argued that the linear connections made by highly influential and widely respected scholars such as Frank Tannenbaum, Stanley Elkins and the earliest works of Pierre L. Van den Berghe had no empirical substantiation. Tannenbaum and Elkins had argued that the social structure and inter-personal relations manifested during slavery would provide a reliable predictor of the nature of race relations after slavery was abolished. In his later works Pierre Van den Berghe disagreed with this idea, observing in *The Ethnic Phenomenon* that 'while all the slave plantation regimes of the Western Hemisphere bore an air of family resemblance, they gave birth after their demise to very different societies with radically distinct types of race and ethnic relations. Even a relatively small area like the Caribbean shows a bewildering internal diversity of systems of race, ethnic and class stratification' (1981:134–5).

The second observation of *The Two Variants* that remains inordinately important to later scholarship is a clarification of the seminal distinction between race and ethnicity. Hoetink accomplished this clarification by his invention of the attractive concept of 'somatic norm image'. A fundamental characteristic of every segmented society, the author defined somatic norm image as 'the complex of physical (somatic) characteristics which are accepted by a group as its norm and ideals'. The timely introduction of the notion of the somatic norm image, like adding active yeast to inert dough, facilitated a clearer understanding of the divergent impacts of race, ethnicity and class within any given social structure. It freed these concepts from rigid, ahistorical and often ambiguous applications. Moreover it made time, place, and locally prevailing circumstances constant considerations in the patterns of social evolution. By establishing a clear distinction between race and ethnicity, Hoetink permitted the more ready acceptance of the notion that the internal social, cultural, political and class dynamics of each society could assume independent logical outcomes. The historical experience of slavery, therefore, while possibly influential in establishing the pattern of race relations did not necessarily become a determinant of such relations. Stated another way, contemporary race relations in any plural, fragmented or segmented society was not the result of a simple linear, teleological process. Race relations remained an intrinsic aspect of social and political relations.

Since the 1960s considerations of race and ethnicity have become far more important in the historical literature dealing with slave systems and their successor societies. But the commonalty of usage has not resulted in any significant diminution of the attendant confusion, ambiguity and obfuscation surrounding the terms 'race' and 'ethnicity'. In most applications, as Hoetink admitted, race is largely a biological concept. In most common usages race conveys a strong connotation of biologically transmitted physical characteristics. *The New Columbia Encyclopedia* points out that:

> Genetically a race may be defined as a group with gene frequencies differing from those of other groups in the human species. However, the genes responsible for the hereditary differences between humans are few compared with the vast number of genes common to all human beings regardless of the race to which they belong. All human beings belong to the same species (*homo sapiens*) and are mutually fertile. The term race is inappropriate when applied to national, religious, geographic, linguistic, or

cultural groups, nor can the biological criteria of race be equated with any mental characteristics such as personality or character (Harris and Levey, 1975:2263).

The last point is an implicit admission that race can be, and has often been, employed with the most imprecise connotations. Moreover, as Julian Pitt-Rivers noted in his discerning article, 'Race, color and class in Central America and the Andes', the connotations of race can shift significantly when moved across cultural frontiers (1967). In Latin America, Pitt-Rivers wrote:

> The word race . . . clearly owes little to physical anthropology, but refers, however it may be defined, to the ways in which people are classified in daily life. What are called race relations are, in fact, always questions of social structure.

But if, as Pitt-Rivers implies, 'race' may be used as a synonym for 'class', then it is quite clear that part of the problem of understanding race relations throughout the Americas stems from a divergence in perception between how some people see themselves and how others see them. Outsiders and insiders will not agree exactly on the importance of race in social relations when they do not share the same somatic norms. And nowhere is this more clear than in the interesting and varied historical literature on the societies of the Caribbean, as Anthony Maingot illustrates in his fascinating essay, 'Race, color and class in the Caribbean' (1992).

The term, 'ethnic' is no less misleading and confusing than 'race' but appears to be less politically charged in contemporary discourse. In its most common usage ethnicity is rather loosely used to designate any group bound together by common ties of language, race, nationality, culture, or pigmentation who might feel themselves to be, or may be considered by others, an ethnic group.

The term 'ethnic' is applied with remarkable inconsistency. In Europe no group is categorized ethnically as 'white', 'European', or 'Christian', but such designations frequently appear in reference to some groups in Africa, Asia and South America. In India, being Indian is not considered a viable ethnic category, but in Singapore Indians constitute one of the principal ethnic divisions. Moreover, throughout Latin America and the Caribbean mestizos and *mulattos* are considered to be generally accepted ethnic categories.

Ethnicity, because it involves so many nuanced connotations, can be a much more elusive – and in many cases a far more acceptable – term than race. In some cases it is merely a synonym for phenotype (another word that *The Two Variants* popularized). In other cases it might represent class rankings, such as the commonly held view in the Dominican Republic that no General is ever 'black'. But in the contemporary Caribbean with its competitive plural political structure, ethnic designations may reflect nothing more than conveniently strategic identifications to attain specific goals.

What is important about the usage of terms such as 'race' and 'ethnicity' – and the same could be said for 'class' and a host of other words – as Oscar Handlin points out in *Race and Nationality in American Life*, is that they are historical, intellectual constructs, not rigid scientific definitions (1957). These terms derive their peculiar genesis from the unpredictable combination of time, place and circumstances. Created at a certain time and influenced by certain circumstances, they change, mutate or alter their definitions by political and intellectual force. Race, ethnicity and class are closely related to what Donald Baker refers to as 'identity, power and psychocultural needs' (1974). Since they are used by groups to define themselves or to define other groups (or to convey a variety of attributes simultaneously), these terms can only be fully understood in the context of political power and social status.

Colonial Cuba

The Cuban experience aptly illustrates the complex relations between race, ethnicity and political power. It shows that culture affects the way social relations are structured, perceived and articulated.

As part of the Spanish American empire, Cuba reflected much of the Spanish colonial attitudes toward race. But these attitudes were never identical throughout the far flung Spanish American empire. Moreover, local conditions always had an impact on social relations. Inevitably, the nature of the society as well as its political and social organization would also be factors determining the ways in which groups in the society acted toward one another. Invariably, economic considerations, demographic representation, and the actual as well as perceived social distance affected personal as well as group behavior.

Colonial society in Cuba began as a form of fortified enclave on the periphery (at least after 1518, when Hernán Cortés discovered gold on the mainland of what the Spanish called New Spain) of the wider American sphere. The principal nodes of settlement – Havana in the Northwest and Santiago de Cuba in the Southeast – were cities constructed as Spanish frontier cities, compactly designed for administration, defense and commerce. Within the walls of the fortifications – and in the case of Havana, within the walls of the original city – all groups lived in close proximity and most often in the same building. In such a situation, animals, servants, slaves and proprietors co-inhabited and coexisted within a single domain. This did not mean that social rank was unimportant. But the presence of slavery blurred some categories, leading the aristocratic *Habanera* Doña María de las Mercedes Santa Cruz y Cárdenas, Montalvo y O'Farrill, the Countess of Merlin, to observe that 'No hay pueblo en la Habana, solamente hay amos y esclavos.'[3] It was not until the eighteenth century that spatial separation and physical distance began to be noted in the architecture and spatial composition of Cuban cities (Marrero, 1972–1988:*passim*).

Like other Caribbean states, the history of Cuba after the middle of the eighteenth century reflected the profound distortions of the development of a socioeconomic system of African slavery based on the expansion of the sugar plantation (McNeill, 1985; Knight and Liss, 1991). The relatively rapid introduction of hundreds of thousands of Africans severely altered the nature of the society in myriad ways: patterns of residence, landholding, demography, economic structure and interpersonal relations.[4] Cuba, somewhat belatedly, participated in the 'sugar revolutions' of the tropical American plantation zone, radically transforming the entire society and exacerbating the pattern of social and ethnic relations. But like elsewhere in the hemisphere (with the notable exception of the United States of America) racial and ethnic discrimination did not lead to physical segregation. As the population moved outside the walls of the old city, creating new neighboring towns and cities and expanding Havana inexorably westward, servants and animals moved outside the principal residences. On rural *haciendas* and *ingenios* slaves and servants had their separate dwelling areas, often contiguous to those of the owners and managerial staff.

Yet the commonality of the general pattern of development of the plantation complex in Cuba should not obscure two important – and intricately intertwined – variations from the other Latin American and Caribbean slave societies. Both of these factors contributed to the accentuated sensitivity to race and social status. The first was that Cuba, having established its slave society after the late eighteenth century, had to confront the mounting international opposition to slavery as well as the increasingly strong and universally generalized political discourse of nationalism in the nineteenth century. The second variation derived from the timing of the demographic transformation.

The sugar revolution did not have quite the same overwhelming impact in Cuba, Puerto Rico and Spanish Santo Domingo as elsewhere in the region. In the tragic and traumatic aftermath of the independence of Haiti, imported slaves were not allowed to inundate the white population in Cuba. Indeed, in Cuba the nonwhite population only surpassed the white population for a very short period during the middle of the nineteenth century – if the available data provided are reliable (Kiple, 1976:47–61). In the spectrum that some writers have created in the Caribbean between the settler and the exploitation society, Cuba retained a considerable proportion of settler characteristics even when it became transformed into a slave plantation, exploitation society (Knight, 1990:66–87, 163–4). The relatively relaxed inter-ethnic relations of the basic settler community remained evident, although somewhat inundated by the more conflictive, more commercialized structure that emerged in western Cuba after 1800.

The peculiar experience of slavery was only one of the factors fashioning the evolving daily interpersonal relations in Cuba. And it ought to be emphasized that Cuban slave society was not a rigid, unchanging structure throughout its existence. Like elsewhere, Cuban society was extremely dynamic, subject to the unrelenting negotiation of status among several elements (Martínez Alier, 1974; Scott, 1985). Race, as well as condition and status, remained circumscribed by the administrative, political and cultural structure of the Spanish colonial state in Cuba. Religion was almost as important to status as genealogy – and religion meant Roman Catholicism. Interestingly enough, Cuba did not develop a pattern of black Christian churches until the middle of the twentieth century. The definition of what was Cuban appeared unclear. But the reality of Cuban race relations was also conditioned by civil war, nationalism, and the large-scale imposition of North American values, especially after 1898 – despite the influence of José Martí, the great, idealistic Cuban patriot (Duke, 1983:85–110). Indeed, it is in this fragmented milieu that José Antonio Saco admitted:

> La nacionalidad cubana de que yo hablé, y de la única que debe ocuparse todo hombre sensato, es la formada por la raza blanca, que sólo se eleva a poco más de 400,000 individuos.[5]

Race during the Republic

The Cuban experience of race relations during the twentieth century when Cuba became an independent state approximated race relations elsewhere throughout Latin America and the Caribbean. Race tended to lose importance to public assertions of national cohesion although for nonwhite groups it assumed greater importance as the central factor in community solidarity and identity. The problem of race has moved beyond mere considerations of somatic norm images. Race has become politicized – and the politics of race has become a model for other groups negotiating political empowerment such as the case of women in Cuba (Stoner, 1991:185–92).

What Emilia Viotti da Costa indicated for Brazil remains equally true for Cuba and the Caribbean:

> In the 1980s scholars were abandoning the assumption that different forms of racism, discrimination and segregation in modern society derived from different slave systems, or that the different

contemporary patterns of race could be explained by reference to traditional differences in the perceptions of race in the Anglo-Saxon and Iberian world. They were also repudiating the notion that slavery had crippled blacks and argued that the problems blacks faced after emancipation had to do with discriminatory practices adopted by the Brazilian elites. The new scholarship favored a more complex historical model, stressing that race was not an objective category but a historical construct that was constantly being shaped and reshaped, within the context of power struggles and the competition for social surplus (1992:147).

Marianne Masferrer and Carmelo Mesa Lago have argued that the situation of nonwhites in Cuba during the Republican period was extremely complex. This seems a normal expectation. While racial discrimination existed, especially in employment and in socially exclusive clubs, hotels, and restaurants, the authors insist that it would be difficult to separate 'discrimination based on race from that based on economic status' (1974:372).

In the public sphere, Cuba was quite comparable to the rest of the Caribbean, to Jamaica, Puerto Rico, the Dominican Republic or Curaçao. Public areas remained open to the public and public services remained available to the entire public, although financial consideration might restrict access of certain individuals.

> There were no black ghettos in Cuba similar to those in the United States. In the lower-class urban areas (i.e., Jesús Maria, Atarés, Luyanó, el Cerro) blacks and whites lived together, although there were greater concentrations of blacks in lower-income areas. However the high-income residential areas, such as Miramar or Biltmore in Havana, were almost completely white.
>
> Access to cinemas, theaters, sports shows, buses, trains, and churches was open to all races. It is important to point out that there were no 'black Christian Churches' in Cuba, although those practicing African rites were largely black. Black athletes were integrated into the national baseball teams, and many represented Cuba abroad in different international sports competitions (Masferrer and Mesa Lago, 1974:372–3).

The revolution of Fidel Castro in Cuba after 1959 scrambled the social as well as the political situation locally, and subordinated considerations of race to other more explicitly articulated goals of the socialist society. A general redistribution of resources took place, administered by a government that had become more bureacratically centralized and ideologically hegemonial. As indicated before, the official rhetoric of the self-admitted socialist state promoted and assumed the equality and inclusiveness of all citizens regardless of race, color, religion, sexual differences (although interestingly enough, not sexual preferences) or national origins (Cuba 1976). For a time the Cuban revolution removed the economic disabilities that inhibited the proportional participation of nonwhites in educational and health facilities, and opened all employment opportunities to the entire society. That was in keeping with the avowed aim to create a 'new Cuba' and a socialist society. The revolution sought to eliminate institutionalized discrimination and in a large measure, it did so in terms of formal relations.

In his original conception, Hoetink proposed two clearly distinct patterns of race relations throughout the Caribbean. One pattern, drawing on a northern European socioracial tradition, tended to be more exclusionist with a narrow dichotomous assumption of 'whiteness'. Anyone deemed to be non-European was de facto, nonwhite. The other pattern, however, drawing on the heterogeneity of the Mediterranean tradition, held that anyone not proven nonwhite was assumed to be white – and created a legitimate social space for persons of mixed ancestry. While at a certain level of considera- tion the perceptual division was tantamount to describing a glass as either half full or half empty (the reality was identical), the operational impact on daily community relations was enormous. The Mediterranean tradition encouraged (and reflected) a greater tolerance of somatic variation.

By the end of the twentieth century these two traditions had basically splintered, as economic and occupational considerations also affected rela- tions between individuals and groups. At the same time, increased literacy and improved technology expanded the facility to construct new myths.

While the rhetoric of absolute equality was important, the reality fell short of the ideal. As Jorge Domínguez (1978:7–8) pointed out, in some respects the revolution was not very different from previous Cuban govern- ments, and Cuba was not very different from the rest of the Caribbean: at the personal level the Cuban government could no better regulate relations than its predecessors. People still act individually in highly variable ways for extremely private reasons. The government was simply not successful in removing gender, race and class considerations from daily intercourse.[6] Cubans, like people anywhere, continually make distinctions between what they ought to do and what they actually do. So in Cuba, as elsewhere, there are probably more than two variants to race relations.

Capturing the essence of race, ethnicity and social structure in Cuba during the contemporary period therefore is not an easy task. No scientific studies exist to establish (or refute) the degree to which fundamental changes in interpersonal attitudes have resulted from the massive social and eco- nomic restructuring that accompanied the revolution. Until the late 1980s the government appeared to have the necessary moral force to impose a sort of conformity that made people aware that overt forms of discrimination were anti-social, and by equating anti-social behavior with anti-government behavior, made deviance punishable by law. At the same time by removing the economic and educational inhibitions that restricted the entry and participation of some Cubans to some areas of the country such as beaches, clubs, hotels, and occupations, the government made public discrimination less noticeable. Cubans, whatever their race, color or condition, did not encounter overt discrimination publicly or privately in their daily lives, and so individual ethnicity, while certainly not abolished, assumed less importance in their daily interpersonal relations.

The problem of increased ethnic sensitivity developed when the Cuban government lost the vital economic support of the Soviet Union in the late 1980s. The government suddenly found itself lacking in many basic consumer items. The drastic changes in the international situation brought about by the disintegration of the Soviet Union and the realignment of international commerce, capital and trade forced the Cubans to reorder their priorities and to make the type of domestic adjustments that modified their centrally controlled economy. Central control was relaxed in some specific cases, allowing for legal small entrepreneurship. After 26 July 1993 the state decriminalized the individual holding of foreign currencies and opened the domestic economy to mixed capital operations. In essence that created a double economy, one dealing in local Cuban *pesos* and the other in *divisas* (foreign currency). Equally important, the dual economy restored a competitive economical market-place in which access to foreign currencies created a new privileged class. Ironically, access to foreign currency is greater for the service classes, especially those working in foreign enterprises and the tourism industry, as well as those with relatives in foreign countries. Formerly, service occupations had lower skills and lower wage rates, and provided employment for a large number of black Cubans. Now these jobs are eagerly sought by opportunistic trained technicians.

The implication of this new political and economic development for racial and ethnic relations in Cuba cannot yet be fully ascertained. Some implications are, however, ominous. An economic hierarchy has replaced the equality that the revolution established. Does that mean that official social equality is also doomed? If the government concedes that it lacks the means to regulate the economy and if the economy becomes the most important aspect of public and private concern, then to what degree will the government be forced to retreat from its long-standing support of the predominantly Afro-Cuban lower orders of society?

A greater proportion of nonwhite Cubans remained and supported the revolution and the Cuban government during the past decades. Nonwhites benefited disproportionately from the changes brought about by Fidel Castro. Indeed, it might be said that their personal situation remains closely aligned with that of the government. By reopening Cuba to those who fled, it is not unreasonable to expect that one of the consequences would be the attempt on the part of the returnees to restore those values and images (including somatic images) that they held before leaving Cuba, or which they acquired in exile in the United States. These are, of course, the values against which the revolution had fought officially for more than three decades.

In *The Two Variants* Professor Hoetink discussed not only the 'somatic norm image' but also the concept of 'somatic distance' – the difference between two somatic norm images (1971:153–60). The theory surrounding both concepts still appears attractive. But the three decades of scholarship since the publication of his exciting book have not permitted us to be more confident about changes in either the concept of the somatic norm image or alterations in somatic distance. The assumption that Cubans in Florida and elsewhere, exiled from their country for more than three decades, have a different view of themselves and of others, remains highly speculative. Just as in Eastern Europe, once the ordered restraint of external administration is removed or altered, the naked atavistic passions of centuries can be easily aroused again. Nevertheless, one intriguing possibility is that with the varied experiences of Cubans who left their country and those who remained, the changes in their respective somatic distance may be as important as changes in their social and economic realities. In this, as in other matters, only time will clarify the situation.

Notes

1. See Bolívar Aróstegui (1991), Fernández Robaina (1990), Nunley and Bettelheim (1988) and Urfé (1984).
2. Davis (1966:264–7), Davis (1984:238–40), Hall (1971), Helg (1990), Klein (1967), Knight (1970), Moreno Fraginals (1978), Scott (1985), Tannenbaum (1992) and Williams (1944).
3. 'Havana has no lower class, only masters and slaves' (Santa Cruz, 1981[1842]:121).
4. See Bergad (1990), Hall (1971), Kiple (1976), Klein (1967), Knight (1970), Marrero (1972–1988), Moreno Fraginals (1978), Murray (1980), Pérez (1988), Scott (1985) and Zanetti and Garcia (1987).
5. 'The Cuban nationality of which I spoke, and the only type that could occur to any intelligent person, is that comprised of the white race, that by themselves amount to a little more than 400,000 individuals' (Torres-Cuevas, 1984:82).
6. See Moore (1988), Nicholson (1974), Reckord (1971) and Sutherland (1969).

References

Baker, D., 1974, 'Identity, Power and Psychocultural Needs: White Responses to Non-Whites', *Journal of Ethnic Studies*, Vol. 1, No. 4, pp. 16–44.
Bergad, L., 1990, *Cuban Rural Society in the Nineteenth Century. The Social and Economic History of Monoculture in Matanzas*, Princeton: Princeton University Press.

Bolívar Aróstegui, N., 1991, *Las Orishas en Cuba,* Havana: Ediciones Union.

Constitution of the Republic of Cuba, 1976, New York: Center for Cuban Studies.

Davis, D.B., 1966, *The Problem of Slavery in Western Culture,* Ithaca: Cornell University Press.

_____ 1984, *Slavery and Human Progress,* New York: Oxford University Press.

Domínguez, J., 1978, *Cuba. Order and Revolution,* Cambridge: Harvard University Press.

Duke, C., 1983, 'The Idea of Race: The Cultural Impact of American intervention in Cuba, 1898–1912', in Silvestrini, B. (ed.), *Politics, Society and Culture in the Caribbean,* San Juan: Association of Caribbean Historians, pp. 85–110.

Elkins, S., 1959, *Slavery. A Problem in American Institutional and Intellectual Life,* Chicago: University of Chicago Press.

Fernández Robaina, T., 1990, *El negro en Cuba, 1902–1958: Apuntes para la historia de la lucha contra la discriminación,* Havana: Editorial de Ciencias Sociales.

Goveia, E., 1965, *Slave Society in the British Leeward Islands at the End of the Eighteenth Century,* New Haven: Yale University Press.

Hall, G.M., 1971, *Social Control in Slave Plantation Societies. A Comparison of St Domingue and Cuba,* Baltimore: Johns Hopkins University Press.

Handlin, O., 1957, *'Race and Nationality in American Life,* Boston: Little, Brown.

Harris, W. and Levey, J. (eds), 1975, *The New Columbia Encyclopedia,* New York: Columbia University Press.

Helg, A., 1990, 'Race in Argentina and Cuba, 1880–1930', in Graham, R. (ed.), *The Idea of Race in Latin America, 1870–1940,* Austin: University of Texas Press, pp. 37–70.

Hoetink, H., 1967, *The Two Variants in Caribbean Race Relations. A Contribution to the Sociology of Segmented Societies,* London: Oxford University Press.

_____ 1973, *Slavery and Race Relations in the Americas. Comparative Notes on their Nature and Nexus,* New York: Harper and Row.

Kiple, K., 1976, *Blacks in Colonial Cuba, 1774–1899,* Gainesville: University of Florida Press.

Klein, H., 1967, *Slavery in the Americas. A Comparative Study of Cuba and Virginia,* Chicago: University of Chicago Press.

Knight, F.W. , 1970, *Slave Society in Cuba During the Nineteenth Century,* Madison: University of Wisconsin Press.

_____ 1990, *The Caribbean. The Genesis of a Fragmented Nationalism,* 2nd edn, New York: Oxford University Press.

Knight, F.W. and Liss, P.K., (eds), 1991, *Atlantic Port Cities: Economy, Culture and Society in the Atlantic World, 1650–1850,* Knoxville: University of Tennessee Press.

Lopez Valdes, R.L., 1973, 'Discrimination in Cuba', *Cuba Resource Center Newsletter,* New York: Center for Cuban Studies, Vol. 2, No. 6, pp. 6–14.

Maingot, A.P., 1992, 'Race, Color, and Class in the Caribbean', in Stepan, A. (ed.), *Americas: New Interpretive Essays,* New York: Oxford University Press, pp. 220–47.

Marrero, L., 1972–88, *Cuba: economía y sociedad,* 16 vols, Madrid and San Juan: Playor.

Martínez Alier, V., 1974, *Marriage, Class and Color in Nineteenth Century Cuba. A Study of Racial Attitudes and Sexual Values in a Slave Society,* London: Cambridge University Press.

Masferrer, M. and Mesa Lago, C., 1974, 'The Gradual Integration of the Black in Cuba Under the Colony, the Republic and the Revolution', in Toplin, R. (ed.), *Slavery and Race Relations in Latin America,* Westport: Greenwood Press, pp. 348–84.

McNeill, R., 1985, *The Atlantic Empires of France and Spain: Louisbourg and Havana, 1700–1763,* Chapel Hill: University of North Carolina Press.

Moore, C., 1988, *Castro, The Blacks and Cuba,* Los Angeles: University of California Press.

Moreno Fraginals, M., 1978, *El ingenio. Complejo económico social cubano del azúcar,* Havana: Editorial de Ciencias Sociales.

Murray, D., 1980, *Odious Commerce: Britain, Spain and the Abolition of the Cuban Slave Trade*, London: Cambridge University Press.

Nicholson, J., 1974, *Inside Cuba*, New York: Sheed and Ward.

Nunley, J.W. and Bettelheim, J. (eds), 1988, *Caribbean Festival Arts*, Seattle: The Saint Louis Art Museum.

Pérez, L., 1988, *Cuba: Between Reform and Revolution*, New York: Oxford University Press.

Pitt-Rivers, J., 1967, 'Race, Color and Class in Central America and the Andes', *Daedalus*, Vol. 96, No. 2, pp. 542–59.

Reckord, B., 1971, *Does Fidel Eat More Than Your Father?* New York: Praeger.

Santa Cruz, M., 1981, [Original French edition, 1842], *La Habana*, Madrid: Bacardi.

Scott, R., 1985, *Slave Emancipation in Cuba. The Transition to Free Labor, 1860–1899*, Princeton: Princeton University Press.

Stoner, K.L., 1991, *From the House to the Streets. The Women's Movement for Legal Reform, 1898–1940*, Durham: Duke University Press.

Sutherland, E., 1969, *The Youngest Revolution. A Personal Report from Cuba*, New York: Dial Press.

Tannenbaum, F., 1992[1946], *Slave and Citizen*, Boston: Beacon Press.

Torres-Cuevas, E., 1984, *La pólemica de la esclavitud: José Antonio Saco*, Havana: Editorial de Ciencias Sociales.

Urfé, O., 1984[1977], 'Music and Dance in Cuba', in Moreno Fraginals, M. (ed.), *Africa in Latin America*, New York: Holmes and Meier, pp. 170–88.

Van den Berghe, P., 1967, *Race and Racism: A Comparative Perspective*, New York: Wiley.
——— 1981, *The Ethnic Phenomenon*, New York: Elsevier.

Viotti da Costa, E., 1992, 'Commentary on George Reid Andrews, Blacks and Whites in São Paulo, Brazil, 1888–1988', *Luso-Brazilian Review*, Vol. 29, No. 2.

Williams, E., 1994[1944], *Capitalism and Slavery*, Chapel Hill: University of North Carolina Press.

Zanetti, O. and Garcia, A., 1987, *Caminos para el azúcar*, Havana: Editorial de Ciencias Sociales.

CHAPTER 7 | 'Constitutionally white': the forging of a national identity in the Dominican Republic

Michiel Baud

Today, national and ethnic identities (and, for that matter, all other collective identities) are routinely interpreted as constructions fashioned in order to create or confirm 'imagined communities', to use Benedict Anderson's now famous term (1991). Authors such as Hobsbawm (1990) and Urban and Sherzer (1992) have developed the argument by showing how political elites have used and manipulated popular beliefs and customs to further their nationalist projects. Still, it may be asked whether this emphasis on the constructed nature of social ideologies is, in the end, satisfying. It leaves two problems unsolved.

First, the symbols and historical interpretations which are chosen to bolster ethnic or national identities are not completely arbitrary, nor is their emotional appeal. It may be true that these symbols are distorted, exaggerated, sometimes invented, but even in this latter case, such inventions do not fall from the sky. They originate in the history or the culture of a given group of people and are only accepted when they do not deviate too far from existing cultural perceptions and social memories (Fentress and Wickham, 1992). These memories are not necessarily true themselves, but they are social facts at the moment of their general acceptance.

Second, the selection and manipulation of symbols do not go uncontested. Actors in the social arena have different interests, which are reflected in the way ideologies are received and interpreted. This process is well-documented for intellectual and political elites, but often ignored in the case of the common people. Superficially, the latter often show a more or less passive acceptance of the constructions of dominant groups, politicians or ethnic leaders, but this is not to say that they necessarily believe all their ideas or accept all the consequences of those ideas. The emphasis on the constructed nature of national and ethnic identities should not close our eyes to the lack of success of many of these constructions.

In this context, Harry Hoetink's *The Two Variants in Caribbean Race Relations*, first published in Dutch over thirty years ago, still provides important insights. The value of Hoetink's analysis is that it presses upon its readers the realization that, while ethnic and racial identities may in part be socially created instruments employed to confirm differences (which may be emphasized or ignored depending on the circumstances), they are also cultural and sociopsychological realities which impose themselves on individuals and groups and from which there is little chance of escape. Hoetink's idea of a 'somatic norm image' leads us into the labyrinths of psychological and social signifying where very few scholars have dared to venture. Social scientists may repeat time and again that racial and ethnic prejudices are scientifically untenable, but they continue to determine the lives of countless people all over the world. As Hoetink (1967:89) poignantly observes: 'The sociologist's exposure of racial prejudices as mere myths will not put an end to their psychosocial reality.' Hoetink's analysis refers more than anything to the unconscious psychosocial necessities of human groupings to give meaning to the, that is, their, world. These necessities clearly have all kinds of social consequences, but Hoetink avoids designating the construction of racial and ethnic images as conscious strategy, either from groups or from individuals. Race or ethnicity may be constructions or even mythologies, but as such they are psychological and social realities, which have dynamics of their own and have, in spite of their constructed nature, unavoidable social consequences.[1] Thus Hoetink's work both precedes and qualifies theories which stress the constructivist nature of national and ethnic identities.

It is not possible here to go into the complex discussion on the concepts of 'race' and 'ethnicity'. However, it is important to note that Hoetink's work is informed by the conviction that ideas about the ethnic organization of the world are 'images', constructions which guide social relations and individual conduct, but at the same time, stresses the structural – cultural and historical – determinants of these images. Human beings are socially and psychologically conditioned and cannot merely deploy those elements of a cultural system which are to their liking. What people like, what they consider esthetically attractive, how they regard the world and human relations, are opinions which are deeply grounded in the cultural and psychosocial systems in which they grow up. These are not unchanging worldviews, and they vary according to the historical circumstances. In this sense, Hoetink appears to attempt a middle course between the 'US' perception of race as a matter of heredity, and the 'Brazilian' point of view of race as phenotype and, above all, color. Whereas in the former, racial and ethnic relations are very rigid, in the latter, there is much more space for the notion of construction and for changing meanings of race and ethnicity (Viotti da Costa, 1992:146).

This perspective, when fully thought through, may lead to a qualification of too one-sided an emphasis on the constructed nature of social identities. At the same time, it suggests that ethnic and racial attitudes are not so prone to manipulation from above as is sometimes suggested. It thus places more emphasis on the resilience of popular world-views and ideologies. These may be 'proto-nationalist', to use Hobsbawm's concept (1990:46ff), enhancing the creation of a nationalist identity, but they may equally well work in the opposite direction, hampering or even resisting the ideological projects of political elites. The analysis of national ideologies thus needs to incorporate their relationship to popular ideologies. It is necessary to confront the schemes and policies of intellectuals and politicians with the daily realities of the population, and to analyze the links between existing somatic norm images and ethnic policies pursued by outsiders. In this article I will attempt to address this problem, taking as an example the Dominican Republic and, in particular, its relations with its neighbor Haiti.

The search for nationhood in Latin America

The social and political history of the Latin American nations in the nineteenth and twentieth centuries is impossible to understand without taking into account the debate amongst the Latin American elite on the roots of the national self. The dominant classes tried to create and shape their societies' culture and to reach acceptable definitions of national identity. This was not an easy task considering the ethnic diversity of most Latin American states and the difficulties they encountered in converting this diverse population into nations. On the other hand, many elite groups feared the destruction of traditional society which often resulted from economic modernization. In a study on Mexican nationalism, Claudio Lomnitz-Adler (1992:248ff) has recently emphasized that nationalism in nineteenth- and early twentieth-century Latin America generally expressed itself by resistance to the modernization of society and the changes it brought. This nationalism failed to recognize, according to Lomnitz-Adler, that nation-states were creatures of modernity. His observation points to a fundamental ambiguity in Latin American movements towards modernization. Most Latin American elites tried to forge their nations in the name of *el progreso*, a concept that symbolized the desire for rapid modernization, but at the same time they feared, and sometimes resisted the destruction of 'traditional' society.

This ambiguity between a modernizing nation-building and a retrospective rhetoric is an interesting starting point for any analysis of nation-building in Latin America. Modernizing liberalism associated the past with backwardness and obscurantism, but at the same time invoked the past to create new patterns of stability and coherence in a world that was threatened by economic growth, labor migration and ethnic confusion. Nostalgic appeals often referred to a mythical past where nationality was supposed to have been unambiguous and unproblematic. This hesitant quest for modernity was also reflected in the ethnic policies of the newly created nation-states. Many Latin American intellectuals had expected that the 'racial question' would resolve itself under the onslaught of modernization. They were bitterly disappointed when they discovered that this was not the case. This was partly the result of the local needs of nascent capitalism. Most large-scale enterprises in Latin America and the Caribbean came to depend on migrant labor which was ethnically distinctive. This was a response to the scarcity of native labor, but capitalist entrepreneurs also took advantage of the resulting ethnic divisions between immigrants and the native population to increase their control over the labor force. According to Greenberg (1980; also Andrews, 1991), they created institutional mechanisms designed to coerce members of racially subordinate groups into entering the wage-labor market and accepting employment on terms dictated by their employers and the state.

Racial and ethnic categories did indeed play an important role in the construction of national identities in Latin America and the Caribbean. Emerging nation-states in the nineteenth and twentieth centuries, confronted by an ethnically diverse population, applied themselves to the task of eradicating the most extreme differences and forging some sort of a national identity.[2] The continuing ethnic diversity in the region and the problems in forging homogeneous nations led to social-Darwinist and racist ideas, and the intellectual pessimism that is often mentioned as a central characteristic of Latin American and Caribbean social thought (Hale, 1986; Lewis, 1983). Most national policies were strongly influenced by European 'scientific racism' and elements from social Darwinism as interpreted by Herbert Spencer. Richard Graham (1990:1) has even argued that the idea of race as it was formulated in nineteenth-century Latin America must be considered a hegemonic ideology, by which the dominant classes maintained or at least justified their economic and political power. The bottom line of these theories was, of course, that the white (or Caucasian or Aryan) race was superior to the other races, and eventually was destined to dominate the world. Although such theories were difficult to apply to the racially mixed Latin American continent, these European ideas were very influential amongst the Latin American elites, who defined themselves as white. Sometimes this led to a deeply felt racial pessimism, directed towards the indigenous or Afro-American population (as for instance in the work of the Argentinean, Carlos Bunge or the Bolivian, Alcides Arguedas), or towards the mixed population which was considered unstable and degenerate (as in the work of the Brazilian, Euclides da Cunha).[3]

It could well be that this racially inspired pessimism was the direct result of the impotence of intellectuals and political elites to obtain full control over the process of social transformation that they were trying to bring about (Smith, 1981:90ff). Many people were appalled by the destruction of traditional society and the consequent disappearance of long-standing social relations and values. They felt betrayed by the Trojan horse which the much-vaunted modernization had turned out to be. Plantations – in many Caribbean and Latin American countries the principal vehicles of modernization – brought economies of scale and much wanted technology to the continent, but they destroyed the order of traditional society. Poverty in the rural areas forced part of the population to migrate or live the unstable life of wage-laborers. This tendency undermined the patriarchal power of the traditional elite and furthered the interests of outsiders, often foreigners. A delegate to the National Congress in the Dominican Republic voiced these sentiments in 1894 commenting on the consequences of the sugar plantations in the south:

> It is certain that the government of the Republic and many others believe that the sugar plantations will enrich the country. I do not agree with them. I do not share the illusion that the plantations will make the country any richer. The progress apparently fostered by them is fictitious. The first time I visited the region, I saw in the countryside many agricultural plots (*conucos*) that provided means of subsistence. But when the plantations came, showers of gold were expected and there was public elation. Today all the people who possessed a *conuco* have sold their land and transformed themselves into *peones* of the plantation owners.[4]

Around the turn of the century, this disillusionment with the consequences of modernization was noticeable everywhere on the continent. This could lead to political resentment, as in the case of the Aprista party in northern Peru (Klaren, 1973). More often it resulted in a romantic nostalgia towards the society destroyed by modernization. This feeling was the breeding ground of the *indigenista* movements in Peru and Mexico, but also of the symbolic glorification of creole society and small-scale peasant production, such as occurred in Cuba, Puerto Rico and, to a certain extent, in the Dominican Republic (Martinez Alier, 1977; Lewis, 1983). We can best understand these nationalist ideologies, and the mobilization of ethnic forces which went with them, when we realize that, in spite of their rhetoric of tradition and unchanging values, they were principally a result of – and a response to – the processes of modernization faced by these countries in the nineteenth and twentieth centuries. I discuss this in more detail by looking at the specific case of the Dominican Republic.

The forging of a Dominican national identity

> But I have to warn you, madam, that the Dominicans are Consti-
> tutionally white, and that is the reason we have established this
> Republic, which you must not confuse with that of Haiti, where
> the people eat human flesh, speak creole French (*patoi*) and
> where voodoo gods abound (Moscoso Puello, 1913:10).

Dominican nationalism had to start from scratch when the country gained
its independence in 1844. After the short period of intensive Spanish colonialism in the sixteenth century, Spain lost interest in its colony, a neglect
which led to the loss of the western part of the island to the French in the
seventeenth century. The French colony, Saint Domingue, became the most
successful plantation colony of its time, bestowing on the population of the
languishing Spanish colony a profound inferiority complex. This feeling
was intensified by the manner in which the Dominican Republic became
independent of Spain. It was, in fact, 'liberated' by the rebellious slaves of
Saint Domingue, who, led by Toussaint Louverture, had put an end to
French rule. Only after being governed by the new Haitian government
from 1822 to 1844 did the Dominican Republic win its independence. The
fact that they had to wrest it from a fellow ex-colony and not from a colonial
power has tainted Dominican nationalism ever since.[5]

The majority of the creole elite – commercial entrepreneurs and landowners – fled the country at the start of the Haitian occupation. Those who
remained were hardly in a position to formulate the tenets of a nascent
nationalism. They were pushed forward by circumstances which, as it were,
thrust independence on them. They felt both a deep fear of the armies of the
neighboring republic and a resentment of French and British intervention
in the island's affairs. While a wave of anti-Hispanism swept the Latin
American continent, the Dominican elite, which based its position on its
possession of land and its Spanish descent, but which by continental
standards was relatively poor and uneducated, fell back on its links with the
Spanish motherland. In the words of the conservative intellectual Peña
Battle (1989[1952]:61): 'We Dominicans formed our national identity fighting to remain Spaniards.' This *hispanofilia* symbolized the desire of the
weak and insecure Dominican elite to hold on to its European ancestry and
to remain part of the 'civilized' world.

Such an ideology was fueled by the repugnance felt for the ex-slave
population of neighboring Haiti. For many Dominicans Haiti became, as we
will see, the antithesis of civilization and the symbol of barbarism. This
contrast between *civilization* and *barbarism* is a common theme in Latin
American intellectual history, but in the Dominican Republic it was inextricably related to the existence of Haiti. Chained as a Siamese twin to a people

whom it despised and feared, the Dominican elite desperately tried to uphold its European identity. This led, in 1861, to an unprecedented step. After unsuccessful negotiations with several European powers (most notably the French), General Santana, then President of the country, placed the Dominican Republic once again under the colonial authority of the Spanish Crown (Domínguez, 1979). No-one knows what would have happened if Spain had grasped its second chance with more enthusiasm and efficiency. In fact Spain did nothing of the kind and its repressive and inept policies provoked immediate protests. In spite of its ideological commitment to European culture, the majority of the Dominican elite was not ready to accept a subordinate status and a new period of Spanish colonialism. By 1863 a resistance movement against Spanish colonialism was already in full swing, ultimately leading to the humiliating departure of Spanish troops in 1865.

The acceptance of Spanish domination by one part of the Dominican elite, and the almost immediate resistance to it by another, clearly demonstrates the dilemmas of Dominican nationalism. The conflicting interests of the various economic and social elites within the country were probably the determining factor in this ideological cleavage. Annexation to Spain had been favored by the southern cattle-holders led by Pedro Santana. This land-owning elite had acquired its properties during Spanish colonialism and hoped to perpetuate its dominant social, political and military position by again linking the country to Spain.

In the northern valley of the country, usually called the Cibao, a completely different situation existed. Here, smaller and larger land-owners took advantage of the end of Spanish colonial rule which, in spite of the subsequent decades of warfare on the island, had opened up the island economy for new commercial contacts. This resulted in the expansion of small-scale export agriculture, especially of tobacco. European (notably German) ships started to anchor off the coast and a regular commercial traffic ensued. It resulted in a dynamic economic development in which all sectors of the population took part (Baud, 1995). The nascent middle classes emerging from the expansion of export agriculture, especially in the Cibao, became the principal bearers of liberal ideology. They advocated commercial freedom and the unhampered traffic of goods, and were quite outwardly oriented. Liberal leaders maintained close contact with congenial spirits in other parts of the Caribbean and even in Europe and the US. They were, in general, critical of Spain as a colonial power (although others, among whom Américo Lugo was the most prominent, always remained *hispanista*) and blamed the former motherland for the weak national identity of the independent Dominican Republic. But they blamed Pedro Santana even more, and his decision to annex the country to Spain made him the hated symbol of treason and *vende-patria*.

The regional difference resulted in a deeply-felt antagonism between the regional elite of the Cibao and the large landowners in the south. This antagonism found its political expression in the ideological struggle between southern conservatives and northern liberals.[6] On several occasions, the elite of the Cibao only just stopped short of declaring its independence. The economic and ideological antagonism between the regional elites was maintained well into the twentieth century and has only gradually lost its importance in Dominican politics.

The Dominican Republic was nominally a presidential democracy, and unless they were temporarily closed, the Congress and the Senate regularly convened. The influence of the sometimes heated, sometimes perfunctory, debates between politicians and intellectuals was very limited, however. Most politicians, and even dictators such as Heureaux and Trujillo, valued the symbolic function of the system, but at the same time were convinced that the real test of strength took place elsewhere. Ideologies hardly mattered in a situation where most politicians were at the same time military men, and in general the political process was decided by military force. The influence Dominican intellectuals could exercise on the political turn of events was very minor indeed. They tried to intervene in domestic politics, but they were hardly in a position to enforce their ideas. Men of learning, like Pedro Francisco Bonó, enjoyed widespread respect, but military men considered their ideas too abstract to be really useful in daily reality. The 'doctors' depended upon the 'generals', as Hoetink (1982:119) observes. The pessimism that is often cited as a basic characteristic of Dominican culture may well be the direct result of this situation. Many Dominican intellectuals felt frustrated because of their impotence to give direction to the political affairs of their country. Nevertheless, in the context of this article it is important to note that we may rightfully doubt that this pessimism was shared by the mass of the Dominican people.

The social gap between the elite and the rest of the population was wide. Because of its emphasis on the differences between social groups, and considering its rigidity and immobility, Hoetink (1970, 1982) labeled Dominican society 'aristocratic'. This is not to say that social differences were wholly static, but that Dominican culture was characterized by an emphasis on social distance. This distance was in part racially based. The majority of the population was of mixed descent and might be described as 'mulatto', although in the twentieth century the term *indio* became normally used. Racial relations in the Dominican Republic were not very polarized, but the dominant classes tried to maintain a clear color line. They were in general distinguished by a lighter complexion and prided themselves on their (alleged) European descent. Periods of temporary social mobility existed, but they were rapidly followed by regroupings of the elite and the creation of new social barriers, which were just as rigid as the former ones.

Hoetink points to the interesting paradox that the growing impact of the world market and increasing market relations initially resulted in greater social mobility, which then rapidly gave way to new forms of rigid social stratification: 'When the new stratification had crystallized and stabilized, the social demarcation lines were more clearly drawn and more difficult to cross than had been the case before these changes took place' (1986:296).

Yet we should not misunderstand the daily reality. The social cleavages never impeded a certain flexibility in day-to-day relations. Multifarious patron–client relations existed between regional powerholders and the peasantry. Both groups had a stake in the maintenance of these links. Landowners and entrepreneurs depended on the peasants to secure labor and political loyalty. At the same time, the loyalties of the rural population were regional and personal more than national. The peasantry had lived in relative isolation for centuries and had been dependent on the protection and occasional support of the economically more prosperous and politically more powerful social groups in their close environment. Peasant existence was built around direct daily needs and rural people placed much emphasis on their good relations with the regional powerholders. These patron–client relations carried over into the urban setting and seem to have been the principal organizing element in Dominican society throughout the nineteenth and early-twentieth centuries.

It is important to understand that this situation gave a special edge to Dominican society. The emphasis on social distance was important and originated in negative elite attitudes towards the Dominican peasantry and the somatically darker, poor population in general. However, the paternalistic relations between rich and poor were used by the elite as an example that these relations had been 'traditionally' good and that the mutual understanding between the Dominican elite and the peasantry had always been a basic characteristic of Dominican culture. This point of view served two purposes. It demonstrated both the paternalistic benevolence and social compassion of the Dominican elite and the peaceful attitude and sense of civic responsibility proper to the native population. This idea of the harmonious character of Dominican culture served the purpose of de-emphasizing the social and ethnic differences within Dominican society. It became one of the essential myths of Dominican national ideology, especially in the northern part of the country.

The Dominican Republic versus the outside world

Dominican nationalism had to confront two principal obstacles: the political and economic underdevelopment of the country and the ethnic and social diversity of the population. To these elements was added the influence of outsiders. In the early decades of the twentieth century, Dominican society underwent drastic social and economic changes resulting in the increasing importance of external relations. Economic development and new links to the world economy made the country more susceptible to external influences. In the second half of the nineteenth century, European interests were gradually replaced by North American investments. US entrepreneurs gained control of the sugar industry and the foreign debt was taken over by the New York-based San Domingo Improvement Company. In the process, the company also took control of the only state-owned railway in the country, the Ferrocarril Central Dominicano which ran from Puerto Plata to Santiago. Thus at the start of the twentieth century the United States became an inescapable presence in Dominican politics. In 1907, when the US government took over responsibility for the Republic's customs houses, national independence became practically non-existent. In hindsight the US occupation of the country in 1916 was probably inevitable. It may be more surprising that it lasted only eight years, until 1924 (Calder, 1984).

Here we are not so much interested in the practical organization of the US occupation as in its sociopsychological and ideological consequences. The ambiguous social and psychological effects of US domination in Latin America have been widely noted (Hale, 1986). These were not unlike those emerging in Africa in the same period as a result of European colonialism (Cooper, *et al.*, 1993; Memmi, 1967). On the one hand, it led to a feeling of inferiority on the part of the Latin American elite, which was politically translated into a lack of confidence in a future for their nations. On the other hand, it found expression in feelings of aggression, envy and hatred vis-à-vis the powerful neighbor to the North. Anti-Yankee feeling throughout Latin America greatly increased towards the end of the nineteenth century. In the Dominican Republic it was compounded by the US occupation of the country. Again, this anti-Yankeeism was deeply ambiguous. Dominican society resisted US influence, but at the same time succumbed to many cultural elements from the US. The persistence of cock-fighting, against the concerted efforts of US officials to abolish this 'primitive' pastime, may be an example of the first attitude; the popularity of baseball of the second (Ruck, 1991). In any case, the encroachment and dominance of US culture inspired a new, more coherent and effective nationalism, which might well have been the most important factor in the relatively rapid departure of US troops.

The second outside influence which deeply influenced Dominican nationalism (and the sense of ethnic identity of the Dominican people) was that of neighboring Haiti (Derby, 1994). After Haiti had attained its independence, the historical development of the two nations were inextricably linked. The economic relations between the two parts of the island remained important and, as we shall see later, there was a flourishing cross-border trade. Haiti was the more populous and ahead in its economic development. It was also the militarily stronger of the two, and the Dominican elite felt profound doubts about the viability of the independence of its country. This ambiguity, and the internal divisions within the Dominican elite, showed clearly when the country annexed itself again as a colony to Spain in 1861. The most likely explanation for this decision was fear of the Haitian menace. Although the military threat of Haiti gradually disappeared, partly because of treaties in 1874 and 1895, the national elite continued to look for outside support. On various occasions politicians tried to annex the country to the United States (Tansill, 1938).

In the twentieth century, fear of Haitian military power was replaced by feelings of disdain for a society with increasing economic and political problems (Vega, 1988). Contempt for the neighboring country became more and more formulated in ethnic and racial terms. The racial differences between the (predominantly) black Haitian population and the (predominantly) mulatto population of the Dominican Republic had always been a factor in relations between the two countries, but the transformation in social and economic structure which occurred after 1870 made the racial factor more important (Hoetink, 1982:192). The rapidly increasing migration of Haitian labor to the Dominican sugar plantations in the beginning of the twentieth century played a determining role in this process. For the first time since the Haitian occupation, major confrontations between the two populations began to take place. The poverty of the Haitian laborers provoked feelings of racial superiority among the Dominicans. These feelings were complemented by a deeply felt disgust at the living and labor conditions of the sugar-cane cutters (Murphy, 1991:129–56). Although many Dominican observers condemned the inhumane conditions inside the largely foreign-owned sugar plantations, the Haitians were implicitly blamed for their passive acceptance of these conditions. Even the more socially conscious elements of society tended to interpret this attitude as evidence of the backward and primitive mental condition of the Haitian migrant laborers. In addition, Dominican workers regarded the Haitian migrant workers as a menace to their position in the labor market. This explains why the incipient labor unions in the Dominican Republic were so critical of Haitian immigration (Cassá, 1990:61ff; Baud, 1992).

In a paradoxical way, the US occupation of the country was another factor undermining the position of Haitian migrants. During the US occupation of both the Dominican Republic (1916–24) and Haiti (1915–34), the labor force of the sugar plantations became exclusively Haitian. Dominican social memory associated the large-scale immigration of Haitian workers directly with US rule. Indeed, many Dominicans specifically blamed the US (and, for that matter, US-owned sugar enterprises) for the uncontrolled invasion of Haitian *braceros*. Anti-Yankee feelings thus confirmed and reinforced anti-Haitian feelings. This negative connection is still maintained in certain nationalist sectors of today's Dominican Republic. In these circles the US is accused of underestimating the cultural differences between the two peoples. Some even suspect the US and other foreign governments of secretly wanting to unify the two countries.[7]

The nineteenth-century tradition of Dominican nationalism and the more recent anti-Haitian and anti-US feeling joined forces in the nationalist movement which arose in the last years of the US occupation. This movement yielded a body of ideas which were put into practice during the six-year term of President Horacio Vásquez and found their most extreme and elaborated expression in the long Trujillo dictatorship (1930–61). The government tried to close the country for Haitian immigrants, except for the seasonal labor migration to the sugar plantations. It started colonization projects in order to 'Dominicanize' the border region. And when that did not work, Trujillo ordered the infamous *matanza* in 1937, in which thousands of Haitian migrants were killed by Dominican troops, causing an international uproar (García, 1983; Prestol Castillo, 1972). Simultaneously, the intellectuals around the dictator molded Dominican nationalism into a true hegemonic ideology. By enforcing existing conservative nationalist ideas with a ruthless system of repression, the more liberal and democratic variants of Dominican nationalism were driven underground.

Historical nationalism: Peña Battle

Conservative Dominican nationalism, as it was formulated during the Trujillo regime, was essentially based on one historical argument; namely, that the origins of the Dominican nation were to be found in the colonial period and that, in *status nascendi*, a national identity already existed in this period. The other elements of nationalist ideology, especially the *hispanismo* and the anti-Haitianism, were derived from this argument.[8]

These historical nationalist ideas were elaborated most profoundly by Manuel Arturo Peña Battle (1902–1954), a Dominican intellectual who after keeping his distance from the Trujillo regime for almost ten years, became one of its principal ideologues (González, 1991; Vega, 1990). He wrote numerous books and articles, all of which were dedicated to the question of national identity. His thesis was relatively simple. The core of the Dominican nation was established in the first century of the Spanish colonization. The Spanish colonists were the direct ancestors of the Dominican people, and Dominican national identity should therefore be traced back directly to the first stage of the Spanish colonization of the island. This vision was in line with early nineteenth-century Dominican nationalism,

with its attachment to the Spanish motherland. The anti-Spanish Black
Legend which played such an important role in continental nationalism of
the nineteenth century, thus acquired a very specific content in the case
of the Dominican Republic. Although Peña Battle does not fail to mention
the *crueldad* of the Spanish colonization and the materialist thirst for
gold of the first colonizers, he was at pains to stress the influential human-
itarian counterforces which also existed among the Spaniards. Stressing
this *formidable corriente de oposición* he wrote:

> Confronted by the greedy gaze of imperialism, there arose in
> America opposing and generous values of those who defended
> the freedom of the Indians and worked for them, and even ad-
> vocated the political autonomy of these recently discovered
> nations. (1989[1937]:28)

This two-sided assessment of Spanish colonialism enabled Peña Battle to
stress the positive influence of the Spanish heritage on Dominican culture
while simultaneously maintaining the necessary distance from the former
colonial master. In addition, it allowed him to affirm the positive characteristics of the native population to the point of historically justifying the
Indian rebellion against the Spaniards in 1520 and juridically defending
the sovereignty of the Indian population. In the view of Peña Battle
(1989[1937]:30–2), Spain could only claim sovereign rights over the island
after the extinction of the Indians.

Peña Battle's analysis of the colonial period is in many ways very
critical of Spain. Although he conceded to Spain the right of colonization,
he delivered severe judgments on its bad administration. In the face of inept
colonialism, resistance was the natural reaction for the population of the
colony. Peña Battle therefore approved very clearly of the illicit commerce
conducted by the island's population. His harshest criticism was reserved
for the Spanish policy towards the western part of the island. By the so-
called *devastaciones* (1605–06) the Spaniards opened up this region to
foreign intruders, eventually leading to the establishment of the French
colony of Saint Domingue. Spanish policy should be blamed for the establishment of Haiti and the division of the island. For Peña Battle one man
was responsible for this situation, the then Governor of the island, don
Antonio Ossorio, 'a debauched and unjust man, a gambler, needlessly cruel,
a nepotist and blackmailer'. He bore all the guilt for the confused identity
of the Dominican Republic:

> Because of his manifest administrative incapacity he compro-
> mised the future and laid the foundation for the extremely serious
> problems that have confronted and will continue to confront the
> island. Don Antonio Ossorio is the father of the social and ethnic

duality into which the island has been divided and of the spirit-less languor which has characterized Dominican nationality. (1989[1938]:105–6)

From a wider perspective, Peña Battle (1989[1938]:118) saw this policy as the symbol of the 'dejected and wavering spirit' of 'the exhausted Spain of Philip III'.

For Peña Battle, the defeatist policy of Spain was thus the essential cause of the problems of the later Dominican Republic. It condemned a vital and healthy national identity to degeneration. 'The systematic and organized destruction of colonial wealth had to produce, fatally, a profound weakening of the population, misery, and consequently, the uprooted nature of the future national identity' (1989[1938]:131). Spanish colonial policy had not only economic and political, but also racial or ethnic consequences. Before the *devastaciones*, Española had a culturally and racially homogeneous population, 'well defined because of its pure roots'. This stood in glaring contrast to the profound racial conflicts which would characterize the island afterwards. Peña Battle concludes: 'The collective life of the Dominicans has to some extent been a case of social pathology from that moment on.'[9]

This analysis of Dominican history served twentieth-century Dominican nationalists in two ways. Firstly, it allowed them to assert their independence without being forced to deny their Spanish heritage. Secondly, it served as a legitimization for the anti-Haitian ideology which developed from the last decades of the nineteenth century onwards. Peña Battle's version of the establishment of Saint Domingue and the origins of the independent republic of Haiti had clear ideological implications. His interest in French colonialism refered to just one element: the importation of hundreds of thousands of African slaves into the French colony. The slave society that came into existence in the western part of the island would have far-reaching consequences for the future of the island, whose problematic history was the direct result of the forced coexistence of two cultures: the African-inspired black culture of the west, and the Spanish-inspired white (or Spanish) culture of the east.

Peña Battle's emphasis on the cultural and racial differences on the island was based on his rejection of the French slave system. The French treated their slaves so cruelly that the latter did not have the possibility of living a decent, human life. The inhuman living conditions had negative consequences for the cultural development of the slave population. In his essay on the origins of the Haitian state, published posthumously in 1954, he wrote: 'They could not count on any of the material facilities needed by a human being to develop himself among his equals' (1989[1954]:152).[10] By denying them both care and a proper religious education, the French slave owners had prevented the slaves from making any moral progress. This conjunction of historical events had disastrous effects on the culture and identity of the slave population:

> As a direct consequence of the lucrative and infamous slave trade by which the protestant powers dishonored themselves in the seventeenth and eighteenth centuries, the great majority of the population in the colony did not develop any culture; neither was it favored by any spiritual guidance or political organization, which would have permitted the beginning of national integration (1989[1954]:155)

When the slaves finally fought their – justified – struggle for freedom, they did not do so out of a sense of national sentiment. After their victory they were therefore unable to join the community of civilized nations.

Peña Battle was not able to finish his analysis of the island's history in the nineteenth century and did not have the opportunity to elaborate his ideas about the development of Dominican nationalism. However, he did indicate the likely contours of his analysis in some shorter studies. It was centered around two persons. The first, not surprisingly, was one of the fathers of independence, Juan Pablo Duarte. Investing him with saint-like dimensions, Peña Battle (1989[1950]:191) presented him as 'the real and only founding father of Dominican national consciousness'. Peña Battle's other hero was less predictable. Indeed, it is difficult to imagine a person more different from Peña Battle, the remote intellectual, than the ruthless warlord Pedro Santana, who was vilified by many Dominicans for selling his country to Spain in 1861. The complexity of Peña Battle's thinking shows itself clearly in his interpretation of this episode of Dominican history. According to him, General Pedro Santana had been fighting Haitian invasions for almost twenty years, before he finally realized, 'with great personal repugnance', that only the protection of a European power could save the infant Republic. His decision to annex the Dominican Republic to Spain should therefore be regarded as a sign of a deeply-felt nationalism.

This historical interpretation of the Dominican Annexation to Spain in 1861 closes the circle of Peña Battle's thinking. It is clear that for him Española should have remained an undivided 'Spanish' island. He envisioned the Dominican people as a nation which has been robbed of its sovereign rights.[11] The creole consciousness which had been developing in the sixteenth century had been thwarted first by Spanish defeatism and later by the political and ethnic division of the island.[12] The existence of Haiti thus was central to his analysis of Dominican nationalism. This was also the ulterior motive for his writing of Haitian history, as is revealed in passing by a short sentence within his erudite interpretation of the Haitian Revolution. He writes: 'We merely wish to determine precisely and as clearly as possible the social and ideological content of this movement in order to relate it to the national formation of the Dominican Republic.' (1989[1954]:177). For Peña Battle and many other conservative nationalists, nationalism in the Dominican Republic was thus inextricably linked to the existence of the Haitian state.

It is interesting to note that in spite of his negative views of the Haitian people, Peña Battle is at great pains to show that this judgment refers only to the poor Haitian masses. For him the Haitian elite was not the issue. As he cynically observed: 'This group does not interest us, because it does not cause problems to us; this one does not migrate.' (1946:89). This attempt to exclude the Haitian elite from anti-Haitian ideology has remained a preoccupation of the Dominican intellectual elite up to the present day. This may be explained by the numerous economic and political contacts between the governing elites of both countries, which, in spite of so much hostile rhetoric, characterized their relations in the nineteenth and twentieth centuries.

Towards a racial nationalism: Joaquín Balaguer

Peña Battle's ideas were shared by many other Dominican intellectuals before and, above all, during the Trujillo dictatorship (Del Rosario Perez, 1957; Sánchez, 1976) but no-one approached his sophistication. During (and after) the Trujillo regime Peña Battle's historical analysis of the origins of Dominican nationalism was transformed into a mechanistic and often overtly racist justification of Dominican superiority vis-à-vis Haiti and the Haitian population. Some recent studies have highlighted the role of Joaquín Balaguer in this intellectual shift (Dore Cabral, 1985; Fennema and Loewenthal, 1987; Zaglul, 1992; Murphy, 1991:135–9). Balaguer was one of the closest allies of Trujillo and held many important posts during the Trujillo regime. He continued to be a prominent politician in the post-Trujillo period, and held the presidency for many years. As such, he became the symbol of continuity within conservative nationalism in the twentieth-century Dominican Republic. His role became even more apparent when his book *La isla al revés* was published in 1983. Here Balaguer repeats, sometimes literally, the ideas he had expounded in 1947 in *La realidad dominicana*. These ideas may be taken as representative of the racially informed nationalism which became so important in twentieth-century Dominican society.

The work of Balaguer touches many of the same themes as that of Peña Battle, and at certain points their interpretations of history are identical (for instance, in their judgment of Pedro Santana and the Annexation to Spain). Nevertheless, there are important differences. All Peña Battle's work is dedicated to unravelling the complicated historical origins of the Dominican nation. Balaguer, on the contrary, takes the existence of a homogeneous Dominican nation for granted. For him the Dominican people have always been characterized by their European culture and Hispanic background. In contrast to Peña Battle's historical vision, Balaguer's interpretation of Dominican culture is inherently static. He makes hardly any effort to analyze Dominican culture, let alone the changes it has undergone. In his eyes, Dominicans are basically Spaniards, whose racial and cultural characteristics have remained the same since the first Spanish colonizers occupied the island. Balaguer writes: 'Santo Domingo is, *por instinto de conservación*, the most Spanish and traditional nation of America.'

All elements of Dominican society, past and present, that do not conform to the ideal Spanish pattern, must be considered the unfortunate result of pernicious extraneous influences, and in the eyes of Balaguer these all boil down to one; that of Haiti. Since he perceived Haiti as the principal enemy of the Dominican nation, his work is one long diatribe against the Haitian people. For him, the cultural conservatism and passivity of the Dominican people was a direct reaction to the cultural and racial threat posed by the Haitians: 'It has nevertheless clung to its Spanish descent as a means of defence against the unnatural labors (*la labor desnaturalizante*) conducted against it by Haitian imperialism' (1985:63).

This leads to another important difference between Balaguer and Peña Battle. Balaguer replaces historical with biological or racist arguments. Where Peña Battle lamented the establishment of another sovereign state on the 'Spanish' island and tried to analyze its consequences for the Dominican nation, Balaguer's work is directed against the black 'African' (or 'Ethiopian') origins of the Haitian people.[13] His entire analysis of the island's history is based on biological and racial assumptions that belong to late nineteenth- and early twentieth-century social-Darwinist and eugenistic thinking. It is based on two interrelated assumptions. First, that it is possible to distinguish a racial hierarchy in the world population, in which the white (or Caucasian) race is at the top and the black (or African) race is at the bottom. Second, that the mixing of race, or *mestizaje* as it was then called, would cause inevitable degeneration and pose a threat to the vitality of the superior race.[14] These two assumptions form the basic foundation of Balaguer's work, as is the case with similar racially-based theories which found support elsewhere on the continent. However, whereas most Latin American elites found this racial hierarchy within their national frontiers, in the Dominican case it was expressed in relation to another nation.

It is not necessary to go deeply into Balaguer's racial discourse. That has been convincingly done by others. It comes down to the following view of history. The Dominican people constitute a white, Hispanic nation, which from the nineteenth century has been threatened by the imperialist tendencies of another nation which, because of its African origins, was in every sense inferior. Because of its primitive nature, the Haitian population procreated much more rapidly than the Dominican population. This was the cornerstone of what Balaguer calls 'Haitian imperialism': the continuous Haitian pressure on the resources of the Dominican Republic. Liaisons between Dominicans and Haitians and race-mixing led to the weakening of the Dominican race. In and of itself this tendency already threatened the Dominican nation, but it was made worse by other factors. The Haitians do not possess any education, carry epidemic diseases and lack moral values (shown above all by their promiscuity). Wherever there is contact with groups of Haitians, a degeneration in the moral and spiritual power of the Dominican population is visible. The indolence of a great part of the Dominican population must be explained by the pernicious influence of Haitian immigrants.

Another source of Balaguer's nationalism was a Dominican form of *campesinismo*. As happened elsewhere in Latin America, both conservative and liberal intellectuals presented small-scale agriculture as the true foundation of national identity. The peasantry was presented as the symbol of creole identity, representing all the essential qualities of *dominicanidad*. The Dominican peasant was simple but honest; poor but content; violent and short-tempered but generous. And, of course, he was a man! In the exalted words of a Dominican journal:

> The peasant is the creole *par excellence*. He loves his cows, his land and his woman, which together form his rustic homeland and his family. His character is straightforward, his manners simple, his affection sincere and his friendship so constant that he makes noble sacrifices to prove his loyalty . . . The peasant is the happiest Dominican. He lives quietly in his rural dwelling, comfortable, innocent, far away from corruption . . . [15]

In the Dominican version of this idyll, there often existed a faint suggestion that this mythical peasant was a creolized Spaniard and white. It therefore appealed to conservative nationalists, especially in the twentieth century when the destruction of traditional rural society provoked a romantic nostalgia for the past. This could lead a loving and attentive observer of rural society like Ramón Emilio Jiménez (1927, 1952) to become a prominent supporter of the Trujillo regime. A clear *campesinista* current is also discernable in the writings (and political program) of Balaguer, which presents the 'pure' peasant as the symbol of traditional Dominican values. It is interesting to note that Balaguer's vision of the spiritual power of the Dominican rural population is strongly colored by *machista* thinking. Nancy Leys Stepan (1991) has rightly emphasized that social-Darwinist thinking usually also implied a specific vision of gender relations and of the female sex in particular. This is certainly true in the case of Balaguer. Dominican men have to guard over their women. They protect them against other men, take them when they wish and generally dominate their lives. The implicit warning in Balaguer's work is that male superiority is an essential element of Dominican identity which is threatened by the degenerating influence of the Haitian incursors.[16]

The importance of Balaguer's analysis is not its sophistication. On the contrary, it is such an idiosyncratic amalgam of opinion, political opportunism and prejudice that it cannot sustain any scientific criticism. The reason why so many people have tried to come to grips with his ideas is that Balaguer has been a very important political figure who has continued to play a central role in Dominican politics until the present day. Fennema and Loewenthal (1987:63) are probably right in thinking that Balaguer takes an extremist position in the racial discussion in the Dominican Republic. At the same time, these ideas have not proved to be any obstacle to widespread political support. The extreme racist position Balaguer has defended during more than fifty years has not hindered his uninterrupted political career. On the contrary, he has enjoyed the support of a large part of the Dominican population and has been elected to the Presidency in two fairly honest elections, in 1986 and 1990. Of course, this support may not be purely the result of his anti-Haitian ideas, but they have clearly not spoiled his chances. It is important then to trace the relationship between his nationalist ideology on the one hand, and the world view of the Dominican population, with its popular notions of nationalism, on the other.

Popular views of Dominican identity

Dominican anti-Haitianism has nowadays become proverbial and most studies on the Dominican Republic stress the racist nature of Dominican nationalism (Sagás, 1993). Such judgments are usually supported by quoting the opinions of Dominican politicians, and more often than not, only those of Joaquín Balaguer (Marquez, 1992). This method of equating the opinions of political leaders with those of the Dominican people is encouraged by the fact that anti-Haitian policies have often been legitimized by reference to the popular will. Intellectuals and politicians throughout Dominican history have sought to make others believe that they spoke on behalf of the people. Conservative nationalists repeated time and again that they were merely voicing ideas alive within the (rural) population. An eloquent example of this tendency can be found in a letter of Balaguer, written in 1945 to Colombian intellectuals, justifying the killing of the Haitians in 1937. Balaguer wrote:

The events of 1937, which the enemies of the Dominican government have tried to present abroad as a merciless slaughter of
enormous numbers of Haitians, were the result of a feeling
of protest in the souls of our peasants against four centuries of
plundering by gangs of Haitian robbers in the northern border
provinces (cited in Cornielle, 1980:244).

Similar remarks can be found throughout the modern period. They are often
taken at face value or at least accepted as evidence of popular anti-Haitianism.

There is no doubt that the existence of Haiti and the differences
between Haitians and Dominicans have always played an important role in
Dominican popular culture. Anti-Haitian feelings already existed in the
nineteenth century. The occupation of the island by Haitian troops and the
danger of invasion after Dominican independence created mutual anti-
pathies and hostile image-building. Dominican animosity was further fuelled
by the superiority of the Haitian economy and the Dominican dependence
on Haitian imports in the nineteenth century. This caused resentment among
politicians and merchants in the Dominican Republic. Anti-Haitianism
became more apparent in recent times with the omnipresence of Haitian
migrant laborers in Dominican society. Whereas Haitian labor was largely
confined to the sugar plantations until the end of the Trujillo regime, cheap
Haitian labor has become essential for today's Dominican economy (Plant,
1987). Agricultural enterprises, public work and industry, have all become
dependent on the labor of Haitian workers.

The presence of Haitian workers in Dominican society is reflected in
daily conversation. References to Haitians and their influence on Dominican culture and society are frequent and commonplace. More often than not,
they are none too favorable. In the countryside it is all too common to hear
children refer to the Haitian practice of eating people (*comegente*). In adult
conversation, Haitians are cursorily blamed with the introduction of AIDS,
unfair competition on the labor market and low morality in Dominican
society. These kinds of derogatory comment about immigrant workers exist
in many parts of the world, but in the Dominican case they seem more
directly linked to the self-perception of the population and its sense of
national identity. Haitian culture is thus widely seen as the very antithesis
of *dominicanidad* (Yunén, 1985:183ff).

However, it must be asked how seriously this everyday anti-Haitianism
should be taken, and whether it has been a constant component of popular
culture. In the same countryside where children scare each other with tales
of Haitian witchcraft, adults work amicably together with Haitian workers.
Such working relations often lead to cordial personal relations. Many
Dominicans have done their best to alleviate the difficult living conditions
of the Haitians. Even in all the detailed reconstructions of the 1937 massa-

cre, there are no indications that any part of the Dominican population spontaneously joined the rounding up and killing of Haitians. On the contrary, Robin Derby and Richard Turits (1993) emphasize that many Dominicans tried to help the Haitian victims. In addition, it is noticeable that in view of this supposedly general anti-Haitianism among the Dominican population, a strong popular anti-Haitian movement never emerged. We have seen the vehemence and verbal violence by which some Dominican intellectuals and politicians expressed their anti-Haitian nationalism, but as far as we can deduce from current research, no militant popular anti-Haitianism has existed or exists in the Dominican Republic.

The explanation of this apparent contradiction is twofold. One part of the answer is that authoritarian nationalism in the Dominican Republic evoked the counterbalance of a more democratic and flexible current of nationalist thought. This liberal nationalism was less powerful and lacked the coherence and elaboration of its authoritarian rival, but it has provided an ideological alternative in the Dominican political arena. A fundamental belief in democratic principles forms the basis of this tendency. Although lack of political success often drove liberal politicians into pragmatic policies and collaboration with authoritarian regimes, this democratic ideology furnished a fundamentally different vision of society. It was complemented by a cosmopolitan attitude which gave Dominican liberalism a quite distinct flavor and clearly distinguished it from conservative nationalism. People such as Gregorio Luperón, José Martí, Ramón Betances, Máximo Gómez and Eugenio Maria de Hostos believed that the social and ethnic problems of the Caribbean nations could only be solved collectively. They advocated a pan-Caribbean nationalism in which color, language and ethnicity did not matter and where nationalist loyalty to one's own country was complemented by (or even submerged in) a regional solidarity (Lewis, 1983:264ff).

This liberal vision also entailed a specific analysis of Dominican society and of the essence of Dominican identity. To describe this identity San Miguel (1992; also Perez Cabral, 1967) suggests the term *mulatismo*, which he sees as the Dominican variant of a wider cosmopolitanism. Where the conservatives implicitly or explicitly favored a hierarchical society in which the classes were more or less strictly constituted along ethnic or racial lines, the liberals tried to incorporate all classes and colors into one project of *dominicanidad*. This democratic and non-racialist view of Dominican society was expressed most clearly in the work of Pedro Francisco Bonó (Rodríguez Demorizi, 1980; González, 1994). He rejected the idea of 'racial exclusivism' which existed both in Haiti and in the Dominican Republic. Instead, he advocated an acceptance of the ethnic heterogeneity of the Dominican nation and of its various cultural, ethnic and racial roots. Its viability was enhanced by the inclusion of a more generally acceptable defense of the Dominican peasantry. Bonó's *mulatismo* showed, just like other liberal ideologies, a benevolent paternalism towards the poorer sectors of society. It favored a national economy based on small-scale agriculture and a more or less equal division of wealth. Subsequent generations of liberals have developed other forms of social and democratic thought, which together have strongly influenced Dominican society. As such they have constituted an ideological reservoir which has served as an inspiration to opponents of authoritarian and conservative nationalism right up to the present day.

Another part of the answer to questions concerning the influence of the dominant anti-Haitian ideology on popular culture can be found in the history of border trade. During the nineteenth and a large part of the twentieth centuries, a flourishing border trade existed involving both Dominican and Haitian merchants. Haitian traders traveled from market to market throughout the Dominican countryside with their merchandise loaded on mules. They swarmed over the entire country and were a familiar sight in cities such as Santiago and Santo Domingo. The majority of these peddlers were women. Their products varied, but they principally sold cheap imported foodstuffs and textiles. Towards the end of the century, when agricultural production on the Dominican side of the border declined, their agricultural produce became particularly important. On the other hand, Dominican landowners sold their cattle in Haiti. This took place at the periodic markets which were organized first around the Haitian capital Port-au-Prince, and later at Croix des Bouquets, twenty kilometers from Port-au-Prince, which became the principal cattle market of the island towards the end of the nineteenth century. Professional merchants also made regular visits to Haiti. It was not uncommon for them to make between ten and twenty journeys a year, a considerable number in the circumstances of the day. Multiple social and political relationships existed across the border and it was just as normal for Dominicans to go to Port-au-Prince for business as it was for Haitian merchants to travel to the Dominican Republic. Beyond the control of the two states, a border society came into existence which followed its own logic and possessed its own dynamics.[17]

The context of day-to-day relations between Dominicans and Haitians started to change slowly in the last decades of the nineteenth century, and relations between the two countries deteriorated further in the twentieth century. This was the result of several interrelated factors. The most important was without doubt the establishment of large-scale sugar plantations along the southern coast of the Dominican Republic, causing marginalization and social and economic crisis in the border region. The displacement of Dominican labor and the simultaneous demographic growth in Haiti threatened the precarious balance in the border region. Dominican politicians tried to take political advantage of the increasing Haitian presence in the border trade in order to reinforce Dominican nationalist identity. It is no coincidence that in this period the first virulently anti-Haitian articles started to appear in Dominican newspapers. This anti-Haitianism accelerated in the 1920s, when the Dominican economy became increasingly dependent on Haitian migrant labor, first in the sugar sector, and later in other agricultural activities and public works. This coincided with vigorous government efforts to end regional autonomy. The southern and northern border regions were the first to feel the effects of this policy, especially after 1907 when United States customs officials created a force of border guards and began to collect custom duties. The increasing presence of Haitian workers in the Dominican economy was thereby accompanied by the fortification of the border as well as by increasing anti-Haitian propaganda. This propaganda culminated, of course, in the Trujillo regime. During that period the Dominican population was bombarded with racist anti-Haitian propaganda.

Nevertheless, the Dominican population seems largely to have ignored the strong anti-Haitian bias which developed in intellectual and political circles during this period. Indeed, we could even hypothesize an alternative popular ideology which rejected the political invocation of the Haitians as the cultural and racial enemy. One argument in favor of such an interpretation is to be found in the popular support which existed for the Haitian occupation between 1822 and 1844 (Vega, 1988:37). Another is that nothing like an aggressive anti-Haitian popular movement has taken root in the Dominican Republic. It may be significant that even the attempts of the nascent labor movement to exploit anti-Haitian feelings at the beginning of the twentieth century were hardly successful (Cassá, 1990).

This is not to say that there is no awareness of somatic differences, but that it goes in a different direction. Although a coherent *mestizo* (or mulatto) ideology was never formulated in the Dominican Republic as it was in Mexico, many Dominicans accept and sometimes pride themselves on their mixed descent. They convert the term *indio*, which has been considered above all as a denial of the African heritage in Dominican culture, into a proof of the specific mixed character of the Dominican population. Few Dominicans hesitate in admitting that, in practice, the Dominican population is a mixed one. It is worth noting that this attitude is especially apparent among the poorer classes living in both rural and urban areas. This suggests that racial attitudes in the Dominican Republic are, at least partly, class-related. While the elite tries to present itself as the representative of a white, European nation, the Dominican poor accept their mixed heritage. In addition, they are all too aware that they live in a society in which racial differences play an important social and political role. They are not convinced by the suggestions of the dominant classes that they live in a homogeneous, 'white' society. For them racial differences primarily accentuate the social differences with which they are all very familiar. Anti-Haitianism is certainly present. Derogatory remarks about Haitians are not unusual and they are often racially colored, but they play a relatively small, and for many people, insignificant, role in their daily lives.

This may lead to a very interesting hypothesis. In contrast to the situation in, for example, Europe, where racist ideas and attitudes originate among the poor or lower middle classes who feel threatened by immigrants, in the Dominican Republic they spring from the elite. Until we have found methods to investigate and analyze the interplay between existing *mentalités* and politically motivated propaganda it will be impossible to tell how firmly these ideas are grounded. Popular world-views are certainly influenced by anti-Haitian ideas and a popular preference for certain 'white' somatic characteristics (or, to use Hoetink's term, a dominant somatic norm image) certainly exist, but popular feeling seems to have developed quite independently of the elite's political propaganda.

Conclusion

In this article I have attempted to describe two different constructions of Dominican ethnicity: one enshrined in the political ideologies of the elite and the other hidden within the everyday assumptions of the population. Such an exercise is very complicated, especially when it involves such deeply ingrained and unconscious mental processes as are implied by the idea of ethnicity and somatic norm images. As Alan Knight (1990:71) rightly observes: 'Measuring the broad impact of ideas within society is notoriously difficult, especially when the ideas themselves – relating to racial equality or inequality – are embedded deep in social relations, may rarely be overtly expressed, and, indeed, may be deliberately disguised or disingenuously denied.' It is especially difficult to establish the interaction between, on the one hand, popular ethnic and racial perceptions, and on the other, political efforts to manipulate these perceptions and construct new ethnic symbols.

This article suggests that historians and social scientists need to be very careful when they interpret the ethnic and nationalist ideologies expressed by elites. Too often these ideologies are taken at face value and more or less implicitly accepted as representative of popular perception. It should be emphasized that the ideas of Latin American elites were shaped by the peculiar conditions from which they emerged. They must be considered as more or less desperate attempts to respond to a rapidly changing world. These elites have supported progress and modernization, but were at the same time appalled by the consequences, which threatened to destroy traditional order and patriarchal authority. This ambiguity has tended to be reinforced by middle-class intellectuals who have felt frustrated at their inability to influence current affairs. Elite ideologies in late nineteenth- and twentieth-century Latin America have therefore combined nostalgia for an idyllic past with a frantic quest for modernization.

In the Dominican Republic this process led to an ambiguous nationalism based around a mythologized Spanish past. The conservative visions of Peña Battle and Balaguer must be considered primarily as denials or even rejections of the social consequences of modernization. Such a 'flight into history' could not, however, resolve their intellectual difficulties. While accepting Spanish culture and ethnicity as the basis for the Dominican nation, Spanish colonialism was at the same time held responsible for the incursion of the French and the eventual division of the island. A similar ambiguity exists vis-à-vis the dominant role of the US in the affairs of the island in the twentieth century. While clearly fascinated by the political and economic opportunities offered by a closer alliance with the US, Dominican elite groups are very sensitive to the cultural and economic differences between the two countries. In addition, there is a lingering contempt for the perceived materialism of US culture. Admiration for US society is therefore precarious and quickly gives way to feelings of anger and scorn.

International charges of Haitian 'slavery' on Dominican sugar plantations and pressure on various Dominican governments from US human rights organizations, such as American Watch, to improve the living conditions of Haitian sugar cane cutters have had mixed results in this respect. On the one hand, they have forced Dominican politicians to put the issue of human rights on the political agenda. Although this has often amounted to no more than rhetoric used for political purposes, it has served to improve the terms in which the Haitian question was discussed within the country.[18] On the other hand, foreign criticism has reinvoked a defensive attitude in the Dominican Republic, especially among the elite, which considers the Haitian question as a threat to Dominican national identity. It confirms the historical suspicion that foreign powers disregard Dominican identity and favor the unification of the island. In this way, it has provoked a more paranoid and vehement anti-Haitianism, sometimes mixed with anti-imperialist rhetoric.

It is my contention that popular anti-Haitianism in the Dominican Republic might well be a great deal less virulent than the Dominican elite and many foreign observers have wanted us to believe. If this is the case, it may be a reflection of the ready acceptance of modernization within the poorer classes of Dominican society. Where the elite have feared modernization and resented the loss of traditional privileges, the majority of the Dominican poor appear to have welcomed the new opportunities offered by social and economic changes within their country. Those who have resisted these changes seem to have been in the minority and most Dominicans show a pragmatic acceptance of new ways of life, which has not stopped short of massive migration. It is noticeable that this pragmatism is very obvious in the case of women (Pessar, 1982; Grasmuck and Pessar, 1991). This again suggests that among the poorer strata too, the willingness to accept change is related to social position and the privileges which go with it.

Of course, in making these judgments we must heed Alan Knight's warning cited above. More research is needed before we can confidently claim to understand popular perceptions. Such research should take also advantage of the 'popular culture' debate among historians. Roger Chartier (1993) has recently suggested that the concept of 'appropriation' could help us to analyze the differences between the cultures of different classes. Popular culture distinguishes itself from elite culture not so much because it is built up from different elements, but because it uses and interprets these elements (ideas and symbols) in its own way. It is, in other words, the construction of meaning that makes popular culture different from elite culture. In Chartier's view, we need a social history of the ways in which popular groups are confronted with ideas and of how they take possession of some, and reject others. This brings us right back to the discussion referred to in the introduction. It is not sufficient to point to the constructed nature of national or ethnic identities. The question should be: What are the content and meaning of these constructions and why are some constructions more powerful or longer-lasting than others? We must analyze the ways in which dominant groups and political elites have tried to create and manipulate national and ethnic symbols. But we cannot ignore alternative versions of nationalism and ethnicity which – implicitly or explicitly – exist.

Such an approach may be recommended for an analysis of Dominican ethnic and national identity. It is impossible to sustain the view that fundamentally different and separated ethnic ideologies exist in a society such as the Dominican Republic (Hoetink, 1967:134). But the meaning and significance given to ethnic symbolism have been quite different at different levels of society. The elite has tried to create the image of an ethnically homogeneous society which was threatened in its most sacred values by racially and ethnically inferior Haitians. In this sense, it has resorted to an ethnic (or racial) strategy which is quite different from what could be called the US and Brazilian models. Conservative elites in the US have not hesitated to 'play the race card' in domestic politics, because the clear racial segregation within US society precluded that their own racial position could become a point of discussion. By contrast, their Brazilian counterparts have generally avoided this tactic, as a consequence of the vague dividing lines between the races in Brazilian society and the danger that they themselves would be implicated in a racial debate (Andrews, 1992:157). The Dominican case presents a third alternative. Here the ethnic or racial differences between the elite and the mass of the population are also quite vague, but, while downplaying the racial heterogeneity of its society, the Dominican elite has 'externalized' the racial argument. The racial argument was exploited to define Dominican identity in relation to the Haitian neighbor.

Despite such attempts to forge a national identity, Dominican conservatives could not in daily life close their eyes to the racially mixed character of the Dominican population. In fact, they often shared the pragmatic – one could almost say 'liberal' – ethnic attitude of most Dominicans. Few Dominicans have favored racial segregation and in spite of existing pro-white somatic norm images, different racial and ethnic groups in Dominican society mingle without too many problems even in conservative circles. On the other hand, conservative ideology tried to conceal, or at least to de-emphasize, the ethnic heterogeneity within Dominican society by the deliberate construction of an external enemy. The anti-Haitianism upon which the Dominican elite based its nationalistic propaganda could not, however, hide the fundamental ambiguity in Dominican nationalism. Its refusal to accept the consequences of modernization and the ethnic diversity of its own population prevented the Dominican elite from creating a coherent ideology of *dominicanidad*. It may be an irony of history that such an ideology may only now be in the process of construction – 'at a distance' – in New York, where Dominicans, just like other Caribbean emigrants, feel an urgent need to define their national identity.[19]

Notes

1. Carter Bentley (1987) uses Bourdieu's idea of *habitus* for a similar perspective. For a critical assessment, see Smith, 1992.
2. We may agree with Urban and Sherzer (1991:8) that the three principal characteristics of the state are: 1) its claim to a monopoly over the legitimate use of force within its territorial boundaries; 2) its assertion of autonomy relative to other states; 3) its gradual development of citizenship as the form of membership of the collective.
3. See Hale (1986:396–404), Schmidt (1978) and Leys Stepan (1991:45ff).
4. Diputado Franco in Congreso Nacional, 14 June 1895, quoted in: *Gaceta Nacional*, 22, 1104, 19 October 1895.
5. In a recent presidential speech marking the 150th anniversary of Dominican independence, 27 February 1994, Joaquín Balaguer again returned to this point, suggesting that this day should be remembered not as Independence Day, but as the Separation from Haiti. See: *El Siglo*, 28 February 1994, p. 3: 'JB cree a consecuencia de próximos comicios podría haber cambios políticos fundamentales.'
6. This is a central theme in Dominican history. See Moya Pons (1977), Yunén (1985: 99ff), also Hoetink (1970, 1980).
7. Such plans have been denounced repeatedly by the current Dominican President Balaguer; for example during the summer of 1993 when a French proposal for the unification of the island was discussed. His recent proposal to celebrate the 'Separation from Haiti' instead of 'Dominican Independence' is by many interpreted as a rebuttal of these projects. See for instance the article by Pedro Manuel Casals Victoria, who supports Balaguer against

this 'objetivo desnacionalizante': *Hoy*, 4 March 1994; 'Un discurso nacionalista'. See also: *Latin American Weekly Report*, 28 April 1994; 'Dominican Republic. Politics'.

8. It could be argued that only anti-communism did not fit this historical myth, but even then it was argued that the Spanish 'Christian tradition' of Dominican society was instinctively opposed to a godless communism. Compare Mateo (1993).

9. It is interesting to note that Hoetink (1967:135) also writes about a society being 'pathological', by which he means that it suffers from a collective sense of non-fulfilment of its somatic norm image.

10. Peña Battle's (1989[1954]:154) version of the French attitude is succinctly summed up: 'El negro esclavo de la colonia francesa era lo mismo que una bestia, y como tal fue tratado.'

11. It is worth mentioning that Peña Battle's idea of the Dominican nation is somewhat confused. In his work on the colonial period Dominican nationalism is embodied by the creole population which traded with the buccaneers against the wishes of Spain. In his later work it is embodied by the Spanish colony struggling against foreign intruders.

12. His emphasis on a 'creole' Dominican consciousness is clear when he describes the resistance of the Dominican population to the Spanish colonial policy of the *devastaciones*. This resistance was, in his eyes, the result of 'un verdadero movimiento revolucionario que determinaron causas puramente criollas, intereses exclusivamente dominicanos' (1989[1938]:125).

13. Few people have noted the absence of racist ideas in Peña Battle's thinking. It is mentioned in Mateo, 1993:175.

14. It is interesting to note that the supposed racial homogeneity of the Haitian population is, in the view of Balaguer, the principal reason why the Dominicans have to fear its influence. For him, the mixed Dominican population is weaker than the Haitian, because 'los haitianos son un pueblo más homogéneo racialmente' (cited in García, 1983:10).

15. *El Diario*, XI, 3063, 16 October 1912; 'Los dominicanos: A los extranjeros, tal como somos' (Julio Acosta). This vision can also be observed in the work of José Ramón López (1975).

16. Balaguer's *machista* vision is most apparent in his novel *Los Carpinteros*, published in 1984 and reprinted numerous times.

17. Palmer, 1976; Baud, 1993a, 1993b. After I finished the draft of this article I read Derby's (1994) article on Dominican–Haitian relations. Her ideas could not be fully incorporated in this text. However, the results of her oral history research seem to corroborate my analysis.

18. Even Balaguer included a denunciation of the inhumane treatment of Haitian sugar workers in his *La isla al revés* (1983:231). Not insignificantly, the book was published when Balaguer was not in power. Since then, his party has repeatedly accused its principal political opponent, the PRD, of having allowed massive Haitian immigration during its period in office (1978–86) (Silié, 1992:180–7). This was also an important issue in the elections of 1994. See: 'Discurso pronunciado por el doctor José Francisco Peña Gomez, candidato presidencial del PRD' (3 March 1994) published in: *Hoy*, 4 March 1994, p. 8B.

19. See Anderson (1992) and Kasinitz (1992).

References

Anderson, B., 1991[1983], *Imagined Communities. Reflections on the Origins and Spread of Nationalism*, London, New York: Verso.

———— 1992, *Long-Distance Nationalism: World Capitalism and the Rise of Identity Politics*, Amsterdam: CASA.

Andrews, G.R., 1991, *Blacks and Whites in São Paulo, Brazil, 1888–1988*, Madison: University of Wisconsin Press.

———— 1992, 'Rejoinder', *Luso-Brazilian Review*, Vol. 29, No. 2, pp. 155–8.

Bentley, G.C., 1987, 'Ethnicity and Practice', *Comparative Studies in Society and History*, Vol. 29, pp. 24–55.

Balaguer, J., 1947, *La realidad dominicana*, Buenos Aires: Imprenta Ferrari.

_____ 1983, *La isla al revés. Haiti y el destino dominicano*, Santo Domingo: Librería Dominicana.

_____ 1984, *Los Carpinteros*, Santo Domingo: Ed. Corripio.

Baud, M., 1992 , 'Sugar and Unfree Labour: Reflections on Labour Control in the Dominican Republic, 1870–1935', *Journal of Peasant Studies*, Vol. 19, No. 2, pp. 301–25.

_____ 1993a, 'Una frontera-refugio: Dominicanos y Haitianos contra el Estado (1870–1930)', *Estudios Sociales*, Vol. 26, No. 92, pp. 39–64.

_____ 1993b, 'Una frontera para cruzar: la sociedad rural a traves de la frontera Dominicano-Haitiana (1870–1930)', *Estudios Sociales*, Vol. 26, No. 94, pp. 5–8.

_____ 1995, *Peasants and Tobacco in the Dominican Republic, 1870–1930*, Knoxville: University of Tennessee Press.

Calder, B.J., 1984, *The Impact of Intervention. The Dominican Republic during the US Occupation of 1916–1924*, Austin: University of Texas Press.

Cassá, R., 1990, *Movimiento obrero y lucha socialista en la República Dominicana (desde los orígines hasta 1960)*, Santo Domingo: Fundación Cultural Dominicana.

Cassá, R. *et al.*, 1986, *Actualidad y perspectivas de la cuestión nacional en la República Dominicana*, Santo Domingo: Alfa y Omega.

Chartier, R., 1993, 'Popular Culture: A Concept Revisited', paper presented at the Erasmus University Rotterdam, 13 December.

Cooper, F., *et al.*, 1993, *Confronting historical paradigms. Peasants, Labor and the Capitalist World System in Africa and Latin America*, Madison: University of Wisconsin Press.

Cordero Michel, E., 1993, 'Documento: Un importante y desconocido acto notarial de la época de la unificación política con Haiti (1831)', *Ecos*, Vol. 1, No. 1, pp. 133–9.

Cornielle, C., 1980, *Proceso histórico dominico-haitiano. Una advertencia a la juventud dominicana*, Santo Domingo: Publicaciones América.

Deive, C.E., 1977, 'El prejuicio racial en el folklore dominicano', *Boletín del Museo del Hombre Dominicano*, No. 8, pp. 75–96.

Del Rosario Perez, A.S., 1957, *La exterminación añorada*, Santo Domingo: s.n.

Derby, L., 1994, 'Haitians, Magic, and Money: *Raza* and Society in the Haitian-Dominican Borderlands 1900 to 1937', *Comparative Studies in Society and History,* Vol. 36, No. 3, pp. 488–526.

Derby, R.L.H. and Turits, R., 1993, 'Historias de terror y los terrores de la historia: La masacre haitiana de 1937 en la República Dominicana', *Estudios Sociales*, Vol. 26, No. 92, pp. 65–76.

Domínguez, J., 1979, *La anexión de la República Dominicana a España*, Santo Domingo: UASD.

Dore Cabral, C., 1985, 'La immigración haitiana y el componente racista de la cultura dominican (Apunte, para una crítica a "La Isla al Revés")', *Ciencia y Sociedad*, Vol. 10, No. 1 pp 61–70.

Fennema, M. and Loewenthal, T., 1987, *Construcción de raza y nación en la República Dominicana*, Santo Domingo: UASD.

Fentress, J. and Wickham, C., 1992, *Social Memory*, Oxford, Blackwell.

Franco, F.J., 1981, *Historia de las ideas políticas en la República Dominicana*, Santo Domingo: Editora Nacional.

García, J.M., 1983, *La matanza de los Haitianos. Genocidio de Trujillo 1937*, Santo Domingo: Alfa y Omega.

González, R., 1991, 'Peña Battle y su concepto histórico de la nación dominicana', *Anuario de Estudios Americanos*, No. 48, pp. 585–631.

_____ 1994, *Bonó, un intelectual de los pobres*, Santo Domingo: Centro de Estudios Sociales P. Juan Montalvo S.J.

Graham, R. (ed.), 1990, *The Idea of Race in Latin America, 1870–1940*, Austin: University of Texas Press.

Grasmuck, S. and Pessar, P.R., 1991, *Between Two Islands. Dominican International Migration*, Berkeley: University Press of California.

Greenberg, S.B., 1980, *Race and State in Capitalist Development: Comparative Perspectives*, New Haven, London: Yale University Press.

Hale, C.A., 1986, 'Political and Social Ideas in Latin America, 1870–1930', in Bethell, L. (ed.), *Cambridge History of Latin America*, Vol. 4, Cambridge: Cambridge University Press, pp. 367–441.

Hobsbawm, E.J., 1990, *Nations and Nationalism since 1870. Programme, Myth, Reality*, Cambridge: Cambridge University Press.

Hoetink, H., 1967, *The Two Variants in Caribbean Race Relations*, London: Oxford University Press.

———— 1970, 'The Dominican Republic in the Nineteenth Century: Some Notes on Stratification, Immigration, and Race', in Mörner, M. (ed.), *Race and Class in Latin America*, New York, London: Columbia University Press, pp. 96–121.

———— 1980, 'El Cibao, 1844–1900: su aportación a la formación social de la república', *Eme Eme Estudios Dominicanos*, Vol. 8, No. 48, pp. 3–19.

———— 1982, *The Dominican People, 1850–1900*, Baltimore: Johns Hopkins University Press.

———— 1985, ' "Race" and Color in the Caribbean', in Mintz, S.W. and Price, S. (eds), *Caribbean Contours*, Baltimore, Johns Hopkins University Press, pp. 55–84.

———— 1986, 'The Dominican Republic, c. 1870–1930', in Bethell, L. (ed.), *Cambridge History of Latin America*, Vol. 5, Cambridge: Cambridge University Press, pp. 287–305.

———— 1994, *Santo Domingo y el Caribe. Ensayos sobre cultura y Sociedad*, Santo Domingo: Fundación Cultural Dominicana.

Jiménez, R.E., 1927, *Al amor del bohío*, Santo Domingo: Virgilio Montalvo.

———— 1952, *Trujillo y la paz*, Ciudad Trujillo: Impresora Dominicana.

Kasinitz, P., 1992, *Caribbean New York. Black Immigrants and the Politics of Race*, Ithaca: Cornell University Press.

Klaren, P.F., 1973, *Modernization, Dislocation, and Aprismo: Origins of the Peruvian Aprista Party, 1870–1932*, Austin: University of Texas Press.

Knight, A., 1990, 'Racism, Revolution, and *Indigenismo*: Mexico 1910–1940', in Graham, R. (ed.), *The Idea of Race in Latin America*, Austin: University of Texas Press, pp. 71–113.

Lewis, G.K., 1983, *Main Currents in Caribbean Thought. The Historical Evolution of Caribbean Society in Its Ideological Aspects, 1492–1900*, Baltimore: Johns Hopkins University Press.

Leys Stepan, N., 1991, *'The Hour of Eugenics.' Race, Gender, and Nation in Latin America*, Ithaca: Cornell University Press.

Lomnitz-Adler, C., 1992, *Exits from the Labyrinth. Culture and Ideology in the Mexican National Space*, Berkeley: University Press of California.

López, J.R., 1975, *El gran pesimismo dominicano: José Ramón López*, Santiago: UCMM.

Marquez, R., 1992, 'An Anatomy of Racism', *NACLA-Report on the Americas*, Vol. 25, No. 4, pp. 32–3.

Martínez-Alier, J., 1977, *Haciendas, Plantations and Collective Farms*, London: Cass.

Mateo, A.L., 1993, *Mito y cultura en la era de Trujillo*, Santo Domingo: Librería la Trinitaria/ Instituto del Libro.

Memmi, A., 1967[1957], *The Colonizer and the Colonized*, Boston: Beacon Press.

Moscoso Puello, F.E., 1913, *Cartas a Evelina*, Santo Domingo: s.n.

Moya Pons, F., 1977, 'La economía dominicana y el partido azul', *Eme Eme Estudios Dominicanos*, Vol. 5, No. 28, pp. 3–11.

Murphy, M.F., 1991, *Dominican Sugar Plantations. Production and Foreign Labor Integration*, New York: Praeger.

Nicholls, D., 1979, *From Dessalines to Duvalier. Race, Color and National Independence in Haiti*, Cambridge: Cambridge University Press.

Palmer, E.C., 1976, 'Land Use and Landscape Change along the Dominican-Haitian Border-lands', unpublished Ph.D. thesis, University of Florida.

Peña Battle, M.A., 1989[1937], 'Enriquillo o el germen de la teoría moderna del derecho de gentes', in Peña Battle, *Ensayos historicos*, Santo Domingo: Ed. Taller, pp. 25–46.

———— 1989[1938], 'Las devastaciones de 1605 y 1606', in Peña Battle, *Ensayos historicos*, Santo Domingo: Ed. Taller, pp. 85–147.

———— 1946, *La frontera de la República Dominicana con Haití*, Ciudad Trujillo: Ed. La Nación.

———— 1989[1950], 'Prólogo a la antología de Emiliano Tejera', in Peña Battle, *Ensayos historicos*, Santo Domingo: Ed. Taller, pp. 183–206.

———— 1989[1952], 'El tratado de Basilea y la desnacionalización del Santo Domingo español', in Peña Battle, *Ensayos historicos*, Santo Domingo: Ed. Taller, pp. 47–83.

———— 1989[1954], 'Origenes del Estado Haitiano', in Peña Battle, *Ensayos historicos*, Santo Domingo: Ed. Taller, pp. 149–82.

Pérez Cabral, P.A., 1967, *La Comunidad Mulata. El caso socio-político de la República Dominicana*, Caracas: Grafica Americana.

Pessar, P.R., 1982, *Kinship Relations of Production in the Migration Process: The Case of Dominican Emigration to the United States,* New York: City University New York.

Plant, R., 1987, *Sugar and Modern Slavery. A Tale of Two Countries*, London: Zed Books.

Prestol Castillo, F., 1972, *El masacre se pasa en pie*, Santo Domingo: Taller.

Rodriguez Demorizi, E., (ed.), 1980, *Papeles de Pedro F. Bonó*, Barcelona: M. Pareja.

Ruck, R., 1991, *The Tropic of Baseball: Baseball in the Dominican Republic*, Westport: Meckler.

Sagás, E., 1993, 'A Case of Mistaken Identity: *Antihaitianismo* in Dominican Culture', *Latinamericanist* Vol. 29, No. 1. pp. 1–5.

Sánchez, R.A., 1976, *Al cabo de los cien años. Tentativa de una justificación histórica*, Santo Domingo: s.n.

San Miguel, P.L., 1992, 'Discurso racial e identidad nacional en la Repúbica Dominicana', *Boletin del centro investigaciones historicas*, pp. 69–120.

Schmidt, H.C., 1978, *The Roots of* Lo Mexicano. *Self and Society in Mexican Thought 1900– 1934*, College Station: Texas A&M University Press.

Silié, R., 1992, 'República Dominicana atrapada en sus percepciones sobre Haiti', in Lozano, W. (ed.), *La cuestion haitiana en Santo Domingo. Migración internacional, desarrollo y relaciones inter-estatales entre Haití y República Dominicana*, Santo Domingo: FLACSO.

Smith, A.D., 1981, *The Ethnic Revival*, Cambridge: Cambridge University Press.

Smith, R.T., 1992, 'Race, Class, and Gender in the Transition to Freedom', in McGlynn, F. and Drescher, S. (eds), *The Meaning of Freedom: Economics, Politics, and Culture after Slavery*, Pittsburgh: University of Pittsburgh Press, pp. 257–90.

Tansill, C.C., 1938, *The United States and Santo Domingo, 1798–1873. A Chapter in Carib-bean Diplomacy*, Baltimore: Johns Hopkins University Press.

Urban, G. and Sherzer, J. (eds), 1991, *Nation-States and Indians in Latin America*, Austin: University of Texas Press.

Vega, B., 1988, *Trujillo y Haiti (Vol. 1: 1930–1937)*, Santo Domingo: Fundación Cultural Dominicana.

———— 1990, 'El Peña Battle sobre el cual no se escribe', in Vega, B., *En la década perdida (Ponencias, conferencias y articulos 1984–1990)*, Santo Domingo: Fundación Cultural Dominicana, pp. 323–5.

Viotti da Costa, E., 1992, 'Commentary on Georges Reid Andrews, Blacks and Whites in São Paulo, Brazil, 1888–1988', *Luso-Brazilian Review*, Vol. 29, No. 2, pp. 145–50.

Yunén Z., R.E., 1985, *La isla como es: Hipotesis para su comprobación*, Santiago: UCMM.

Zaglul, J.M., 1992, 'Una identificación nacional "defensiva": El antihaitianismo nacionalista de Joaquín Balaguer – Una lectura de "La isla al revés" ', *Estudios Sociales*, Vol. 25, No. 87, pp. 29–65.

CHAPTER 8	The somatology of manners: class, race and gender in the history of dance etiquette in the Hispanic Caribbean

Angel G. Quintero Rivera

> *Si hay baile en algún CASINO*
> *Alguno siempre se queja,*
> *Pues a la blanca aconseja*
> *Que no baile con negrillo.*
> *Teniendo, aunque es amarillo,*
> *'El negro tras de la oreja.'*[1]

¡El que no se ría es cafre![2]

It is illustrative of changes in Hispanic Caribbean societies that one hundred years after the Dominican popular singer, Juan Antonio Alix, wrote this *décima* advising white Caribbean women against dancing with light-skinned mulattos ('though yellowish, with the black behind his ear'), it was, precisely, a yellowish mulatto who became most famous for his advice on manners. In 1987, the new comedy program *Sunshine's Café*, with its many sketches on manners, achieved the highest ratings in advertising surveys for Puerto Rican television.[3] Comedian Emmanuel Logroño, significantly nicknamed *Sunshine*, was already quite notorious for his participation in popular street theater – *Anamú, la yerba que el cabro no mastica* (Anamú, spiny grass that not even goats chew) – and for his musical talents in *Nueva Trova* (left-wing sociopolitical song) and in avant-garde (John Cage-style) music. Though he rapidly became quite a popular character, and Anamú's performances were well received by trade unions, ecologists and other popular social movements, he was mainly appreciated at that time by progressive intellectual circles. In 1987 he shocked even those circles with a humorous TV program which was considered by many 'too vulgar' and in 'bad taste', *chabacano*. Nonetheless, popular acclaim was widespread, especially amongst young people (people in their late teens and young adults) from the middle and lower-middle social strata.

Sunshine's Café combined satirical music with theatrical sketches, dealing with everyday situations, laughing primarily at established taste and manners. One of the most popular characters Logroño created was *Iván Fontecha,* named after a notorious socialite – Iván Frontera – who wrote magazine accounts of upper class social gatherings. Through this character, Logroño created and popularized a distinction between what he called *avantismo* or *caché* (avant-garde, refined taste), caricatured by *Fontecha,* and *cafrería* (taste – or manners – conventionally considered bad by the dominant culture, characterized by striking colors and vulgar kitsch). Apart from the sketches, in his on-air conversations with the public (the program set was a mock-up of a cosy varieties bar), *Sunshine* frequently proudly declared himself a *cafre: Soy cafre ¡¿y qué?!* (I am *cafre* and, so what?!), and the participating public enthusiastically joined him in this festive dislocation of values around the socially very touchy issue of manners.

The comedy of manners, which has been very important in the history of English literature and theater, but which in that context generally refers to witty comments by members of the upper classes, was, to the best of my knowledge, a new phenomenon in the Hispanic Caribbean. Its emergence is not associated in the Caribbean with communication within the ranks of the upper classes, but rather with phenomena in the mass media (with which it has also become associated in England and most countries). It was not, as in the original English tradition, ironical, but satirical; not charmingly witty, but harsh. *Sunshine's* sketches were in fact clearly transgressive. They provoked the fiery criticism of a very conservative and religiously oriented pressure group named Morality in Media, and in spite of the program's popularity and wide audiences, it was finally taken off the air after several years.

A decade after the birth of *Sunshine's Café,* Puerto Rican fiction writer Juan Antonio Ramos published a comic work entitled *El manual del buen modal* (A manual of good manners; 1993). Ramos was already quite famous among contemporary writers, mainly through a book of short stories, *Papo Impala está quitao* (Papo Impala is out of drugs; 1983), in which he humorously rewrites in popular or lumpen language great literary works, be they international (like Kafka or *La celestina*), Latin American (such as García Márquez) or Puerto Rican (Zeno Gandía, *La charca*). These stories have been transformed into theater with great success. Like *Sunshine's* sketches, *El manual* provoked the most acrimonious and destructive reviews from the Establishment's literary critics (Trelles, 1993). In spite of that, it has maintained its position as one of the top bestsellers in Puerto Rico since its publication. The book's launching, which took place in October 1993, consisted of a dramatic reading of some sections of *El manual* by some young actors headed by the notorious *Sunshine* Logroño.

The audience, which filled the theater to capacity, laughed and applauded like mad, turning this intellectual event into a memorable social happening.

Besides the histrionic merits of *Sunshine*'s sketches and Ramos's writings, one could ask what explains this new widespread and enthusiastic interest in manners. Why does this interest take the form of bitter humor? What views of interpersonal relations are being questioned; which new views are being put forward? What does this phenomenon tell us about Caribbean culture and its transformations?

Like many other important contemporary social processes, this new interest in taste and manners has not been approached yet by Caribbean social scientists.[4] The first attempt in Puerto Rico at an interpretation in print also came from a fiction writer. The Hungarian-born, Argentinean-raised, Puerto Rican writer Kalman Barsy, combining both an outsider's and an insider's view, advanced a suggestive class interpretation of this social phenomenon in his essay *Reivindicación de Iván Fontecha*.[5] His argument goes more or less as follows:

> An emerging urban middle class, recently risen from the lower social echelons – and /or the countryside – needs to distinguish itself from its origins, which it achieves through manners. But it has rapidly matured enough to be able to laugh at its own attempt at 'refinement', and even to give itself the luxury of establishing a new norm for *caché: ¡el que no se ría es cafre!* (It's darky vulgar not to laugh!).

This breaks the previous norms of refinement of *the* recognized Hispanic Caribbean book on etiquette of one hundred years ago:

> The custom of always speaking in humorous or mocking terms is intolerable, and what is even more intolerable is the behavior of those who always try to appear funny (Carreño, 1894:75).

Barsy's identification of manners with class, and the importance he attributes to the emergence of an urban middle class for the analysis of contemporary Caribbean culture is, of course, very important, but he misses two points of great significance.

First, the sexual identity of *Iván Fontecha,* paladin of *avantismo* and *caché*, is not at all clear in *Sunshine's* sketches. *Fontecha* is formally a man, as men are supposed to have the authoritative voice in our society. However, it is significant that many elements of the sketches puzzle the audience to the point where the spectator is not certain whether *Fontecha* is a homosexual (as apparently – though it was never accepted – Iván Frontera was in real life) or a woman; women are supposed to be more concerned than men with manners. Second, Barsy neglected that *Sunshine* Logroño is a light-skinned mulatto, and that when he is proudly declaring himself a *cafre,* he is not only redefining, in class terms, a judgment of taste, but simultaneously bringing to the surface his black origins. *Cafre*, which came to mean vulgar taste and manners, was originally a derogatory term for blacks of a particular African tribe (Kafir, or black Muslims).

I would here like to analyze some elements of the historical sociology of manners in the Hispanic Caribbean; the forms and codes of interpersonal relations in societies constituted by a particular type of colonialism, which grouped people from different ethnic origins within the dialectics of plantation–counterplantation through which Caribbean societies developed. In these societies, social distinctions and identities intermingle ongoing socio-economic processes with ethnic (historical) backgrounds, which represent, in this case, not only different cultural behavior patterns, but also, as Hoetink has emphasized (1967), distinctive physical traits, that raise special difficulties for socialization by amalgamation.

It could be argued that class analysis is always inseparable from history; but, when history makes itself present not only in culture, but also in the skin, its continuous presence is more clearly overwhelming. Since gender relations (which also exhibit – as race – evident somatic manifestations) are of such importance in the reproduction of physical traits, their multi-phased presence in any class–cultural analysis is of paramount significance for all interpersonal interchange in racially segmented societies.

I will therefore attempt to examine some of the complex relations between class and gender in the forms and codes of interpersonal interchange embodied in manners within what Hoetink called the Iberian variant of race relations in the Caribbean. The nature of these processes requires a broad Hispanic Caribbean approach, but most primary sources and documents I was able to work with are Puerto Rican. The focus will therefore be on Puerto Rico, drawing on other Hispanic Caribbean material for the necessary (but admittedly incomplete) broader perspective.

Words and body of evidence

In the eighteenth century, European countries competing for control of the Caribbean – Spain, England, France and the Netherlands – all adopted the word *etiquette*, formerly a French term for *label*, as 'conventional rules for conduct or behavior' (Bonhart, 1988). If behavior patterns are conventional, why do they have to be labeled? The definition for *etiquette* in the *Oxford Dictionary of English Etymology* (Onions, 1969) is revealing in this respect:

'prescribed or conventional code of behavior'. A tension is evident within the meaning: we could again ask, if it is conventional, why does it have to be prescribed?

The history of the word *manners*, taken from the same authoritative source, is also very significant. In the twelfth century, it meant *kind* or *sort*, as in Spanish *manera* or *modo*, the origin of our contemporary *modales*; in the fourteenth, it began to refer to *way or mode of action – customary practice*, and in the plural, *moral character and outward bearing*; in the seventeenth, it was also used for *method* or *style* (Onions, 1969), which in the eighteenth came to be coded or labeled in the French *etiquette*.

The *Encyclopedia Britannica* (1985), which under the heading of *manners* includes only a reference to the *comedy of manners*, reminds us, under *etiquette*, of its origin in certain Italian works of the sixteenth century known as *courtesy books*, overlooking the fact that the word *etiqueta* was used in Spain during the same century to mean *protocolo real* (court protocol) (Corominas, 1987). Interestingly enough, the word *protocol* was to be used later in France as *State etiquette* or etiquette for State activities or ceremonies. Though *courtesy* comes from *court*, the *Britannica*'s connecting of the modern meaning of *etiquette* with Italian courtesy books and not to the Spanish state protocol is correct, as Italy was the birthplace of modern civility. Moreover, *etiquette* in the modern sense is identified with the shifting of perspective with regard to social stratification that Western European countries experienced in civil society some centuries later (eighteenth and nineteenth), that is from ranks to social classes. The bourgeoisie, a segment of the common people (the third estate or rank) displaced the nobility (first estate) and clergy (second) and came to occupy the highest echelon of the social hierarchy. New forms of distinction and differentiation developed. It is no coincidence that a French word was used to designate the hegemonic new code of conduct under class stratification (as opposed to rank stratification), since the shift in stratification parameters was much more dramatic in France (through the French Revolution) than in other countries, where this transformation generally occurred in a more gradual way. It was also in France where, with the Revolution, new units of measurement were developed within an attempt at a completely different *Weltanschauung* (world-view): the bourgeoisie introduced the rationality of the decimal system for measuring space, which spread all over the world, and made an unsuccessful attempt at a new – supposedly more rational, but unreal – (decimal) subdivision of time.

It is not surprising that courtesy books were first written in Italy, where the hegemony of an urban culture over the countryside was first developed, and with it, the predominance of an inchoate bourgeoisie.[6] It is no coincidence either that the Spanish word *urbanidad*, which originally referred to urban life, also came to mean courtesy and good manners (Echegaray,

1889). This nineteenth-century Etymological Dictionary adds to *cortesanía y buen modo*, as a definition of *urbanidad*, the concepts of *comedimiento y atención*, both of which refer to moderation and civility. The countryside, identified with nature, was associated with physical impulses, and the city with the human control over them, a supposedly necessary requisite for social interchange. The nature-based distinction underlying the model of stratification based on rank – the hereditary nobility of blood – had to be displaced by the conquest of men over nature, that is *cultivation*. As a noun, this came to mean civilization, and as an adjective, education, with a fairly common association with taste and manners (Williams, 1976:81). These were therefore not natural, but learned; not something you were born into (like nobility), but achieved (within the achievement ideology of the bourgeoisie).

It is important that it was also during the eighteenth century that *taste*, originally a physical sense, was turned into an

> abstraction of a human faculty to generalized polite attribute, associated . . . with the notion of Rules, and elsewhere with Manners (which was itself narrowing from a description of general conduct to a more local association with etiquette . . .). Taste became so separated from active human sense and became so much a matter of acquiring certain habits and rules [that] Taste became equivalent to discrimination; 'the word taste . . . means that quick discerning faculty or power of the mind by which we accurately distinguish the good, bad or indifferent' (1784) (Williams, 1976:264–5).

The emergence of the modern meaning of etiquette as the code of behavior, taste and good manners is thus strongly related in European history to modes of stratification within a particular (bourgeois) transformation of what Tönnies (1963[1887]) analyzed as the movement of human interchange from community to society, characterized by the hegemony of city life, the rule of law, the nation-state and commercial transactions. Manners – not natural, but artificial or learned patterns of relations – were a means for the bourgeoisie, formerly part of *the people* (the third estate), to differentiate itself; adopting forms or manners of the aristocratic order but as *rules* of taste that would establish distinctions from the rest of its former *rank*. Codes flourished for many areas of life, sometimes replacing and on some occasions combining customs with new learned behavior; but the coding of manners had a special importance for cultural analysis, as these always represent a threshold between the public and private spheres of personal intercourse.

The emergence of civility in the Hispanic Caribbean, of a society (beyond communities) organized around a distinctive civic culture which could serve as basis for nation-building processes, shares important elements with European history, but was marked, in the private–public threshold of personal relations, by the peculiar nature of its development or genesis as a human conglomerate. Examining the writings of one of the first Caribbean social analysts, José Antonio Saco, Cuban historian Manuel Moreno Fraginals – who later published one of the most important books ever written on Caribbean slavery, *El ingenio* (1978) – in one of his earliest works presents the distinction between *nation* and *plantation* as the great political dilemma in the emergence of a Caribbean civic culture (1953). Since the first half of the nineteenth century, shortly after the Latin American wars of independence, Saco had been arguing that the plantation system, around which Caribbean economies had been built, was the most important factor hindering nation-building processes in Cuba. It was an economy which hampered the formation of an internal market and responded to exogenous forces; it generated an ideology which vilified[7] *work,* the basis of modern economic rationality; and, most important, it helped to cause insurmountable social cleavages (see also Pérez de la Riva, 1978).

Saco argued against slavery, not basically because of sympathetic feelings towards blacks, but mainly out of fear of the Haitian solution to a severely divided society. He proposed the whitening of the population as the main basis for the establishment of a nation, forbidding the slave trade:

> The solution and future happiness for Cuba depends on the ending of the slave trade. The day on which that occurs, we will be able to say: *we have a fatherland* (1974:71, my emphasis).

He fostered European immigration and the slow and cautious incorporation of blacks into civil ('white' creole) life. He even argued in favor of sexual unions between white immigrants and native women of color;[8] but never vice versa – colored men with white women – a point to which I will return later in this essay.

Free men of color in the Hispanic Caribbean were, in fact, already incorporating themselves into civil life, perhaps not so slowly or cautiously. They were not only *being incorporated* (in Saco's terms), but were becoming a fundamental element in the constitution of civility.[9] In contrast to the European bourgeoisie, the Hispanic Caribbean *hacendado* plantocracy was rural-based, while the free coloreds, who were mostly independent skilled workers (artisans), were city dwellers. In the Cuban census of 1862, for example, with around 80 per cent of the population living in the countryside – in Puerto Rico and Hispaniola the percentage was even higher – 53 per cent of the free coloreds lived in urban centers (Moreno, 1983:52). While cities represented an opening for *hacienda* or plantation life to the world, they were the normal arena of daily life for artisans, who were therefore much more involved in current debates and more conversant with new ideas in the international artistic or intellectual world than the rural-based classes.[10] The merchants, though urban-based, also rejected modern ideas because of the conservatism typical of their identification with a Spanish colonial authoritarianism that granted them economic interests and political privileges (Quintero Rivera, 1977). Artisans, the majority of whom were colored (free blacks or mulattos in the main) became one of the most *cultivated* social sectors by the late nineteenth century.

Their interest in education was praiseworthy. Some of the best libraries in Puerto Rico at the time were in the artisans' *casinos* (club houses) (García, 1982:21). In 1886, a Spanish traveler visited one of these *casinos de negros* and was astonished by the quality of its books (Peris Menchieta, 1886:76). Figures presented in the 1899 Puerto Rican census clearly show the artisans' high levels of literacy. While Puerto Rico's general rate was 22.7 per cent, printers scored 100 per cent, tailors 87.5 per cent, barbers 79 per cent, carpenters 69 per cent, and cigarmakers 60 per cent (US War Department, 1899). Literacy rates alone perhaps underestimate the artisans' real level of education, most of which was acquired through oral tradition, as in the institution of the *reader* in cigar-making establishments (Pérez, 1984).

The plantation legacy strengthened an old Spanish cultural tradition of disdain for non-agricultural manual labor, the product of white Christians' interest in not being taken for Moors or Jews, who were famous for their gifted craftsmanship. Skilled work, which came to be known as *manual arts*, was left to the free coloreds. The word *maestro*, which is now almost exclusively used in relation to intellectual activity to designate a professor or a teacher, was then used indiscriminately for other *saberes* (forms of knowledge), and very frequently for musicians and craftsmen. A Cuban nineteenth-century dictionary also identifies the word as a term of distinction for cultivated people of color: 'Term that is used for those who practice some art or craft, especially . . . for *people of color'*.[11] The combination of *artes y oficios* (arts and crafts) was very frequent amongst free coloreds. Already in 1831, Saco was pointing to the fact that

> . . . it was to be expected that no white Cuban should dedicate himself to the arts . . . thus it was that all the arts became the exclusive preserve of people of color (quoted in Deschamps Chapeaux, 1971:127).

The 1862 Puerto Rican census presents statistics for race within occupations. While the colored population accounted for 23.7 per cent of all agricultural laborers, 13 per cent of land owners, 0.8 per cent of merchants and 0.3 per cent of store clerks, it accounted for 68 per cent of musicians.

Most of these combined music work with other artisan trades (Carpentier, 1946; Díaz Ayala, 1981; Galán, 1983; Quintero Rivera, 1988). It is no coincidence that the main male colored character in the most important nineteenth-century Hispanic Caribbean novel – *Cecilia Valdés* – was both a musician and a refined tailor (Villaverde, 1981). Campeche, the first important Puerto Rican painter, was a colored tailor and musician.[12] The artisans' *casinos* in Puerto Rico became important centers of artistic activities, such as concerts, *veladas lírico-literarias* (literature reading evenings), theater, and conferences (see, for example, García, 1982:20). Mulatto artisans were definitively one of the most refined sectors of late nineteenth-century Puerto Rican society.

The *hacendado* plantocracy's economic activity was oriented towards export (unlike the European bourgeoisie at the time), in contrast with the artisans' commodity (or service) production, which involved them in a whole set of endogenous social interrelationships, and generated a vision of the importance of civil interchange.

> . . . let us hope that the tailor comes to realize that to his elegant creation the shoemaker must contribute for its maximum glory; to them both, the hatter will add his work; the same goes for the blacksmith, and then each in turn for the carpenter and the mason. And once convinced of the need of each for the other, with the desire of entering the pathways of Progress, may all Artisans grasp hands and recognize each other for what they are, brothers. And then may they strive to create 'Centers' where it will not be the pretension to shine in this or that way that brings them together – *as in balls* – but the desire to learn from one another, to perfect themselves in the knowledge of our political, social and religious duties, so that marching on the road of virtue and enlightenment we may better fulfill our earthly mission, so that we may be good citizens deserving well of society, serving our *Patria* (Fatherland) (*El Artesano*, 1874, in Quintero Rivera, 1976:185–6).

Refinement (as education, civil interchange and social manners) not only distinguished, in interpersonal relations, the upper (propertied) classes from peasants (which included many poor whites) and plantation blacks, but also differentiated colored artisans from these 'lower' sectors of society based in the rural world. The establishment of a civic culture, which was of fundamental importance for the emergence of the coding of manners, or etiquette, in the metropolitan colonial powers, involved, in the Hispanic Caribbean colonies, the fundamental participation of sectors still considered 'second class' by the dominant social strata.

To this indirect challenge to social hegemony, the propertied classes responded through the plantation heritage. In order to maintain in the threshold of the public–private sphere an *aristocratic* – as opposed to a *democratic* – social structure, using Hoetink's terms borrowed from Mannheim (Hoetink, 1982:165), the upper classes had to somatize manners: organize etiquette with reference to the body and the body's movements, though in European etiquette references to the body are secondary to table manners (Elias, 1978). The Pygmalion phenomenon (in reference to Shaw's play, 1962), where Liza Doolittle as a woman of working class origin could pass as a member of the upper classes if she learned to speak and behave, was not possible in an aristocratic racially segmented society, as workers (in our analysis, especially artisans) carried their class origins in their skin.

El Carreño

European etiquette was not enough. In the second half of the nineteenth century, during the constitution of a Hispanic Caribbean civic culture, the Caribbean upper classes developed their own book of manners: *El Carreño*. This was not just an imitation of European bourgeois etiquette; it was also written with a different *otherness* in mind: the strong cultural vitality of Negroes who had been stripped or deprived of their language, their geography and power, but never of the polyrhythmic movement of their bodies.[13] A special emphasis was placed on a 'refined' (in Spanish, *fino*) way of referring to and representing the body. While in Spain it was absolutely natural and *correct*, for example, to make reference to *el culo* (anus or buttocks), in Caribbean Spanish this represented an inexcusable vulgarity. A physical trait which came to be identified with colored female sexual attractiveness was stigmatized as unrefined, and no direct mention of that part of the body was socially admissible.[14]

> It is not admissible in society to name the different parts or areas of the body, with the exception of those which are never covered up (Carreño, 1894:72).

El Carreño was written in Venezuela, the first Hispanic Caribbean region to experience a state-centered nation-building process; but it soon became *the* established book of manners throughout the Hispanic Caribbean and was also used in other Latin American countries. In Puerto Rico, the very conservative press *El Boletín Mercantil* published an authorized abridged version for school education in 1894. *El Carreño* was clearly written for the upper classes, as, for example, the passages on how to treat domestic servants show (91). But, while the Caribbean upper classes were mostly rural-based, it was written for city life, which suggests that it also had in mind other classes (nearer to the menacing otherness) that could be seen as questioning the patriarchal social hegemony over the establishment of civility, a process, as already discussed, associated with the urban culture.

El Carreño is divided into two parts. The first is devoted to men's moral duties as the basis for good manners:

> The possession of religious and social principles and the recog-
> nition and the practice of those duties which follow from these
> principles, will always constitute the firm basis . . . of good
> manners (23).

It was very important for the constitution of modern civility (associated with the nation-state) to base the prescribed forms of social intercourse on duties and not on privileges. The moral duties discussed in the book are (in this order) those to God, those to society, and our duties to ourselves. Social duties are (in this order) those towards our parents, those towards the Fatherland (Patria), and duties to other people, significantly using the Spanish word *semejantes*, which refers to *equal others*. *El Carreño*'s discussion of duties combines bourgeois ideology with a patriarchal *Weltanschauung*, typical of the *Junker*-like *hacendado* plantocracy of the period.

The discussion of duties to ourselves is very important, because it relates all duties to a process of education, of *cultivation*, which represents a civilizing process over our nature (the body, our passions). Carreño's summary of this whole first part is as follows:

> The educated man will know God, will know himself and will
> know other men: he who looks after his health and his existence
> will live for God, for himself and for his fellow men; *he who
> curbs his passions* will please God, will fashion his own tranquility
> and his own happiness and will contribute to the tranquility and
> the happiness of others. Here therefore, in sum, are . . . *all* the
> duties and all the virtues (24, my emphasis).

Duties are presented as a learned way of *taming the body*[15]

> In order to please God . . . and to be good citizens . . . we must
> dedicate our whole existence . . . to establishing in our hearts the
> gentle empire of *continence* (23, my emphasis).

A cultivated control over the body and its (natural) desires is presented as the basis for civility, that is to say, continence, which is 'self-restraint especially in the matter of sexual appetite' (Onions, 1972).[16]

The second and most important section of *El Carreño*, to which the first part is a prelude, is directly devoted to manners, using as its subtitle the Spanish word *urbanidad*. Its upper-class character is again evident in its conservative emphasis on social order, present throughout the book, but stressed in the first, introductory, chapter:

> Manners (*urbanidad*) are an emanation of moral duties and, as such, all the principles of manners tend to the preservation of order and that true harmony that must reign among men (25).[17]

But the *hacendado* plantocracy in the Caribbean, besides maintaining an order from which to sustain its position of dominance, was involved in an active struggle of social transformation, that is, in the development of a civil society distinct from the metropolitan colonial order, a civic culture where it could exercise its own class hegemony. The previous quotation concludes:

> *and to tighten the bonds that unite them* through means of the agreeable impressions that they make on each other (25, my emphasis).

Faced with the tacit (indirect) competition of a highly cultivated colored artisan class, its social hegemony in the emerging civility was to be based on its somatic refinement as well. It is a common idiomatic phrase throughout the Hispanic Caribbean to refer to Caucasian physical traits as *facciones finas* (refined features). Immediately after the introductory chapter, *El Carreño*'s discussion of *urbanidad* starts with body hygiene (*aseo*), and the refined representation of the body and body movements permeates the whole book.

The third chapter is devoted to manners in the home, the fourth to conduct outside the house. The urban nature of civility is again evident: the chapter is subdivided into manners in the street, in church and at school. The horror of bodily proximity and the concern for body movement are stressed in all situations:

> It is vulgar and uncivilized in conversation . . . to touch the clothing or the body of those whom one is addressing (74).
>
> We should never get so close to the person with whom we are speaking that he can smell our breath (40).
>
> We should ordinarily walk neither too slowly nor too fast . . . our footsteps should be soft (59–60).
>
> . . . we will then proceed to sit down . . . making sure that we

are not too close to our neighbor's seat (79).

> . . . nor should we lean on the back of the seats of those persons who are next to us, nor should we touch their arms . . . nor should we execute any other movements than those . . . that are absolutely necessary (85).

> . . . let us not forget that delicacy in particular prevents us from having recourse to others in the performance of any of the operations necessary for the cleanliness of our person (107).

> . . . when we take off our clothes . . . to get into bed, we must proceed with honest demureness, so that at no moment do we appear uncovered, either to others *or* to ourselves. How *horrible* is the spectacle when through some *accident* that occurs in the middle of the night, a person appears totally uncovered (49, my emphasis).

El Carreño was clearly written from a masculine perspective and references to women are always directed towards stressing the reinforced restrictions which are placed upon them. His dictates are openly explicit:

> Women will have as a clear guide the fact that the rules of manners apply, with regard to their sex, with greater severity (30).

From the Hispanic Caribbean patriarchal perspective, there are several reasons to explain this difference. One, which is general to any patriarchal vision, is the identification of women with the household and the importance of the domestic sphere in manners:

> These rules are perhaps more important for the woman than for the man, since her destiny calls her to the management of the house and to the immediate running of domestic matters (47).

Another general consideration is associated with the active assertive role men are supposed to play in social interaction, while women are relegated to passive behavior:

> Thus if a man were to adopt the bearing and customs of a woman, he would appear timid and withdrawn, while if a woman, in the same way, were to take on the open demeanor of a man, she would appear immodest and excessive (30–1).

But a third reason has a special importance in racially segmented societies: it is in women that the responsibility of transmitting physical traits lies. Though childbirth is a product of the relation of both sexes, as a symbol of the household, women's procreation is always part of the family, while this is not seen in the same way for men: children born out of marriage are not necessarily part of the man's family unless he specifically takes action (*reconocer*, literally to recognize his parenthood). Somatic inheritance (color as a factor of distinction) is thus a responsibility of women, and the refined representation of the body and body actions is therefore seen as more important in them. *El Carreño* mentions, for example, that it is always unrefined to spit, but while this habit could be tolerated in men, in women it is a repulsive vulgarity which 'undoes *all* her attractive characteristics' (35–6, my emphasis). The importance of body posture is specifically mentioned regarding women (54). Women are a sort of incarnation of nature and their human transformation or refinement embodies special sacrifices and privations. In a very compromising eulogy to women, *El Carreño* dictates:

> Woman contains within her everything that is most beautiful and interesting in human *nature*; and since she is essentially disposed towards virtue, through her *physical* and moral make-up and through the gentle life that she leads, in her heart the most eminent social qualities can find a worthy resting-place. But *nature* has bequeathed on her this privilege only through great privations and sacrifices, through the most serious compromises with morality and with society; and if the gifts of a good education appear in her with added lustre and splendor, by the same token there show up in all her acts, like the slightest stain on a glass, even those insignificant defects which, in a man, might sometimes pass unnoticed (29–30).

¡Baile que está muy bueno! ¡baile en el jaleo![18]

A mi me gusta bailar apambichao
con una negra retrechera y buena moza
a mi me gusta bailar de medio lao
bailar bien apretao
con una negra bien sabrosa.[19]

El Carreño never directly mentions blacks, nor the act of dancing. Race, especially within gender relations, is subtly but very clearly present through the somatization of manners. It is not surprising that if manners were somatized – especially in the inter-gender relations so important for the maintenance of sociosomatic distinctions – the main concern of the Hispanic Caribbean *hacendado* plantocracy, in terms of morals and etiquette in everyday descriptions of social intercourse, focused on the public act *par excellence* of body movement and proximity: dancing as a couple.

Dancing as a couple, associated in 'primitive' societies with fertility rites, did not form part of European ballroom dancing until the late eighteenth century; first through a combination of figure group dancing with couples in the *contradance*, and later through the development of the *waltz*, which was danced entirely in couples. The displacement of the *minuet* by the *contradance* and the *waltz* is analyzed in the classic, scholarly book on the history of dance as being part (like modern etiquette) of the bourgeois transformation of aristocratic culture (Sachs, 1943:399). In the eighteenth-century Hispanic Caribbean, dancing in couples was rare in popular sectors of society, and if done at all, with only the lightest embrace, since in the African tradition embrace signifies the climax of fertility rites: copulation (Jahn, 1963:122). Dancing as a couple holding each other was introduced in upper-class ballrooms (*bailes de sociedad*) at the beginning of the nineteenth century as, in the words of Puerto Rico's first *costumbrist* literature, 'a repeated echo of those from Europe' (Alonso, 1968:33–4); from there it moved, in a more generalized way, to the popular sectors.

By the middle of the nineteenth century in Puerto Rico and Hispaniola, and some two or three decades earlier in Cuba, a new ballroom music with a distinctive Caribbean character emerged. These were the creations of mulatto artisans who were already the most important musicians. They derived from the European *contradance* and had European melody and harmony, but incorporated African elements, especially at the level of rhythm (Henríquez Ureña, 1984:150–1), the most developed element of the African musical tradition. Since colored artisans were involved in a struggle for civic recognition (in their aspiration to be recognized as part of the emerging civil society which, in fact, they were helping to form), this new ballroom music (suffused with popular elements) had to appear refined, as a deferential tribute to the upper classes. For that matter, rhythm was not usually conveyed through percussion instruments, which would clearly show their black origins, but through melodic instruments; in Puerto Rico basically through the euphonium (*bombardino*), a bass brass instrument which was incorporated into dance ensembles from military bands (Quintero Rivera, 1986).[20]

It is significant that the most acclaimed of these new forms of ballroom music came to be called simply *danza*, which is not only a shorter version of *contradanza (contradance)*, but a term that also has a very significant history in the Spanish language. There are two words for dance in Spanish: *baile* and *danza*. This distinction apparently developed in Italy by the time of the emergence of courtesy books. While *ballo* had varied rhythms, suitable for individual display of virtuosity or group spectacles, *danza* had a uniform rhythm throughout and was thus considered more courteous and appropriate to ballroom dancing. A very detailed study of seventeenth-century leisure activities in Spain points towards a similar distinction:

> We should distinguish *danzas* from *bailes* since the former were more measured, honest and aristocratic, whilst the latter were more brazen and plebeian. *Bailes* . . . caused arousal . . . whilst *danzas* . . . as an expression of *gallardía* (elegance) . . . *were accepted without censure* (Deleito, 1944:69, my emphasis).

Deleito adds another important element: in *bailes* the dancer could move both hands and feet with greater freedom, while in *danzas* only the movement of feet was acceptable, in a more measured way. This would eventually facilitate dancing in couples.

Though Caribbean *danzas*, as the adoption of that term indicates, were created by the free coloreds to denote *gallardía* – refinement – and in order to be accepted in upper-class ballrooms (as they were, in fact), the incorporation of elements of the black music tradition[21] gave this new dance wide popularity among all members of the common people, where the black presence was stronger. The 1849 Cuban dictionary starts its definition of *danza* in the following way:

> A favorite dance throughout this Antillean island and which is generally performed in the most solemn functions in the capital as well as in the most indecent *changüí* in the remotest part of the island (Pichardo, 1953:258).

Such a *changüí* was defined as a 'dance and meeting-place for the common people; like a *cuna*'. (Pichardo, 1953:240). *Cuna*, in turn, is defined as a 'meeting of *creole people of color* or common people to dance and often to play; small house, a few musicians, harp and guitar, etc.; everything small and *without etiquette*'.[22] While admittance to an upper-class *casino* (ballroom or club house) was forbidden for mulattos, except as members of the music ensemble, young upper-class white males used to attend these *cunas*.

> The dance was one of those which, although its origins were unknown, were called *cuna* in Havana. We only know that . . . individuals of *both sexes* from the colored class entered freely, and that young white men who *would honor them* with their presence were also not denied entry.[23]

The new Caribbean *danza* consisted of two parts: an introduction, with a clearly European character, called the *paseo* (walk), where men would invite their chosen partners to dance and after a few elegant walking steps would make a courteous salute, followed by the dance proper, which was longer and rhythmical, called the *merengue*. There is a controversy over the origins of this term. Haitians argue that *merengue* originated in the French colony of *Saint Domingue*. and that its name derives from an African dance from Mozambique the *tomton mouringue* (Fouchard, 1973:40). There are, on the other hand, many mid-nineteenth-century documents in the Hispanic Caribbean which directly or indirectly relate the term designating this second, rhythmical part of the *danza* to symbolism associated with *meringue*, 'sweet music'. It is the last section of the dance, just as desserts come at the end of banquets. It is not stiff, but fluffy, like the body movements of the new dance. In this mixture, egg whites and sugar lose their original identity. Through vigorous beating a new thing emerges, just as European and Caribbean musical elements get all mixed up in this new music, and as European whites lose their stiffness in the movement, mixing with Caribbean sugar. Moreover, eggs are associated with fertility, which brings to mind the fertility rites of dancing in couples. In Spanish, eggs are primarily associated with male sexuality, while sweetness is associated with femininity.[24] Most probably, both arguments have some element of truth. The spread of the *contradance* throughout the Hispanic Caribbean in the early nineteenth century is connected by historians of music with the immigration of French families from *Saint Domingue* after the Haitian Revolution (see Díaz Ayala, 1981:31; Urfé, 1982:154). It is probable that this *contradance* had already incorporated some African elements of the *tomton mouringue*, which colored artisans developed in the dance part of their new *danza*, but that the name *merengue* was kept because of its multiple symbolism.

In any case, the black tradition in *danza* rhythm, though camouflaged through melodic instruments, can be clearly seen in the body movements of *merengue* dancing, which was soon considered lascivious, emphasized by the fact that it was danced in couples. Public arguments arose regarding this new dance and the word *voluptuosa* (voluptuous) was constantly used in both sides of the controversy. In 1849, the Spanish Governor of Puerto Rico explicitly prohibited the dancing of *merengue,* a prohibition which had no effect because people of all classes 'stubbornly adhered to this malicious fad'.[25] A politically liberal, but morally conservative writer on the anti-prohibition side of the controversy argued that the State prohibition had the opposite effect of making anti-authoritarian people more eager to try it out (Morales, 1895:55–6). There was a general consensus among upper-class writers that *danza* was at least potentially dangerous. This view was colored by the patriarchal image of women as an incarnation of nature, and as a source of passions in the myth of Eve.

> In its origins, dance was religious and warlike . . . the dancer was always a man. Woman did not take part in dance until it became popular and festive. Even after woman entered the dance, she was *danced* at rather than dancing herself. Dance became profane but not licentious because there was no occasion for licentiousness. It was only when woman came down from her goddess pedestal and

became an *actress* that *the danger of dance* could begin . . . woman, who is beauty and grace personified, descends from her throne, where she was the object of the dance, and begins to dance herself with an ever greater beauty and grace; and since these attributes can only be found in her, this previously unknown beauty and grace could only be revealed *fatally in the exaggeration of the grace* and beauty that the soul and *body* of the woman possess. Thus dance is more innocent and pure when woman plays a smaller part in it and becomes more profane and licentious when feminine beauty and grace hold greater sway (Castro, 1878:403, emphasis added).

A similar argument may be found even in liberal attacks on the *merengue* prohibition:

Dance is the natural state of instinct . . . the fair sex dancing is the saddest sight . . . vice is engendered and virtue is banished. A woman who has danced just once cannot be perfect. She has had to lose her modesty for a few minutes; she has had to *become detached from formality*; she has had to be immodest and vain through the *exaggerated* gallantries of her partner. Dance is the cathedral of vice (Morales, 1895:46, emphasis added).

Faced with these perils, some, like the colonial government, would have preferred to suppress *danza* completely; but, as part of its hegemonic struggle, the *hacendado* plantocracy presented an alternative: to enhance the positive elements which the development of its own national music represented, while countering the potentially chaotic threats to morality through the somatization of manners, through dance etiquette. As *El Carreño* pointed out, this dance etiquette would be especially severe on women.

Danza is not a dance of *mastery* but rather one of *union*, of intimate union, so intimate that it seems designed to give rise to inevitable touching and encounters. People who see this dance for the first time might wrongly judge it as free and dangerous, but I must say, in just and deserved deference to the ladies of Puerto Rico, that, conscious that their modesty could conceivably be in jeopardy, they clothe their movements and bathe their features with a veil of demureness and decorum which not only brings forth their beauty and habitual modesty but which also instills respect and consideration. Never in these dances of select society does one see a gesture, a pose or the slightest action that might indicate illegitimate intentions or inappropriate carelessness. Thus it is that this dance is in general use throughout the island (Anonymous, 1858:34–5).

But particular body movements respond to specific types of musical stimulus:

> The music of these dances, which bears the significant and sweet name of *merengues*, is also very special and delicious in its rare composition . . . and in the modulations of its musical tempos and periods. We can assure you that when a *danza* is played, everyone dances it, and even those who, because of age or for other reasons, do not want to go onto the dance floor, either move their bodies slightly or nod their heads or, at the very least, accompany with rhythmic and light taps of their cane those harmonious sounds which not only please the ear but also affect and sweetly disturb the nervous system through their special character and the very particular nature of their harmonies, cadences and consonances (Anonymous, 1858:35).

The curbing of lascivious movements through dance etiquette also implied possible changes to the music itself.

> It seems that the polemic is not yet over and there is no doubt that both sides of the dispute are putting forward arguments which, in the end, are reaching a form of agreement due, perhaps, to the fact that music has such a great influence on developing souls just as these souls, in turn, influence the dances that are subsequently created (Anonymous, 1878:412–13).

As part of the development of a dance etiquette, the *hacendado* plantocracy launched a campaign to suppress the black elements of the music that colored artisans had created 'for them'. Alejandro Tapia y Rivera, probably the most renowned Puerto Rican intellectual figure of his time, commented on what was becoming our national music, the *danza*:

> Still today some abuse it . . . giving it an affected rhythm to bring out the influence of *voodoo* or of the African tango. *It should be purged of all this*, as Tavarez has done . . . and *the way in which it is danced should be changed* when it is danced by people *comme il faut* for *once it is cleansed of its voluptuous elements*, there will always remain . . . poetry . . . which characterizes our way of feeling (Tapia, 1928:103, my italics).

The suppression of black elements in *danza* was quite a difficult task, partly because composers were mainly mulattos:

> The authors of the *danzas* are in the main sick souls who still retain the traces and the consequence of the times of slavery (Anonymous, 1878:412).

Moreover, Hispanic Caribbean culture still bore the strong imprint of slavery:

> The influence of another race oppressed for three centuries has been more influential . . . the African slave who could not bring learning like the Greeks, has modified our character in an unfavorable way; he has bequeathed us his guttural intonation in speech, his loose movements in dance, the voluptuous sadness of his music, his lack of deference and indolence (Morales, 1895:57).

While the other Latin American countries were involved in (tortuous) nation-building processes, Cuba and Puerto Rico were still colonial societies. The *hacendados*' claim for self-government, a prerequisite for the development of their still incomplete and fragile class hegemony, required showing the world of nations, the First World of *civilized* capitalist countries, that their societies were part of the modern world. Modernity was associated with rationality: science was the basis of progress, and progress required the profitable use of time. The triumph of civilization over barbarity implied the suppression of passions by reason, of leisure by work; the control of the body and natural bodily drives (*urgencias*) through the cultivation of the mind and labor. In interpersonal relations, *El Carreño* stresses the importance of method over spontaneity:

> Method is indispensable for the organization of all acts of social life, if there is to be order and precision in our acts and for us to make good use of our time and not to become tiresome to others through continuous . . . informalities. (44)

In plantation societies, where work had been vilified by slavery

> *A mi me llaman el negrito del batey*
> *porque el trabajo para mí es un enemigo . . .*[26]

and leisure was identified with the untamed ('passionate, voluptuous, barbarous') movements of the body – Negro dancing – it was especially important for the *hacendado* plantocracy to show the world its formidable efforts against the enemy within, against the corrupting presence of the menacing *otherness*.

> We are walking with giant strides towards a bottomless abyss with these dances of *one hundred and twenty beats* of the MERENGUE with which today the good society of Puerto Rico amuses itself. Not only are modesty and virtue the best shield for our beauties; we must also avoid the supremacy of a passion the sad effects of which might affect us very soon. Dance . . . is an honest and

legitimate pastime in itself; but it is more susceptible than any other to degenerate into a guilty and dangerous state.

Either the *danza*, the *voluptuous* dance of the country, must be reformed in a way that makes it more in keeping with good manners, or else foreigners, who visit us in the future, will have the right to suspect us and the habits that have become infiltrated into our way of being, without our being able to build a dike strong enough to correct them (Morales, 1895:42–3, emphasis in the original).

'*Me distrae el eco de una música dulce y no puedo trabajar . . .*' is the opening sentence of another upper-class article warning the *hacendado* plantocracy against the perils of *danza* to reason and the work ethic, because of its 'predisposition towards voluptuosity'.[27] The founder of the distinguished Puerto Rican learned institution of intellectual refinement, El Ateneo, a prominent Liberal, an Autonomist (pro self-government) patriarchal politician, speaks out against a music of the senses: the curse of our plantation heritage. '*Danza* music reminds us of women', he argues, which are the reason for men's downfall, of their sins, the triumph of nature, of passion, over the intellect.

Oh *Danza*, sad canto of my country, be silent! With those cadences, you intoxicate, with those chords you lull, with those inflections you fashion dreams. You convert the *interior* into a camera obscura where there are reflected . . . faces of all kinds which bewitch and call out and provoke, because as soon as you raise your voice, you conjure up pictures of women, awakening the most refined voluptuousness and always draining the spirit of its *energy* . . . How much voluptuous depression do you contain . . . a gentle but terrible echo if we study your causes and your effects . . . you were born only as a punishment! A slow punishment!! And more punishment!!! . . . how softly you insinuate yourself like a devil into our senses to *still our sleeping energy* (Elzaburu, 1878:407, emphasis added).

Salvador Brau, the most articulate spokesman of *hacendado* ideology at the turn of the century, considered by many to be the founder of Puerto Rican sociology and modern historiography,[28] agreed with Elzaburu on the importance of the study of *danza* in its pernicious effects on the rationality and work ethic of modernity. He wrote of its 'intoxicating softness which, by producing a physical wasting, leads to moral weakness' (1956:205). In a nation-building process, it is important, he argued, to analyze defects and vices, in order to overcome them. He recognized that *danza* had come to be the national music, but as a mulatto creation it embodied the shortcomings of colonial history; *hacendado*s should therefore replace this 'effeminate dance of softness' by 'the sacred beat of work and progress, to the rhythm of the solemn harmonies of science' (206).

Danza is so dangerous because it is associated with the body movements of mulatto women, the wellspring of sin, which serve to bewitch *respectable* men. Mulatto women are the forbidden fruit, rejected rationally, but passionately longed for as the *ideal somatic norm image*, the bewitching passion which etiquette cannot contain. The intoxicating bewitchment of the *Leonardos Gamboas* by *Cecilia Valdés* and her likes was the crucial concern of the Hispanic Caribbean patriarchy with regard to interpersonal relations, which must be prevented through manners organized as the control of reason over the body's passions. *Cecilia Valdés* is the great myth of nineteenth-century Hispanic Caribbean interpersonal relations. The white creole *hacendado*, Leonardo, is fascinated by his illegitimate sister, the daughter of his Spanish father and a creole slave. Cecilia bewitches because she is *mulata*, that is because of her color (body movement, polyrhythm), but also due to her being female (that fabulous embodiment of the senses).

> Study that music, dear readers. But do not study it in the dance hall. There the warm density of the atmosphere . . . the dazzling irradiation of the lights, the pungent stimulation of the perfumes, everything, everything producing physical excitement will lead us to *psychological disturbance*; and when you clasp in your arms the *woman*, sometimes loved, *always desired*, when you are in contact with *the expressive softness of her form*, when you inhale her breath and hear from her lips some words of hope, a promise so long sought after, of ineffable delights, inhibited by the *mysterious force of irresistible sorcery*, you will not be able to appreciate the complete transcendence of that music which responds in harmony with the derangement of your reason. But . . . taking refuge in the solitude of thought . . . try to put into play your intellectual faculties . . . if, in those instants, the chords of a *danza* vibrate beneath your balconies, if those languishing, *sensual*, *intoxicating* notes manage to fly up to you, you will feel them taking control of your organism, like the tentacles of a formidable polypus and invading your heart with a wave of grief and sapping your will . . . you will see *all the past of your history* ebbing away (Brau, 1956:202, my emphasis).

In 1882, only three years before Brau wrote his essay on *danza*, Luis Bonafoux had shocked Hispanic Caribbean society with his publication in a Madrid journal of the following description of this *voluptuous* dance, displaying to European eyes our (Caribbean) simultaneous (superego) re-

pulsion and (libidinous) fascination with mulatto women, through whom all
etiquette is overcome.

> Lewd and happy pairs give themselves up with the voluptuous-
> ness of satyrs, to an orgiastic dance called *merengue* due to its
> exquisite taste. And you will see there the brazen and sensual
> mulatta, her hair loose, her lips pursed in a paroxysm of pleasure,
> her eyes moist and very tender, her palpitating breast threatening
> to burst out of its thin and indiscrete confinement, impressing on
> her hips lascivious girations, panting, sweating, burning, thinking
> only of pleasure and living for pleasure, beginning that dance
> . . . which is voluptuous like no other, exhausted in the arms of
> her lover (1882:110–11).

This scene did not take place (and could not have taken place) either in an
upper-class ballroom or in an artisans' *casino*; but rather in a popular
carnival where, as in festivities for patron saints, 'slaves and masters, ladies
and rogues jostled in a motley mixture' (Brau, 1909:325). It was in popular
festivities, like the supposedly religious *Fiestas de Cruz*, where these scan-
dalous scenes could frequently be seen: 'Some man intertwined with some
woman of wholesome contours, swayed loosely to the plangent tones of the
sensual *merengue*' (Brau, 1956:244). In 1845 in the Dominican Republic
the police even prohibited dancing in *Fiestas de Cruz* because of the danger
to good manners (Rodríguez Demorizi, 1971:67).

In 1875, a yellowish (almost *whitish*) mulatto journalist, Ramón Marín,
the illegitimate son of a distinguished *hacendado* and a slave woman, who
had to leave his hometown and move to the progressive city of Ponce to
become, with his father's help, an important spokesman of the *hacendado*
plantocracy, published the most detailed description (a whole book) of the
popular festivities of this important city, the *hacendados*' urban center *par
excellence* in Puerto Rico.[29] He makes the distinction between three types of
dancing parties: the upper-class *bailes de confianza*; dance meetings in
artisans' *casinos;* the open-entrance street or public square festivities (*bailes
públicos*). In the first two, dance etiquette was strictly followed. With
regard to artisans' *casinos*, Marín emphasizes the rule of 'moderation and
order' of this 'respected and respectable' class (1875:51). But 'public'
dances were licentious and immoral:

> These so-called public dances are unedifying centers, which
> morality repels, and at which good manners blush for shame. We
> do not wish, nor should we, to paint this scene because the vigor
> of its tones would hurt the eyes of decorum and good sense (44).

Stressing the importance of manners for social order, he adds:

It is of the upmost moral importance that the necessary measures are taken to ensure that these dances do not degenerate into centers of dissipation and cause an eruption which would lead us to the chaos of dissoluteness (44).

Though, as mentioned before, young white upper-class males used to attend these festivities, Marín emphatically points out that artisans did not dare to get mixed up with this *crápula*.

Contrary to what some people think, *[these places] are not visited by honest artesans nor by women who respect themselves: this class* which merits every consideration and respect, *has its own decent and civilized clubs* (44, my emphasis).

A common saying all over the Hispanic Caribbean, which applies mainly to colored artisans, is '*negro, pero decente*' (black, but decent). In their struggle to be recognized as part of the emerging, respectable civility, but also because of their popular origins, artisans had to be especially cautious in circumstances where manners were at stake. In his elegant description of *La Habana Artística*, published in the official government press, Serafín Ramírez shows no concern at the enjoyment of dance, including 'mulatto artisans, who are those best at *Danzas*' (1891:9); but he appears horrified at the possibility that this enjoyment

would be converted into a mad and vehement passion . . . to the turbulent and hot rhythm which accompanies this degeneration of our *contradanza* called *danzón* characterized by the rough scraping of the *guayo* and the *numbing noise of the drums* (1891:29, my emphasis).

The echo of drums could play a bad trick on the most 'respectable' mulatto who dropped his guard for a minute:

The *bombardino* establishes the rhythm . . . As the beer and rum are now taking their effect . . . any *traces of etiquette have disappeared* and the couples *hug and squeeze each other at will*, with great pleasure *on both sides*.
What did you think of the dance?
Be quiet woman! I will not allow to be fooled again. Just think of my daughter mixing with the Martinez girls who are good-for-nothing! *One can't dance in society anymore . . .*
And don't you know that the woman speaking in this way is a direct descendent of the blackest black ever known on these islands? (González, 1893:192, my emphasis)

In order to be accepted as part of civil society of the emerging nationality, colored artisans had to suppress any bodily manifestation of emotions. In one of its closing statements, *El Carreño* explicitly rules that

> We should become accustomed to exercise over ourselves what-
> ever control is necessary to *suppress ourselves* in the midst of the
> strongest sensations. Excessive shouts of pain, of surprise or of
> fear, jumping *and other demonstrations of happiness and enthu-
> siasm* . . . are entirely characteristic of vulgar and badly educated
> people (109, my emphasis).

And he concludes his book of manners with a whole section criticizing jokes and laughter.

Epilogue

It would be beyond the 'decent' limits of an essay to attempt an analysis of the development of dance etiquette from *danza* to present-day festivities, but I hope to have shown that the recent comic revival of an interest in manners cannot be interpreted only in terms of the consolidation of a new urban middle class. Barsy's class hypothesis regarding the necessity of that new urban middle class to distinguish itself from its supposedly popular or rural origins should receive serious consideration, but it needs to be refor-mulated. I hope to have demonstrated that race and gender must be incor-porated into any attempt at a class analysis of this phenomenon, as probably of any social process in Caribbean societies. Race, gender and class rela-tionships in the Caribbean are not separate spheres of social life, but differentiated and intermingled aspects of a socio-historic reality, and none can be seen in this context independently of the others.

All the authors quoted in the picture I have tried to present of dance etiquette in nineteenth-century Hispanic Caribbean society wrote from a clearly white upper-class masculine perspective. In the first decades of the twentieth century new books on manners were published within the then new 'academic' field of Home Economics, and were all written from a feminine perspective (for example, Ferguson, 1915).[30] It is significant that the stories of Ramos' *El manual del buen modal* constantly shift from male to female characters, and that the gender identity of Iván Fontecha in *Sunshine's* TV sketches is not at all clear. Both Ramos' book and *Sun-shine's* sketches do not reveal a vision of a class with hegemonic aspira-tions, like the nineteenth-century *hacendado* plantocracy. They show no orientation towards a social order; on the contrary, both are directed to disrupting order, which is manifested in their use of humor. They are plebeian[31] transgressions of an order constituted by both the patriarchal *Weltanschauung* and the artisans' deferent prudence and decorum.

The analysis of contemporary social transformations which could help us explain the plebeian character of this trangression, like most of the questions posed at the beginning of this essay, will have to wait for another paper. However, this long historical detour will help, I hope, to delimit the kind of problems which we need to address.

Danza, described in the nineteenth century as an embodiment of voluptuousness, is now considered a very refined music and seigniorial dance form (see, for example, Acosta, 1989:41, Blanco, 1935:106). The traditional white upper class concern with morality now focuses on an overtly mulatto music, where rhythm need not be camouflaged, but is openly presented, developed and enhanced. The concern is greater when lyrics lose all inhibitions with reference to the body and to sexual delights, as in a contemporary genre named *erotic salsa*. We indeed have loose etiquette while dancing, but since our bodies are contested fields of struggle, negotiations and transactions within our contradictory history, we Caribbeans very strongly feel . . . fire in our skin.[32]

Notes

1. 'If there is a dance in some CASINO,/Someone always complains,/Because the white woman is always advised/Not to dance with the young black./For even if he is yellow, he has/"Black behind his ears." ' Juan Antonio Alix, 1883 (quoted and translated in Hoetink, 1982:190).
2. 'It's darky vulgar not to laugh!' Translations from Spanish in this article, unless where otherwise stated, were kindly provided by Professor John King of Warwick University, England. I express my deepest thanks for this help.
3. It was the program with the highest rating for six consecutive months.
4. For other social contexts see Bourdieu, 1984.
5. Included in one of the most important books of essays of recent Puerto Rican literature, which also contains essays by Ramos (Vega, 1991). The only other social analysis of the comedy TV program *Sunshine's Café,* though not focusing on manners but on other issues, came from the new academic field of social communication (Colón, 1991). Colón also stresses the transgressive character of *Sunshine's* sketches through the analysis of his parodic representations of official culture and his festive, carnivalesque defense of alternative popular values, specifically regarding the image of the body. As will be seen, this has many points of contact with my analysis of taste and manners.
6. *Bourgeois* were first citizens or freemen from burghs – *bourg* in French (Onions, 1972).
7. In Caribbean Spanish we would use the world *denigrar*, which comes, in fact, from 'nigger'.
8. See Ortiz' prologue in Saco (1974:72).
9. See Deschamps Chapeaux (1976), Duharte (1984), Quintero Rivera (1988, 1983) and Hoetink (1982:165–92). Earlier, Cuba had a much stronger free colored urban culture than Puerto Rico or Hispaniola. For example, the population of Havana represented around 15 per cent of the island's total population during the nineteenth century, while San Juan

represented only 3.5 per cent during the same period in Puerto Rico and Santo Domingo around 4 per cent (Morse, 1971:5a, 78; Quintero Rivera, 1988:39–41; Hoetink, 1982: 19–46). This process of colored participation in the establishment of Cuban civility developed to such an extent that the white *hacendado* plantocracy considered it necessary to curtail it violently. In 1844, in an incident significatively named *La escalera* (ladder), the free colored population was accused of conspiring with plantation slaves to bring about a general black revolt, and a terrible repression was launched in which many distinguished free coloreds were killed or jailed (Deschamps Chapeaux, 1971). This was a tremendous setback. By the late nineteenth century, the process was therefore probably stronger in the two other Hispanic Antilles.

10. This is evident in Puerto Rico from a comparison of late nineteenth-century artisans' periodicals, such as *El Porvenir Social*, *La Miseria*, or *El Pan del Pobre*, with the rest of the newspapers in the country (Quintero Rivera, 1983).
11. Emphasis in the original, Pichardo, 1955[1849]:442.
12. Rodríguez Juliá (1986a) has a very suggestive socio-cultural analysis of his paintings.
13. Benítez Rojo (1989), in his section *Del ritmo al poliritmo*, offers very suggestive observations in this respect.
14. On the unnamed Caribbean obsession with buttocks see Rodríguez Juliá (1986b). Recent sociological research on sexual practices confirms this obsession (Cunningham, 1989–92).
15. Carreño, 1894:21
16. This is the meaning in Carreño's text, but it is significant that in Spanish it has a second (related) meaning: 'graceful bow in dancing' (Amador, 1971:778) or *Especie de graciosa cortesía en el arte del danzado* (Vox, 1986:426), as will be discussed later.
17. See also pp. 14–15, 17, and 19.
18. 'Dance, it's good to enjoy it! Dance, while mixing up!' (in the most rapid and voluptous section of *merengue*). Phrase in the famous Dominican *merengue, Compadre Pedro Juan* (Alberti, 1973).
19. 'I like to dance a slow *merengue* / with an attractive, good looking black girl / I like to dance it sideways / holding her tightly / with a delicious black girl.' Famous 1950s Dominican *merengue, El negrito del batey*; music by Medardo Guzmán, lyrics by Héctor J. Díaz.
20. In Cuba the same phenomenon is found but through other instruments (Galán, 1983:135; Carpentier, 1946:112, 185; Grenet, 1939:xxi). This process was also important in Hispanic Caribbean peasant music, as I have analyzed elsewhere (Quintero Rivera, 1994). Bebey (1969) describes as an African tradition the search for and/or creation of instruments which could simultaneously provide melody and rhythm.
21. More details in Álvarez (1992:36–40).
22. Pichardo, 1953:228. First emphasis in the original, second emphasis added.
23. From the fourth chapter of Villaverde, 1981, emphasis added. The usual meaning of the world *cuna* is cradle; probably the adoption of the term for the kind of dance described above comes from its association as a place to mate; it could also be related to the term *baja cuna*, which refers to persons of 'ignoble' social origin.
24. Though the gender identity of sugar is ambiguous – mostly *el*, but in some circumstances *la*.
25. Pedreira (1929:136) quotes the entire text of the prohibition order. Coopersmith (1974: 26–7) examines the close relationship between Dominican *merengue* and *danza* and describes the strong moral reaction to *merengues* in Dominican society around 1855. See also Nolasco (1956:324).
26. 'They call me the little forecourt black / because work is an enemy to me . . .' Famous Dominican *merengue*.

27. 'I am distracted by the echo of a sweet music and I cannot work . . .' (Elzaburu, 1878: 406–7).
28. A more detailed analysis of his works is included in Quintero Rivera (1988), particularly the fourth chapter.
29. Quintero Rivera (1988), particularly the first chapter.
30. See Ortiz Cuadra, n.d. Ortiz's historical research has been very important for the development of all the ideas presented in this essay, as have been the stimulating conversations and discussions we have shared on this subject.
31. González (1980) presents a very provocative analysis of contemporary Puerto Rican *plebeyismo*, focusing on the visual arts.
32. ¡Fuego en la piel! 'Fire in the skin!' is a frequently used slogan of Eddie Santiago, one of the main creators of erotic *salsa*, in his LP *Atrevido y diferente*, TH AMF 2424, 1986.

References

Acosta, L., 1989, 'From the Drums to the Synthesizer', *Latin American Perspectives*, Vol. 16, No. 2, pp. 29–46.

Alberti, L.F., 1973, *Método de tambora y güira*, Santo Domingo: Ed. Cultural Dominicana.

Alonso, M., 1968[1849], *El Gíbaro*, San Juan: Cultural.

Álvarez, L.M., 1992, 'La presencia negra en la música puertorriqueña', in González, L.M. (ed.), *La tercera raíz, Presencia africana en Puerto Rico*, San Juan: CEREP, pp. 29–41.

Amador, 1971, *Diccionario manual inglés-español-inglés*, Barcelona: R. Sopena.

Anonymous, 1858, *Descripción de las fiestas reales que celebró la muy noble y muy leal ciudad de Puerto Rico con motivo del fausto natalicio del Serenísimo Príncipe de Asturias don Alfonso*, San Juan: Imp. Acosta.

Anonymous, 1878, 'El baile y la música de nuestra danza', *Revista Puertorriqueña*, Vol. 30, No. 10, pp. 412–13. [José Gautier Benítez or Manuel Fernández Juncos.]

Bebey, F., 1969, *Musique de L'Afrique*, Paris: Horizons de France.

Benítez Rojo, A., 1989, *La isla que se repite. El Caribe y la perspectiva posmoderna,* Hanover: Ed. del Norte.

Blanco, T., 1935, 'Elogio a la plena', *Revista del Ateneo Puertorriqueño*, Vol. 1, No. 1, pp. 97–106.

Bonafoux, L. [1882], 'El Carnaval en las Antillas', reprinted in Coll y Toste, C., (ed.), *Boletín Histórico de Puerto Rico*, No. 12, pp. 110–11, San Juan: Tip. Cantero, Fernández y Co. 1914–27.

Bonhart, R.K., 1988, *The Bonhart Dictionary of Etymology*, s.l.: H.W. Wilson.

Bourdieu, P., 1984, *Distinction: A Social Critique of the Judgment of Taste*, Cambridge: Harvard University Press.

Brau, S., 1909, *Hojas caídas*, San Juan: Tip. La Democracia.

––––––– 1956, *Disquisiciones sociológicas*, San Juan: Universidad de Puerto Rico.

Carpentier, A., 1946, *La música en Cuba*, México: FCE.

Carreño, M.A., 1894, *Manual de urbanidad y buenas maneras*, San Juan: Imp. del Boletín Mercantil.

Castro y Serrano, J., 1878, 'El baile', *Revista Puertorriqueña*, 1 October, pp. 400–5.

Colón, E., 1991, 'La hora del cuerpo: recepción y consumo de la comedia en Puerto Rico', *Diálogos de la Comunicación*, No. 30, pp. 64–75.

Coopersmith, J.M., 1974, *Música y músicos de la República Dominicana*, Santo Domingo: Dirección General de la Cultura.

Corominas, J. and Pascual, J.H., 1987, *Diccionario crítico de etimología castellana e hispana*, Madrid: Gredos.

Cunningham, I., 1989–92, *Comportamiento de riesgo al VIH y factores asociados*, San Juan: Universidad de Puerto Rico.

Deleito y Piñuela, J., 1944, . . . *También se divierte el Pueblo (Recuerdos de hace tres siglos: Romerías/Verbenas/Bailes/Carnaval/Torneos/Toros/Academias políticas/Teatro)*, Madrid: Espasa Calpe.

Deschamps Chapeaux, P., 1971, *El negro en la economía habanera del siglo XIX*, La Habana: UNEAC.

_____ 1976, *Los batallones de pardos y morenos libres*, La Habana: Ed. Arte y Literatura.

Díaz Ayala, C., 1981, *Música cubana del Areyto a la Nueva Trova*, San Juan: Cubanacán.

Duharte, R., 1984, *Dos aproximaciones a la historia de Cuba*, Santiago: Casa del Caribe.

Echegaray, E. de, 1889, *Diccionario etimológico de la lengua Española*, Madrid: Ed. José María Faquita.

Elias, N., 1978, *The History of Manners*, New York: Pantheon.

Elzaburu, M. de, 1878, 'La música de nuestra Danza', *Revista Puertorriqueña*, Vol. 20, No. 30(10), pp. 406–7. [Pseud. Fabián Montes.]

The New Encyclopedia Britannica, 1985, Chicago: University of Chicago Press.

Ferguson, G.J., 1915, *Home Making and Home Keeping*, San Juan: Bureau of Supplies, Printing and Transportation.

Fouchard, J., 1973, *La méringue, danse nationale d'Haiti*, Ottawa: Ed. Leménc.

Galán, N., 1983, *Cuba y sus sones*, Valencia: Pre-textos.

García, G.L. and Quintero Rivera, A.G., 1982, *Desafío y Solidaridad, breve historia del movimiento obrero puertorriqueño*, San Juan: Huracán-CEREP.

González, J.L., 1980, *El país de cuatro pisos*, San Juan: Huracán.

González García, M., 1893, 'El baile', *La Ilustración Puertorriqueña*, Vol. 2, No. 24, p. 192.

Grenet, E., 1939, *Popular Cuban Music*, Havana: Corosa y Co.

Henriquez Ureña, P., 1984[1929], 'Música popular de América', *Boletín de Antropología Americana*, No. 9, pp. 137–57.

Hoetink, H., 1967, *The Two Variants in Caribbean Race Relations*, London: Oxford University Press.

_____ 1982, *The Dominican People, 1850–1900. Notes for a Historical Sociology*, Baltimore: Johns Hopkins University Press.

Jahn, J., 1963, *Muntu: las culturas neoafricanas*, México: FCE.

Morales, J.P., 1895, *Misceláneas*, San Juan: Suc. de J.J. Acosta.

Marín, R., 1875, *Las fiestas populares de Ponce*, Ponce: Tip. El Vapor.

Moreno Fraginals, M., 1953, 'Nación o plantación. El dilema político cubano visto a través de José Antonio Saco', in Le Riverend, J. *et al.*, *Estudios históricos americanos. Homenaje a Silvio Zavala*, México: El Colegio de México, pp. 241–72.

_____ 1978, *El ingenio, complejo económico social cubano del azúcar*, La Habana: Ed. de Ciencias Sociales.

_____ 1983, *La historia como arma y otros estudios sobre esclavos, ingenios y plantaciones*, Barcelona: Crítica.

Morse, R.M., 1971, *The Urban Development of Latin America 1750–1900*, Stanford: Stanford University Press.

Nolasco, F. de, 1956, *Santo Domingo en el Folklore Universal*, Santo Domingo: Imp. Dominicana.

Onions, C.T. (ed.), 1969, *The Oxford Dictionary of English Etymology*, Oxford: Clarendon Press.

_____ 1972, *The Shorter Oxford English Dictionary on Historical Principles*, Oxford: Clarendon Press.

Ortiz Cuadra, C.M., n.d., 'Apuntes sobre *Home Making and Home Keeping* de Grace J. Ferguson', unpublished manuscript.

Pedreira, A.S., 1929, 'El Merengue', *Indice*, Vol. 1, No. 9, p. 136.

Pérez de la Riva, J., 1978, *El barracón. Esclavitud y capitalismo en Cuba*, Barcelona: Crítica.

Pérez Velasco, E., 1984, 'La lectura en los talleres de tabaco en Puerto Rico', *La Torre del Viejo*, Vol. 1, No. 2, pp. 37–8.

Peris Menchieta, F., 1886, *De Madrid a Panamá; Gigo, Tug, Tenerife, Puerto Rico, Cuba, Colón y Panamá*, Madrid: s.n.

Pichardo, E., 1955[1849], *Pichardo Novísimo o Diccionario provincial casi razonado de vozes y frases cubanas*, La Habana: Selecta.

Quintero Rivera, A.G., 1976, *Workers' Struggle in Puerto Rico: A Documentary History*, New York: Monthly Review Press.

_____ 1977, *Conflictos de clase y política en Puerto Rico*, San Juan: CEREP-Huracán.

_____ 1983, 'Socialist and Cigarmaker: Artisan Proletarianization in the Making of the Puerto Rican Working Class', *Latin American Perspectives*, Nos. 37–38, pp. 19–38.

_____ 1986, 'Ponce, the *Danza* and the National Question: Notes Towards a Sociology of Puerto Rican Music', *Cimarrón*, Vol. 1, No. 2, pp. 49–65.

_____ 1988, *Patricios y plebeyos: burgueses, hacendados, artesanos y obreros*, San Juan: Huracán.

_____ 1994, 'The Camouflaged Drum, Melodization of Rhythms and Maroonaged Ethnicity in Caribbean Peasant Music', in Béhague, G.H. (ed.), *Music and Black Ethnicity: The Caribbean and South America*, London: Transaction Publishers, pp. 47–64.

Ramírez, S., 1891, *La Habana artística*, La Habana: Imp. de la Capitanía General.

Ramos, J.A., 1983, *Papo Impala está quitao*, San Juan: Huracán.

_____ 1993, *El manual del buen modal*, San Juan: Ed. Universidad de Puerto Rico.

Rodríguez Demorizi, E., 1971, *Música y baile en Santo Domingo*, Santo Domingo: Lib. Hispaniola.

Rodríguez Juliá, E., 1986a, *Campeche o los diablejos de la melancolía*, San Juan: ICP.

_____ 1986b, *Una noche con Iris Chacón*, San Juan: Antilla.

Sachs, C., 1943, *Historia universal de la danza*, Buenos Aires: Ed. Centurión.

Saco, J.A., 1974, *Contra la anexión*, La Habana: Ed. de Ciencias Sociales. [Compiled with a prologue by Fernando Ortiz, 1928.]

Shaw, G.B., 1962, *Complete Plays*, New York: Dodd, Mead.

Tapia y Rivera, A., 1928, *Mis memorias (1826–1882)*, New York: De Laisne and Rossboro.

Tönnies, F., 1963[1887], *Community and Society*, New York: Harper.

Trelles, C.D., 1993, 'Manual de un autor en decadencia', *El Nuevo Día*, 15 August, p. 14.

U.S. War Department, 1899, *Census for the Island of Porto-Rico*, Washington: Government Printing Office.

Urfé, O., 1982, 'La música folklórica, popular y del teatro en Cuba', in *La cultura en Cuba socialista*, La Habana: Ed. Letras Cubanas, pp. 151–73.

Vega, A.L. (ed.), 1991, *El tramo ancla*, San Juan: Ed. Universidad de Puerto Rico.

Villaverde, C., 1981[1882], *Cecilia Valdés, o La loma del Angel (novela de costumbres cubanas)*, Caracas: Bib. Ayacucho.

Vox, 1986, *Diccionario general ilustrado de la lengua española*, Barcelona: Bibliografía SA.

Williams, R., 1976, *Keywords. A Vocabulary of Culture and Society*, London: Fontana.

CHAPTER 9
Jamaican decolonization and the development of national culture

Colin Clarke

When Jamaica achieved independence in 1962, in the aftermath of a referendum over its membership of the West Indies Federation, this was more an
expression of distrust of the other British Caribbean colonies than an
upwelling of latent nationalism. That some sections of the middle stratum of
its society were developing a sense of Jamaican (as well as West Indian)
identity, through politics and the arts, is not in doubt; but Jamaica's 'no' to
Federation was largely an expression of its insularity and its unwillingness
to be burdened with responsibility for the smaller and economically weaker
territories, as distinct from a burning desire to be independent on its own.
Prevailing Jamaican attitudes at that time were insular and colonial; put
pejoratively, they were parochial and imitative. If these isolationist views
were more extreme than those expressed elsewhere in the Federation, it was
because Jamaica was more isolated from the rest than they were from one
another; it was larger, and had, so it seemed, more to lose and less to gain
from Federation than its temporary bed-fellows.

Blockaded but not captured by the Axis Powers during World War II,
unlike many European colonies in South-east Asia, the British West Indies
of the 1940s and 1950s were prized at the UK Colonial Office for their
loyalty to the Crown and their swift acceptance of gradual, constitutional
decolonization. Colonialism had been an established fact in the Caribbean
for more than three centuries; virtually no antecedent peoples or cultures
remained; scarcely a pre-European archaeological site worth visiting could
be found. British West Indian societies were entirely creations of empire,
and more especially of the systems of forced labor that had been deployed
during the seventeenth, eighteenth and nineteenth centuries to operate the
sugar plantations. Local political elites, increasingly elected after 1945, had
been socialized to treasure Pax Britannica, and to appreciate and imitate
British institutions and values. As the distinguished black Barbadian,
Sir Hugh Springer (1960:253), observed, 'our culture is rooted in Western
culture and our values, in the main, are the values of the Christian Hellenic
tradition'.

This view, while a faithful reflection of the opinion of the black and brown middle stratum from Georgetown, British Guiana to Kingston, Jamaica, failed, of course, to take into account the culture and values of the black and Indian masses, the descendants of the slaves and indentured laborers who were imported by the planter class, under imperial regulation, to work on the sugar estates. Writing on a similar theme almost twenty years ago, I noted that 'colonialism is a state of mind as well as a political fact, and a striking feature of West Indian identity is the low esteem in which it is locally held' (1976:12). Denigration of Caribbean peoples and products has been a major colonial theme which has persisted into the post-colonial period. 'They will forever consume,' the Trinidad novelist, V.S. Naipaul once wrote, 'they will never create. They are without natural resources, they will never develop the higher skills. Identity depends on achievement; and achievement here cannot but be small' (1972:250). However, when a tiny ex-colony such as St Lucia can boast two Nobel Prize winners in the last quarter century (Sir Arthur Lewis for economics and Derek Walcott for literature), Naipaul's pessimism seems excessive.

This chapter concentrates on Jamaica's decolonization and the development of the plastic and performing arts in the first three decades after independence; inevitably, it also focuses on the experience and achievements of two generations of Jamaicans, who, with the assistance of a handful of Britishers during the 1920s and 1930s, laid the foundations for the flourishing of creole culture (the culture of the brown and black population) as national culture after 1962. The chapter opens with a brief account of Jamaica's post-independence experience of statehood, and the need to forge a national identity instead of relying on the imitative provincialism of white colonial culture. It then looks at the cultural complexity of Jamaica, drawing attention to distinctions in family, religion, education and language between the three principal social strata, in the lower two of which the modern arts movement has been embedded.

The focus is subsequently placed on the plastic arts – sculpture, wood carving and painting; literature, poetry and the novel; pantomime, dance and plays. The final section concentrates on popular music and the creative role of the Rastafari movement in the development and diffusion of reggae, one of the quintessential expressions of Jamaican national culture. Here low-status black culture has been not only a national unifying focus for all (or almost all) sections of society, but also a vehicle for projecting a Jamaican black identity on to the international stage.[1]

A major feature of Jamaican national culture is that it is creole, or local to Jamaica. However, it is also a plural culture, in that virtually all branches of the arts are divided into tutored and untutored versions: Cooper (1993) uses the terms 'book' and 'long head', reflecting the involvement of the middle and lower strata, respectively. Furthermore, this plural national culture has evolved almost exclusively in the crucible of urban living in Kingston, the capital, with a population now in excess of three-quarters of a million or one-third of the Jamaican total. Here, the West Kingston ghetto has played a vital part in the evolution of black Jamaican culture, notably, but not exclusively, in the shape of reggae music. As Cooper notes, 'the brash revisionism of the ghetto youth's cries for social justice challenges the wisdom of the conservative peasant culture' (1993:4). So the terms used by Cooper, 'down-town' and 'up-town', as they relate to modern cultural forms, are rooted in distinct socio-cultural strata which have been developing in specific geographical localities in Kingston since the 1920s (Clarke, 1975).

Two final preliminary points require emphasizing. First, although this chapter celebrates the creativity of Jamaicans in the arts, it is also true that Jamaica since independence has become an intensely politicized and violent society. These conditions have been woven into the sense of national identity that has been achieved since 1962. Second, it is important to resist the temptation to portray achievement in the arts as uncontested in the broader society or to infer that collaboration between tutored and untutored artists can be treated as symptomatic of middle- and lower-strata co-operation and mutual approval. A distinction must be made between the artists, who frequently supply mutual support across the tutored–untutored divide – 'one culture's "knowledge" is another's "noise" ' (Cooper, 1993:4) – and the broader society whose conservative middle stratum still rejects 'folk' achievements and prefers its tutored arts to be based upon traditional and recently imported elements of European and US provenance.

Jamaica since independence

Since independence in 1962, and more especially since 1972, Jamaica's material achievements have – to echo Naipaul's words – indeed been small. The balanced export economy of the 1950s, involving sugar, rum, bananas, coconuts, coffee, and cocoa, all of which were produced by planters and peasants alike, diversified by bauxite mining, modern manufacturing and tourism, has spun out of control. Sugar and banana output barely meet the quotas set by the European Community under Lomé; US hostility to Jamaican socialism under Michael Manley destabilized manufacturing and bauxite in the 1970s, the latter being rescued only by government intervention; and the tourist industry, shored up by government purchase in the late 1970s, was a decade later denationalized and identified as the only economic sector with any real growth potential. The net result of these shifts is that GDP has been characterized by negative growth for much of the period since 1975, and it is only since the late 1980s that modest economic improvement has been re-established, though under a dubious regime of structural adjustment. In relation to its population size, Jamaica has one of the largest national debts in the world.

Unemployment, now measured at about 15 per cent, coupled to the burgeoning expansion of the urban and rural informal economy, has created a necessitous citizenry. Some of the worst conditions are found in Kingston, the capital, where there is a massive dependence on illegal activities, epitomized by the 3 g's – gangs, guns and ganja (marajuana). This urban electorate, tribalized by the People's National Party and the Jamaica Labor Party, has come to depend for succor on political patronage – in the form of jobs and housing. Robbery has emerged as a basic technique for the redistribution of material wealth, and while some gangs are free of political involvement, many have important links to the political class who provide protection for their clients. The brew is a potent one, since these gangs, in turn, are often deployed for political purposes, especially at election times, when the West Kingston slum is divided, not by race – it is uniformly black, but by party political affiliation (Payne, 1991).

There have also been several gains since independence. Democracy has been firmly established, though the electoral system came close to breakdown in 1980, when more than 600 deaths accompanied the hustings. Nevertheless, seven post-independence national polls have taken place, and the government has changed hands three times in thirty years. Attempts have been made to confront or challenge dependency, but the results, while boosting national awareness, have resulted in an anti-Jamaica backlash in the US, which damaged the open economy in the 1970s – a condition from which it has not subsequently recovered. But one of the clearest gains so far has been in the formation of a distinctive post-colonial national identity through the elaboration of a national culture.

The uniqueness in this respect of Jamaica, among the plethora of post-colonial societies in the Third World, has been signalled by Rex Nettleford (1989:291–2):

> Long before it became universally mandatory to view 'culture' as integral to national development strategies and certainly before the United Nations felt that the subject deserved a decade, Jamaica strove to give form and purpose to the idea of its people's creative energies and cultural achievements, informing nation-building and the shaping of the new society. The country has long developed a cultural policy, formally dating back to 1959 but harking back to 1938 with a well thought out updating in the 1963 Five Year Development Plan. . . . Long before [the 1930s] there were ancestral sources of artistic, religious and linguistic discovery as well as innovative designs for social living. These have .

left Jamaica with a rich legacy of original and distinctive music and dance, rituals and belief systems as well as Jamaica Talk, which remains a vibrant dynamic means of communication, challenging poets and playwrights to creativity and certain educators to unnecessary anguish.

Jamaican national culture is a creole counter-culture, elaborated in opposition to the British provincialism toted by the white elite during the last half century of colonialism. Describing Jamaica, to which he returned from Britain in the early 1920s, Norman Manley, Michael's father, admitted that he was 'surprised and a little shocked. Few, if any . . . were interested in anything except the daily round of events in Jamaica, and even as to that the range of interest was extremely narrow. You talked, or tried to talk, about important events in other countries, but hardly anyone was interested. Books and drama were barren gambits – music was worse.' (quoted in Nettleford, 1971:cv). Of necessity, it was the creativity of the colored and black sections of the society that filled the post-colonial vacuum created by the overturning of 'European' culture, values and images. The elevation of brown and black culture as national culture was facilitated by the virtual extinction of the white urban community by emigration during the socialist years of the 1970s. Twenty years after independence, the white population of Kingston, obviously less rooted than the small landed class in the rural areas, had declined by 90 per cent to about 2,000.

Cultural pluralism

Historically, however, white culture was dominant throughout colonial times, and non-European features, in language for example, were subordinate and denigrated. Mervyn Alleyne, Professor of Socio-Linguistics at the University of the West Indies, has commented that, 'in Jamaica the form of speech – mainly rural – commonly called "creole" still shows clear links to field slave speech, of which it is the modern representative' (1988:137). It is common to treat Creole and Standard English as poles, separated by an intervening register.

> Taken together, these levels form what is called Jamaica's linguistic continuum. These intermediate variants can generally be ranged, in terms of their formal characteristics and grammatical structure and in terms of speakers' reaction to them, along a scale of degrees of approximation to either the 'target' (Standard English) or to the base ('creole'). This scale may also be calibrated in terms of degree of continuity (or loss) of West African features. West African features prevail at the 'creole' end of the

continuum and are progressively replaced by forms approximating more and more to Standard English (137).

These language registers – according to the Jamaican anthropologist M.G. Smith – have direct analogues in the cultural institutions (family and kinship, religion, education, property and recreation) practised by the Jamaican population (1965). The cartographic depiction (Figure 1) of socially crucial combinations of these institutions in Kingston, based on the 1960 census, reveals a close, systematic relationship between European culture, based on grammar school education, formal marriage and high-class suburban living; and between Afro-Jamaican matrifocality and serial polygamy, illiteracy, Afro-Christian cults and residence in low-class inner-city neighborhoods, especially in the West Kingston slum. In addition, there was an interstitial 'brown' and black middle class that integrated features of the subordinate and superordinate cultures and strata, and acted as a social and geographical buffer between them (Clarke, 1975). Field work carried out in 1961, the last year of the colony, suggested that language variations correlated closely with the spatial patterning of culture/color/class attributes. In short, the geography of Standard English/intervening register/Creole distinctions would have been banded, from the northern suburbs to the southern slums, in ways reminiscent of the maps, but with two distinctions: first, the middle stratum, in keeping with its hybrid nature already alluded to, was notably bilingual; second, most of the upper and lower strata would be able to move away from the polar extremes of the register, thus facilitating inter-class (or inter-cultural) communication.

It will now be clear why the evolution of a post-independence national culture in Jamaica has been so necessary and so challenging. Necessary, because of the historic domination of white culture, values and the English language, which marginalized the mass of the new Jamaican citizenry; challenging, because of the need to seek a national identity that was non-European, authentic rather than imitative, and based on the characteristics of 'the other'. That Jamaica has been able to go a long way to forging such an identity, in the face of economic adversity (or perhaps, in part, because of it, since the tribulations of the 1970s involved standing up to the US), has been due principally to the artistic creativity of the people and to the establishment, during the late colonial period, of programs and institutions that made this flowering of talent possible.

The plastic arts

Jamaican national culture did not spring into life with independence in 1962, but had been nurtured in embryo by a few white and nonwhite

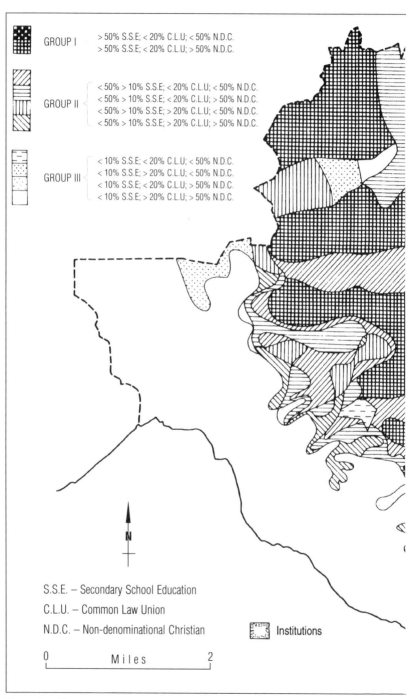

Figure 1. Kingston, 1960: combinations of cultural institutions – aspects of education, family and religion.

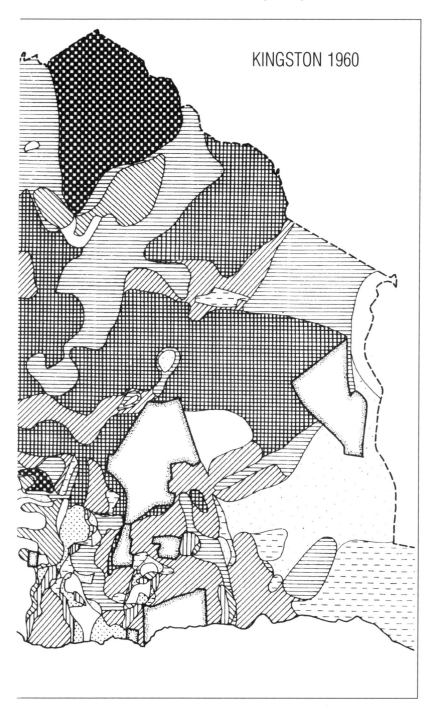

KINGSTON 1960

Jamaicans since at least the 1920s and 1930s, after which its leaders merged with the directorate of the People's National Party. The interaction between this political party and the modern art movement is important, and is personified in the husband and wife pairing of Norman and Edna Manley. Norman was Jamaica-born and -reared, and Oxford-educated, while Edna, Norman's cousin, was British-born but with a Jamaican mother. They married in Britain in 1921, after Norman's training as a barrister was completed, and settled in Kingston, Jamaica, in 1922. A sculptor and wood carver trained in London at the St Martin's School of Art, Edna Manley immediately set to work in a Cubist style, producing her now-famous small bronze figure, *The Beadseller*. By 1925, according to David Boxer, 'she had abandoned the planar and rectilinear and formulated a new style based on curvilinear forms – earthy carvings invariably devoted to women' (1983:13).

As late as 1934, by which time her own work was quite well known in Britain and France, Edna Manley exposed the general dearth of artistic activity in Jamaica in an article published locally in the *Daily Gleaner* (13 September):

> Who are the creative painters, sculptors, engravers and where is the work which should be expressions of its Country's existence and growth? A few anaemic imitators of European traditions, a few charming parlor tricks, and then practically silence. Nothing virile, nor original, nor in any sense creative, and nothing, above all, that is an expression of the deep-rooted, hidden pulse of the Country – that thing which gives it its unique life. To go into the cause for this barrenness is too big a subject for a newspaper article – perhaps it is a still unrealized Island consciousness; of one thing I am sure it is not – that there is nothing to be expressed.

Stimulated by the arrival in Jamaica of the young Armenian painter, Harootian, Edna Manley formed the nucleus for a small group of creative artists – the photographer, Gick, the furniture designer, Webster, and the sculptor, Marriott. They began to exhibit their work as a group in various combinations. By 1936, Edna Manley was ready for her first solo exhibition in London, but, determined that it should have its premiere in Kingston, she arranged for it to be displayed in the offices of a local life insurance company. Retrospectively reviewing the exhibition, Boxer (1983:15) has noted:

> In the works which she unveiled it was clear that two stylistic tendencies of her formative years, the 1920s, had found resolution. The voluptuous masses of *Eve* were now tamed by the underlying Cubist geometry that had surfaced in *The Beadseller*.

There seemed to be a further resolution: with her new style she had forged a personal iconography rooted in the physiognomies, the physiques, the stances, and the gestures of working-class Jamaicans. She caught the movement of the Digging Songs, the rhythm of the market vendors balancing their heavy loads on their heads, the circular movement of the Pocomania cultists as they swayed and jumped 'in the spirit'.

Key items in the exhibition were *Negro Aroused* (sculpted 1935), *The Prophet* (1936), *Young Negro*, *Pocomania* (1936) and *The Diggers*. Receiving good reviews in Jamaica, but a mixed response in London, the Director of the Jamaican National Gallery has subsequently said of the exhibits, '[they] have truly become the icons of that period of our history, a period when the black Jamaican was indeed roused, ready for a new social order, demanding his place in the sun' (Boxer, 1983:15).

Indeed, it might be thought that *Negro Aroused* was both a response to the Jamaican Marcus Garvey's program of black upliftment, embodied in his Universal Negro Improvement Association (founded 1914), and a harbinger of the riots of 1938. The latter were to propel Norman Manley into Jamaican politics for three decades and to curtail Edna's creativity after another bout of productivity in the 1940s, during which she carved *Horse of the Morning* (1943). However, Edna Manley's support for the plastic arts, and the arts in general, was to continue, if less directly, through her teaching and inspiring presence.

The link between the political and the cultural, so obvious in a small society such as Jamaica, was rapidly perceived by Norman Manley. In 1939, the year in which the People's National Party was founded with him as leader, he argued,

> It takes political action to stir a country into a state of national consciousness . . . This political awakening must and always goes hand in hand with cultural growth . . . Around us and before our very eyes are stirring the first shoots of a deeply felt 'national' artistic and intellectual life (quoted in Nettleford, 1971:109).

The riots of 1938 had precipitated a movement for decolonization. It was clear, even to an Oxford-educated barrister such as Manley, that

> we can take everything that English education has to offer us, but ultimately we must reject the domination of her influence, because we are not English and nor should we ever want to be. Instead we must dig deep into our own consciousness and accept and reject only those things of which we from our superior knowledge of our own cultural needs must be the best judges (quoted in Nettleford, 1971:109).

If 1938 was the *annus mirabilis* of Jamaican protest and politics, 1937 has the same legendary status in the arts. It is not only the year of the Edna Manley exhibitions, but of the emergence into the Manley circle of the teenage painter, Albert Huie, of the visit to Jamaica of the famous British painter, Augustus John, who was to have such an influence on the early career of Carl Abrahams, and of the 'discovery', by the Secretary of the Institute of Jamaica, of John Dunkley, Jamaica's first Primitive or, rather, Intuitive, painter. Dunkley, who had traveled to Latin America and Europe as a young man, was running a barber's shop when his pictures were seen by the Englishman, Delves Molesworth. Dunkley has been called 'the Samuel Palmer' of Jamaican art: 'dark, mystical landscapes, populated by strange creatures, jerboas, spiders, crabs, birds, they are paintings that would have delighted the Surrealists had they known them' (Boxer, 1983:16). Dunkley's best-known work is *Banana Plantation*, painted in the mid-1940s.

The distinction between tutored and untutored art, reflecting European technique and folk innovation, respectively, is an enduring dichotomy in the development of Jamaican national culture. Untutored work has been especially important in wood carving, pioneer figures being David Miller Sr and Jr, both of whom were taken up by the Manley Institute of Jamaica group in the late 1930s. David Miller Sr, the more innovative and mystical of the two, taught his son, and for a time their artistic identities merged. Later, the younger Miller embarked upon a series of heads – explorations of black physiognomy – of which the best known is *Girl Surprised* (1949). An even more extraordinary intuitive, carving in wood, was the Revival preacher, Kapo (Mallica Reynolds), who from the late 1940s to the late 1960s produced an enormous body of work. 'The inspiration for these carvings came out of Revivalism: the work was imbued with the movement, the rhythms, the whole intense emotionalism of this religion that is at once African and Christian' (Boxer, 1983:22).

If the roots of the modern art movement in Jamaica are in sculpture, painting has not been neglected. David Boxer (1983) has divided early painters into 'the Institute group' and the independents. The former attended art classes at the Junior Centre of the Institute of Jamaica and took part in informal gatherings at the Manleys' home. If their style was modeled on European post-Impressionism, their themes were local, even nationalistic – Jamaican life, landscapes and faces. While Albert Huie concentrated on rural life (his *Crop Time*, 1955, is justly famous), Ralph Campbell and David Pottinger depicted the street life of the tenement area of down-town Kingston.

Most important among the independents are Carl Abrahams, Gloria Escoffery and Namba Roy. Carl Abrahams, since the mid-1950s, has concentrated on religious themes in *The Last Supper*, *Man of Sorrows* (1965), and *Judgment Day* (1973), and has produced a commentary on the internecine political violence of the late 1970s in *The Angels are Weeping* (1977). Active as a journalist, teacher and painter, Gloria Escoffery was educated at McGill University, Montreal, and the Slade School in London. Her best-known work was carried out in the 1950s, and involved figure compositions. Namba Roy, the most unusual of the three, was born into the Maroon community at Accompong in the centre of Jamaica. After service in the Royal Navy during World War II, he settled in London and became a novelist and ivory worker, having been taught by his father to carve (Boxer, 1983).

Many of these mainstream figures continued to be productive into the 1960s or 1970s. Indeed, Edna Manley herself had a second flourishing after the death of her husband in 1969, and her release from political duties, which had included that of wife of the Chief Minister (1959–62). During the second phase of her career, Edna Manley sculpted religious and mystical themes, as well as turning to political and social topics. In 1965, her figure of Paul Bogle, commissioned by the Jamaica Government, was unveiled in front of the Court House in Morant Bay: Bogle was a 'bold man' (Manley, 1989:68) and had burnt down an earlier version of the building in 1865, at the outset of the Morant Bay Rebellion. Later, in 1981, Edna Manley completed *Ghetto Mother*, a tribute to the motherly qualities of the women of West Kingston, many of them heads of household, in their struggle against poverty and the political violence of the 1970s (Boxer, 1990).

The mainstream was, however, greatly strengthened by the return to Kingston in 1962 of European-trained Barrington Watson, to head the newly created Jamaica School of Art, and by the prominence accorded to the US- and Mexico-trained Karl Parboosingh. Watson has been especially successful with traditional Jamaican subjects, such as fishermen gathering their nets, washerwomen on the banks of a river, urban water carriers, as expressed in *Conversation* (1981), and household scenes, exemplified by *Mother and Child* (1968). In recent years he has become Jamaica's premier portrait artist. Parboosingh, an eclectic expressionist, became attracted to Rastafarianism shortly before his death in 1975, and this inspired some of his best work, including *Brother Man* (1973).

While the Jamaica School of Art has trained many local artists and provided a gateway to foreign instruction – as well as giving employment to local practising painters and sculptors, the intuitive tradition has continued. Kapo, the wood carver mentioned above, Gaston Tabois, Sidney McLaren, Clinton Brown, Everald Brown, and Albert Artwell, have created national, in some cases, international reputations. In the latter category are Gaston Tabois, who became established in Jamaica (*The Road Menders*, 1956) during the 1950s, and Kapo, 'best known for his landcapes, lush

Jamaican hills dotted in rhythmic fashion with red-roofed huts and orange groves' (Boxer, 1983:22). McLaren, too, boasts an international reputation. Discovered at the age of 75 when he had already retired from cultivating, he won first prize in the Institute of Jamaica's Self-Taught Artists Exhibition held in Kingston in 1970. Buoyed up by this success, 'his paintings became more and more ambitious, and soon his sparkling and intricate compositions of the streets of Kingston and Morant Bay – full of the hustle and bustle of city life, always teeming with motor cars – became sought after by local and foreign collectors alike' (Boxer, 1983:23).

Since the early 1970s, the Rastafari cult has had a substantial impact on intuitive art. Everald Brown's symbolism, the religious themes of Artwell, and the topics selected by Clinton Brown are markedly informed by the spiritualism or social radicalism of Rastafari. William Joseph (Woody), on the other hand, seems to have drawn the inspiration for his carvings directly from a personal, mystical connection with Africa. The entire body of untutored work stretching back from the Rastafarians to Dunkley and the Millers, and first brought together in an exhibition entitled *The Intuitive Eye*, held at the National Gallery in 1979, undoubtedly forms 'an impressive counterbalance to the increasingly cosmopolitan mainstream artists' (Boxer, 1983:23).

The unique contribution made to Jamaican national culture by the intuitives – who clearly draw their subject matter *and* their technique from folk traditions and experience, is neatly summarized by Edward Seaga, Prime Minister in the 1980s. Extolling the virtues of Kapo in 1982, in words that might have been been used by his political opponent, Michael Manley, he remarked:

> The best intuitive art has the ability to animate us because it makes us see things as if we were looking at them for the first time. Between the artist and the medium there seem to be no inhibitions and the imagination is set free to relate what it sees with an immediacy which brings us to the heart of the artistic experience (quoted in Boxer, 1983:22).

There are some artists, however, who have traveled the spectrum from folk-artisan to trained artist, thereby synthesizing, so to speak, the two ends of the creole register in their lives, apprenticeship and output. Such an extraordinary person is the potter, Cecil Baugh.

Born in 1908 into a peasant family in Portland, on the north-east coast of Jamaica, Cecil Baugh became a regular visitor to Kingston in his childhood. Falling in with women potters who lived on what is now Mountain View Avenue, he later reminisced, 'I would get a bit of clay for myself and from that bit of clay I would instinctively roll some coils' (Baugh and

Tanna, 1986:3). The women worked without a potter's wheel, using the walk-around method, and they eventually taught him how to make yabbas (earthenware bowls), garden pots and water jars, called monkey jars. By the mid-1930s Baugh had a small pottery: 'I used to sell pottery door-to-door in Kingston and because I made something different from the rest of the potters, people would buy my things like hot cakes. My works were glazed with colors and designs. I didn't just remain making yabbas and monkey jars, but moved on to making vases, often glazed in Egyptian blue' (Baugh and Tanna, 1986:5).

Migrating to Montego Bay, Baugh was given his first book on pottery and some manganese oxide, and he started to experiment with glazes. In 1938 he entered an Arts and Crafts Exhibition in Kingston and received an award: it was at this event that he met Albert Huie. Edna Manley, later a close friend and associate, was also a participant. Service in the British forces during the war was followed by Baugh's successful entry in the Jamaica Arts and Crafts Exhibition in 1947 and by a spell in Britain during which he worked briefly with the distinguised potter, Bernard Leach. Returning to Kingston in 1949, he joined Edna Manley and Albert Huie, part-time, in setting up the School of Arts and Craft, and eventually became full-time when the Jamaica School of Art was placed on a more secure foundation with independence. An inspiration to two generations of pupils, Baugh has been a prolific potter of earthenware and stoneware, famous particularly for the colors of his slips and glazes.

Baugh's genius was to transcend the limitations of his culture–class background through creative work, self-education, emigration (and return) and the support of others. In colonial times it was rare: but with independence it has become more common, as will be illustrated below. Moreover, with the passage of time, the significance of the folk ingredient in the contemporary arts has, if anything, increased, as the evidence for literature indicates.

Literature

While Jamaica has not produced a novelist of the stature of Trinidad's V.S. Naipaul, authors are numerous, and poets particularly distinctive. Indeed, Jamaica's men and women of letters are drawn as much to the oral as to the scribed tradition, which, given the historic significance of recitation – notably Anancy stories of Ashanti origin – is hardly surprising. Remarkable in this respect has been Louise Bennett, Miss Lou, author of Anancy stories, dialect verse, and star of pantomime and radio. A student at the Royal Academy of Dramatic Art in London in the late 1940s, she built up a formidable reputation as a dialect poet – in Mervyn Morris's telling words, 'the only poet who has really hit the truth about the society through its own language' (quoted in Nettleford, 1966:9). Two examples must suffice: the first deals with the smallness of independent Jamaica on the world map (Bennett, 1966:180); the second with Jamaican emigration to Britain in the early 1960s (169).

> She hope dem caution worl'-map
> Fe stop draw Jamaica small
> For de lickle speck can't show
> We independantniss at all!
>
> Wat a devilment a Englan!
> Dem face war an brave de worse,
> But I'm wonderin' how dem gwine stan'
> Colonizin' in reverse.

Since independence, poetry has been a vehicle for the expressions of artists as diverse and creative as (to name but two) the Oxford Rhodes Scholar, Mervyn Morris, who lectures in English at the University of the West Indies and writes in Standard English and Creole, as did Thomas Macdermot, 'Tom Redcam', Jamaica's first Poet Laureate (1870–1933), and the 'dub' poet, Michael Smith, who, during his brief career, before being stoned to death in the political violence of the early 1980s, spoke his verse to the rythm of reggae.

> Its dubbing out the little penta-metre and the little highfalutin business and dubbing in the rootsical, yard, basic rhythm that I-an-I know. Using the language, using the body. It also mean to dub out the isms and schisms and to dub consciousness into the people-dem head. That's dub poetry (Oku Onuora, quoted in Cooper, 1993:81).

Influenced by Marcus Garvey, Walter Rodney and the Rastafari movement, Smith spoke for rebellious (anti-Babylon) and violent West Kingston (where he was born), when he declared (1986:91):

> I an I alone
> ah trod tru creation
> Babylon on I right
> Babylon on I left
> Babylon in front of I
> an Babylon behine I
> an I an I inna de middle
> like a Goliath wid a sling shot

Unfortunately, the lyrics are no guide to the non-verbal aspects of a performer such as Smith, who used 'melody, rhythm, the body in dance and the dancefloor itself as a space of spectacle and display' (Cooper, 1993:5).

Almost contemporaneous with the poet, Tom Redcam, was the novelist, H.G. de Lisser, editor of the *Daily Gleaner*, one of the dominant figures in public life between the wars, and a Fabian who veered politically to the extreme 'right' with age. De Lisser was the author of several books ranging from the naturalistic and much admired *Jane's Career* (1913) to the comparatively lurid *The White Witch of Rosehall* (1929). Jane's integrity, in *Jane's Career*, enables her to overcome her handicaps and to travel from the rural peasantry via domestic service, factory work, rent-yard dwelling and love in Kingston to the lower-middle class bliss of respectable marriage and semi-suburban living. The Victorian missionary ideal of sex within an early and stable marriage, to which low status Jamaicans aspired in Edwardian times and for long afterwards – but rarely achieved – is also Jane's. When advised that she should take a male friend to protect her in Kingston, she refuses, saying, 'I promise me fader to keep meself up, and I gwine do it. Perhaps I may married one of these days; who is to tell' (1981[1913]:11). But de Lisser's treatment, though full of interesting local color and descriptive authenticity, is essentially an outsider's view. Ultimately, it is also a moralizing one, for it elaborates the elite and middle-class view that only moral perseverance will lift the deviant black lower stratum out of their deformed cultural existence – an attitude that, though attenuated, has persisted way beyond independence.

Urban poverty set in the slums of Kingston, blackness, social protest, religious revival and the cult of Rastafari have all been the topics for a number of Jamaican writers over the decolonization–independence decades, ranging from Roger Mais, with his trilogy published between 1953 and 1955, *The Hills Were Joyful Together*, *Brother Man*, and *Black Lightning*, to Orlando Patterson, who, shortly before he became a lecturer at the University of the West Indies, wrote *The Children of Sisyphus* (1964). Although Andrew Salkey continued with his books – after independence largely for children – organized around people's responses to Jamaican hazards, no major novelist has emerged, though Olive Senior has added to her repution as a poet with her collection of short stories, *Summer Lightning* (1986). With the exception of the extraordinary edition of women's oral testimonies to growing up in male-dominated Jamaica, *Lionheart Gal* (Sistren with Honor Ford Smith, 1986), transcribed in a range of Creole-English registers, and elicited from members of the famous Sistren Theatre Collective, creative writing in prose has been overshadowed by poetry and the other media. If the strength of the Jamaican creative urge has been channelled elsewhere, it has gone, above all, into various forms of the theater and into popular music.

The theater

As in the case of poetry, so in the case of the theater, performance has been the key factor. Crucial in the development of the indigenous theater has been The Little Theatre Movement, started by the Fowlers in the 1930s. The Little Theatre, itself, was opened on Tom Redcam Avenue near Cross Roads in 1961. Since 1940, the Little Theatre Movement has put on an annual pantomime at the Ward Theatre in central Kingston, running from Boxing Day to Easter. Watched by an audience of as many as 70,000 per annum, the pantomime has nurtured a wide range of local amateur-cum-professional talent – comedians, dancers, musicians, actors, actresses and singers. The pantomimes at the very end of colonialism, in 1959, 1960, and 1961 are thought of as definitive, because they led to a very successful tour to North America, and the subsequent foundation of the National Dance Theatre Movement.

Directed in its first years by the immensely talented Rex Nettleford (a Rhodes Scholar at Oxford and now a Professor at the University of the West Indies) and Eddie Thomas, who had trained in the US, the National Dance Theatre Movement has been one of the most successful artistic creations of the Jamaican post-independence period. Classical ballet and modern dance – especially the Martha Graham School – have been its principal inspirations, and it now has an international reputation throughout the Caribbean and beyond. Described in its early years by a Canadian critic as 'not just another group of ethnic dancers' (quoted in Nettleford, 1969:28), it draws on Jamaican history and contemporary life as well as addressing modern abstract themes; moreover, dances are choreographed to local and international music. Having myself seen productions over a period of more than 25 years, I have been struck by the increased sophistication of performers and audiences – in 1961, middle-class spectators had broken out in embarrassed laughter when a convincing version of ritual dancing was staged in a number named after the Afro-Christian cult, *Pocomania*.

The 'legitimate theater' has been less vibrant. Trevor Rhone has made a name for himself as a playwright, and as the script writer of the famous 'Jamaican' films, *The Harder They Come*, directed by Perry Henzel and starring the reggae singer Jimmy Cliff as the ghetto hero-anti-hero, and *Smile Orange* – set among the black staff and white clients of a beach hotel on the north coast. But the theater in Kingston has come to depend on sex-comedies analyzing the foibles of black, working-class life played in Creole to middle-class audiences. Two theaters catering to this genre are located near Cross Roads and the third at Halfway Tree, both areas located as near 'downtown' as most 'respectable' citizens are prepared to go. (The Ward Theatre in central Kingston is hazardous to visit and requires advanced planning of some complexity.)

Despite these caveats, the Sistren Theatre Collective, founded at the instigation of working-class women and now directed by Honor Ford Smith, a lecturer at the Jamaica School of Drama, has recorded a remarkable achievement in bringing a sense of critical consciousness to Jamaican women. Male dominance has been challenged through the women's active participation in theatrical productions, sometimes improvised, sometimes scripted by Ford Smith, such as *Bellywoman Bangarang* and *Domesticks*. Sistren play to working-class audiences all over the island, and have had a substantial impact on how ordinary people – especially women – see themselves. Important though Sistren are, they have, however, had nothing like the impact that modern music has had on the black lower-class; for reggae, and its dance-hall version ragga, emanating from the black, West Kingston ghetto, seized the attention of the masses, and projected anti-culture as national culture for popular consumption, in Marcus Garvey's words, 'at home and abroad'.

Music

By the early 1960s, popular music in Jamaica was still influenced by American rhythm and blues, but the general appeal of Cuban music, so frequently used to accompany the pantomimes, was on the wane. Rhythm and blues in the Kingston dance-halls developed into ska, and ska into rock-steady and then reggae. In 1967, Toots and the Maytals had sung 'Do the reggay!' Reggae – meaning, according to Toots Hibbert, *regular* people who are suffering (Davis and Simon, 1979:17) – was directly influenced by Rasta music, which was characterized by its use of fundeh, repeater and base drums to create an insistent, penetrating slow beat (Nagashima, 1984). Indeed, it is impossible to overestimate the significance of Rastafari, the cult of the divinity of Haile Selassie, Emperor of Ethiopia, itself an expression of *négritude* and black creativity, in the development of reggae. Reggae music and lyrics, often composed by the performer and/or backing group, imbibed the culture-class-color complex of post-independence Jamaican society, and the analysis of it provided by Rasta ideology: namely, that the blacks were the true Children of Israel, carried into captivity by white and brown Babylonians; that Ras Tafari (Haile Salassie) was God – and Marcus Garvey John the Baptist; and that the ways of the white man were bad, especially for the black. As Davis noted, 'from the beginning reggae was slum music and was disdained by all but the lowest classes of black society' (1979:18).

By no means all reggae performers were members of the Rastafari movement, but two of the principal stars were – Bob Marley and Burning Spear. Born in the rural parish of St Ann and raised in Trench Town, Marley was to rocket to international fame and fortune – through the efficient marketing strategy of Island Records – with a whole series of 1970s hits, including the rivetting 'Get Up, Stand Up, Stand Up For Your Rights' and 'Redemption Song' (quoted below from Cooper, 1993:124). Singing in a language close to the standard end of the linguistic spectrum, but with 'clearly rootsical vibes' (Cooper, 1993:5), Marley urged:

> Emancipate yourselves from mental slavery
> None but ourselves can free our minds
> Have no fear for atomic energy
> Cause none a them can stop the time.
> How long shall they kill our prophets
> While we stand aside and look?
> Some say, 'it's just a part of it,
> We've got to fulfil the book.'
> Won't you help to sing
> These songs of freedom?
> Cause all I ever had
> Redemption songs

Burning Spear, voicing Rasta conceptions that Jamaican blacks are the true Israelites, that slavery was 'captivity' and white imperialism Babylon, sang (quoted in Boot and Thomas, 1976:70):

> By the rivers of Babylon
> Where we sat down,
> And there we went
> When we remembered Zion.
> But the wicked carried us away, captivity
> Require from us a song,
> How can we sing King Alpha song
> In a strange land.

Many Rastas envisaged redemption through repatriation to Africa, but this fixation was to wain as its impracticability became evident during the 1960s. The sense of dog-eat-dog deprivation among the migrant poor in the West Kingston ghetto, riddled as it was after independence by political factionalism, drugs, violence and a dream-wish, get-rich-quick fixation on materialism, has never been better expressed than by Jimmy Cliff in 'The harder they come', the theme song (1986:63) from the film in which he appeared:

> So as sure as the sun will shine
> I'm gonna get my share now, what's mine
> And the harder they come, the harder they fall
> One and all
> Ooh the harder they come, the harder they fall
> One and all

Reggae was inspired by the beat of the Rasta drummers, the tradition of oral poetry performance, and the socio-economic and race–culture problems pointed up by the Rodney Riots of 1968. These disturbances were precipitated by students at the University of the West Indies in Kingston – and rapidly taken up by the urban poor, when Walter Rodney, a Guyanese lecturer in African history was refused re-admittance to Jamaica. The responses to these issues provided by the performers were as varied as the singers themselves. Marley aligned himself, loosely, with Manley's mid-1970s democratic socialism, thereby indirectly obtaining the legitimation of reggae as a national cultural expression. Burning Spear retreated to Hafrica (sic). Jimmy Cliff was to play the film character Ivan O. Martin, a prototype gangster, Rude Boy or Rudie of the type immortalized (many were soon to die of gunshot wounds) by the Slickers in 'Johnny Too Bad' (quoted in Davis and Simon, 1979:17–18):

> Walking down the road with a
> pistol in your waist
> Johnny you're too bad
> Walking down the road with a ratchet
> in your waist
> Johnny you're too bad
> You're jesta robbing and a stabbing
> and looting and shooting
> Y'know you're too bad
> One of these days when you hear a voice say come
> Where you gonna run to?
> You gonna run to the rock for rescue
> There will be no rock

For more and more black youth, drawn into the violent lifestyle of the Rudies, the only way out was 'via a hit single or a police bullet. The ethos of Rude Boy was pure punk – being the most relentless, outrageous, rudest, best-looking, baddest character on the gullybank' (Davis and Simon, 1979:17).

Since 1980, reggae has been usurped by a surge in the popularity of DJ (disc jockey) dance-hall music – a long-established but previously over-shadowed art. Whereas dub poets performed to reggae, only to have the music dubbed out and the rhythmic voice left behind, the DJs improvise to the record they are playing.

> To the uninitiated much of the 'noise' that emanates from the DJs is absolutely unintelligible. The insistent sing-song of fixed rhythmic structures conspires to obscure meaning; individual words become submerged in a wash of sound . . . The lyrics of the DJs define the furthest extreme of the scribal/oral literary con-tinuum in Jamaica. Unmediated by a middle-class scribal sensi-bility, DJ oracy articulates a distinctly urbanized folk ethos (Cooper, 1993:136).

Artificially isolated for scrutiny, the words of the DJs evidence 'slackness', which has been defined by Gilroy as 'crude and often insulting wordplay pronouncing on sexuality and sexual antagonism' (1987:188). Although 'slackness' has been construed as conservative, Cooper argues that 'it can be seen to impart a radical, underground confrontation with the patriarchal gender ideology and the pious morality of fundamentalist Jamaican society. … [I]n its invariant coupling with Culture, Slackness is potentially a politics of subversion. For slackness is not mere sexual looseness – though it is certainly that. Slackness is a metaphorical revolt against law and order; an undermining of the consensual standards of decency. It is the antithesis of Culture' (1993:141).

Cooper categorizes DJ songs as falling into five groups: celebrating DJing; dance songs; social commentary songs; songs about sexual/ gender relations – the majority; and songs about the Slackness/Culture dialectic (1993:142–3). Yellowman, one of the more scurrilous of the DJs, reports on an amorous adventure that founders when Paulette, a wordly-wise young woman, rebuffs his advances – an anti-*macho* gender theme unlikely to have been celebrated some years ago (1993:164):

> Becau meet up a gyal las week Satiday
> Mi ask ar we shi name, shi name Paulette.
> Mi se if shi love mi, di gyal se, 'Gu we!
> Cool Yellowman, mi an yu bredrin de.
> But di someting we mi ave, im never get
> Di Bwoy waan come mek love right away.'

As Cooper, a Lecturer in English at the University of the West Indies in Kingston, succinctly notes, 'the Culture/Slackness antithesis that is medi-ated in the dance-hall is one manifestation of a fundamental antagonism in

Jamaican society between up-town and down-town, between high culture and low, between literacy and oracy'. But she adds, tellingly, 'that the lyrics of the DJs should be identified as an appropriate subject for literary analysis is in itself evidence that Culture is in hot pursuit of fleet-footed Slackness' (1993:171). Her observation provides a vital link in my argument, that culture/slackness and Standard/Creole dichtomies, rooted literally in the social and linguistic geography of Kingston, have contributed, sometimes antagonistically, sometimes harmoniously, to the development of Jamaican national culture.

Conclusion

While the culture of Europe, distant, post-imperial and less oppressive, has provided a constant frame of reference for Jamaican national developments in the arts, it is equally true that the flourishing of national, creole, culture has been facilitated by decolonization – it is as though a lid which had been clamped down on a pressure cooker has been released. This local 'culture an' tradition an' birthright is being refined in the revisionist work of native Caribbean intellectuals – both "folk" and "academic" – who are remapping the boundaries of "margin" and "centre" ' (Cooper, 1993:174).

Few other countries in the Third World can boast of national achievements in the arts to compare with those of Jamaica. This is largely due to the up-town/down-town dichotomy, rooted as it is in two distinct creole class-culture-color complexes: the up-town Standard-English culture of the 'colored' middle class which has orientated itself to local people, landscapes, townscapes and values, as never before, but employs or modifies European techniques in painting, sculpture and dance, and writes in Standard English yet with reference to the Creole register, which dominates oral performance of poetry and the theater; and the down-town creole culture of the black lower class (the majority of whom are engaged in 'informal' employment, much of it illegal), which is characterized by intuitive contributions to painting and sculpture, dub poetry, reggae and DJ music.

Although 'down-town' is still disparaged, and greatly feared by 'up-town' polite society, several factors have worked together to harmonize the artistic impulses of the two. The first has been the need to fill the void created by decolonization; the second is local awareness of the 'authenticity' of each cultural complex – easier now that the white arbiters have gone; the third is the fact that both national political parties are multi-class, multi-culture coalitions and each, while in power, has given support to the arts, broadly conceived; and finally, the fact that artists, irrespective of social or cultural characteristics have mutually recognized one another's worth.

No one is better able than Rex Nettleford (1989:327) to assert:

The performing arts . . . have facilitated the lowering of social barriers if not their total removal. One thing is certain: a person is judged on his or her merit and his or her creative ability; and the respect that ensues from that has served as a basis for the personal development of scores of Jamaicans since Independence. The race-class 'war' is boldly addressed by the test of talent in the arts. The eminence of the best of the reggae artists who will be remembered long after the barely competent imitators of the music of former masters are duly forgotten, is a lesson for the future.

The gains of the last thirty years, however, have not only to be consolidated but extended. The role of Creole vis-à-vis Standard English, and the educational context in which one replaces, or runs parallel with, the other, require careful evaluation. Referring to the capacity of practicioners of 'Jamaican orature to write and perform a script of cultural resistance to the hegemony of anglocentrism', Cooper argues that 'these talented writer/performers challenge the smug equivalence of class/language/intelligence so zealously espoused by the uncunningly ignorant' (1993:9). It can no longer be said that Jamaicans – in the popular sense of the term – have no 'culture'.

I conclude that Jamaicans enjoy a plural national culture, in which the major artistic ingredients interact positively with each other, though 'uptown' takes precedence in 'polite society' where 'down-town' is emphatically disparaged. This plural national culture needs not only to be nurtured, but to be protected now that Jamaica is fully under the influence of US films and television (Nettleford, 1993:122); and, even more insidiously, US revivalism is making massive inroads into traditional Afro-Christian sects and cults.

Note

1. I am indebted to Gillian Clarke, my wife, for sharing with me her interest in Jamaican art, and for making critical comments on the text; and to my Jamaican-born colleague, Patricia Daley, who has alerted me to several important issues that were inadequately discussed in an earlier draft of this chapter.

References

Alleyne, M., 1988, *Roots of Jamaican Culture*, London: Pluto Press.
Baugh, C. and Tanna, L., 1986, *Baugh: Jamaica's master potter*, Kingston: Selecto Publications.
Bennett, L., 1966, *Jamaica Labrish*, Kingston: Sangster's Book Stores.

Boot, A. and Thomas M., 1976, *Jamaica: Babylon on a Thin Wire*, London: Thames and Hudson.

Boxer, D., 1983, *Jamaica Art: 1922–1982*, Kingston: National Gallery of Jamaica, Washington: Smithsonian Institution.

—— 1990, *Edna Manley: Sculptor*, Kingston: National Gallery of Jamaica and the Edna Manley Foundation.

Clarke, C., 1975, *Kingston, Jamaica: Urban Development and Social Change, 1692–1962*, London, Berkeley: University of California Press.

—— 1976, 'Insularity and Identity in the Caribbean', *Geography*, No. 61, pp. 8–16.

Cliff, J., 1986, 'The Harder They Come', in Burnett, P. (ed.), Th*e Penguin Book of Caribbean Verse in English*, Harmondsworth: Penguin Books, p. 63.

Cooper, C., 1993, *Noises in the Blood: Orality, Gender and the 'Vulgar' Body of Jamaican Popular Culture*, London: Macmillan.

Davis, S. and Simon, P., 1979, *Reggae Bloodlines*, London: Heinemann.

de Lisser, H.G., 1981[1913], *Jane's Career*, London: Heinemann.

Gilroy, P., 1987, *There Ain't No Black in the Union Jack*, London: Hutchinson.

Manley, R. (ed.), 1989, *Edna Manley: the Diaries*, Kingston: Heinemann.

Nagashima, Y.S., 1984, *Rastafarian Music of Contemporary Jamaica*, Tokyo: Institute for the Study of Languages and Cultures of Asia and Africa.

Naipaul, V.S., 1972, 'Power?', in *The Overcrowded Barracoon and Other Articles*, London: Andre Deutsch, pp. 246–54.

Nettleford, R., 1966, Introduction in Bennett, L., *Jamaica Labrish*, Kingston: Sangster's Book Stores, pp. 9–24.

—— 1969, *Roots and Rhythms*, London: André Deutsch.

—— 1989, 'Cultural Action in Independence', in Nettleford, R. (ed.), *Jamaica in Independence: Essays on the Early Years*, Kingston: Heinemann Caribbean, London: James Currey, pp. 291–328.

—— 1993, *Inward Stretch Outward Reach: A Voice from the Caribbean*, London: Macmillan.

Nettleford, R., (ed.), 1971, *Manley and the New Jamaica: Selected Speeches and Writings, 1938–68*, London: Longman.

Payne, A., 1991, 'Jamaican Society and the Testing of Democracy', in Clarke, C. (ed.), *Society and Politics in the Caribbean*, London: Macmillan, pp. 31–46.

Sistren with Honor Ford Smith, 1986, *Lionheart Gal: Life Stories of Jamaican Women*, London: The Women's Press.

Smith, M.G., 1965, *The Plural Society in the British West Indies*, Berkeley, London: University of California Press.

Smith, M., 1986, 'I and I alone or Goliath', in Burnett, P. (ed.), *The Penguin Book of Caribbean Verse in English*, Harmondsworth: Penguin Books, pp. 91–3.

Springer, H.W., 1960, 'Oriens ex Occidente Lux', *Caribbean Quarterly*, No. 6, pp. 246–57.

CHAPTER 10

Ethnicity, nationalism and the exodus: the Dutch Caribbean predicament

Gert Oostindie

In his seminal writings on 'race' in the Americas, Harry Hoetink opened new horizons for the understanding of how ideas about race, color and ethnicity are constituted and then become self-evident elements of the frame of reference of particular groups and cultures.[1] Even if there are evidently political dimensions to these processes of establishing ethnic boundaries around and between peoples, his explicit perspective was more of a social-psychological nature. In this contribution, while subscribing to most of Hoetink's ideas on the subject, I attempt to give the discussion a twist by directing it towards the ways in which young and ethnically heterogeneous nations have used race and ethnicity in the process of nation-building.

While taking all of the Caribbean as a frame of reference, I specifically discuss 'Dutch' Caribbean experiences. This geographical focus aims to correct the cursory neglect of this part of the region in writings on the Caribbean. More importantly, it should underline the theoretical relevance of including these cases in comparative studies. In Hoetink's writings, comparisons of Curaçao and Suriname provided additional credibility to his approach of disentangling metropolitan backgrounds and systems of slavery, and of severing the erstwhile seemingly self-evident link between the specific nature of slavery in a given colony and its subsequent record of race relations. The following analysis, through its focus on Dutch Caribbean experiences, ultimately addresses wider dimensions of ethnicity, nation-building, and the frustrated experiences of decolonization in the region.[2]

Post-World War II decolonizations

The contemporary Caribbean differs in a myriad of ways from the region it was in the early 1960s, when Harry Hoetink started to develop his theories on race relations in the Americas. An increasing economic and hence political marginalization has negatively affected most of the region. Standards of living, the functioning of democracy, and guarantees of civil rights may still be relatively high in the Caribbean, especially if one were to take the so-called Third World as a frame of reference. However, in much of the region, the relevant comparison is not the one with the 'Mother Continents' of Africa or Asia, or with geographically and historically nearby Latin America, but rather with the old metropolises in Europe, and the dominant new one, the United States. From that perspective, the economic and political development of the last decades has been disappointing. The high hopes of decolonization that were once nurtured contrast sharply with the present sense of uncertainty and conservatism – sometimes bordering on despair – in the smaller countries of the region.

Caribbean decolonization obviously dates back way beyond the post-war period. In a sense, the Maroon communities established in most of the larger colonies during the early eighteenth century prefigured the establishment of independent states. Maroons in Suriname, once a Dutch colony whose authorities had found no other recourse than to pacify the Maroons by way of granting them autonomy, have indeed claimed that their independence dates back to these peace treaties of the 1760s rather than to 1975, when all of the country became a republic. The more conventional approach, however, dates the beginning of Caribbean decolonization to the slave revolution of Saint-Domingue, leading to the proclamation of the Republic of Haiti in 1804. The emergence of this second independent nation of the Americas – the first black state, and the first one to abolish slavery – triggered the hesitant Dominican secession from the Spanish state, started in the 1820s but only fully accomplished in 1865. The remnants of Spanish empire in the Americas dissolved at the turn of the century with the independence of Cuba and the renewed colonization of Puerto Rico, this time by the US.

Formal decolonization in the region stagnated for the next six decades. After World War II, the constitutional status of the French and the Dutch colonies as well as Puerto Rico was brought up to date in a liberalizing move which at the same time consolidated and even strengthened these territories' links to their metropolis. Yet around 1960, two major developments seemed to open up new perspectives for the region. The Cuban Revolution promised finally to fulfil the promises of independence frustrated during the US-dominated period of what would soon be termed the *pseudorrepública*. At the same time, the British West Indies embarked on a route to full decolonization which, after the collapse of the West Indian Federation, resulted in the individual independence of most territories between 1962 and 1983.

In the early 1960s, nationalist avant-gardes in the non-independent Caribbean nurtured high hopes of the benefits of independence. Not only would full decolonization restore dignity to peoples colonized for centuries in an imperialist framework, but there would be more tangible results too. Once in control of their own destiny, the new Caribbean states would be in a better position to ensure sustained economic growth, fuller political participation of the masses, and the development towards a more equitable society. Somewhat ironically in view of its previous role in the region, Western Europe provided a highly influential model of social democracy. There was an awareness of the disadvantages of scale and the limited scope for independent action in a region where few former colonies could ever hope to be more than micro-states. Yet, according to nationalist rhetoric, this should not keep Caribbean populations from accepting the challenge. In the words of the influential British Caribbean scholar and activist, Lloyd Best (1967:28): 'what I am arguing is that social change in the Caribbean has to and can only begin in the minds of Caribbean men'.

Three decades on, one cannot escape the conclusion that expectations at the time regarding the economic potential of the region were inflated, whereas the process of marginalization in the world economy was underèstimated. The days when, to take the most obvious case, the British West Indies could generate the wealth which made them 'darlings of empire' are long gone. Of course, economic growth was achieved. In many parts of the region, per capita incomes improved considerably between 1960 and 1990, as did standards of education and health. Only notorious exceptions such as Haiti and Guyana remained among the poorest countries of the hemisphere. Moreover, most Caribbean economies made the transition from primary to secondary and particularly tertiary sector producers. Yet the industrial and service sectors have remained volatile. The high unemployment and emigration figures suggest that the economic transition has been partially successful at best, as have been development strategies based on external financing and aid. Radical new strategies such as the Cuban model have proved to be even less rewarding. Many Caribbean policy-makers must have sympathized with Michael Manley's desperate characterization of the development process as a struggle 'Up the Down Escalator' (1987). The limitations of scale already apparent in the 1960s have continued to haunt planners. Moreover, the ongoing restructuring of the world economy left the entire Caribbean in an ever more marginal position within an Atlantic economy itself struggling to retain some of the gravity which had seemed unbeatable decades ago.

In this perspective, it is hard not to characterize the postwar economic development as disillusioning. Moreover, an intra-regional comparison suggests that the very process of decolonization has been a crucial factor. Just over 85 per cent of the Caribbean's 33 million people live in independent states. The remaining 14 per cent live in what are sometimes thought of as 'not yet fully decolonized' territories. Standards of living in this last group of countries are significantly higher than in the independent states. This comparison yields only marginally more positive results if the Spanish-speaking Caribbean and Haiti are excluded. On average, living standards in the independent Commonwealth Caribbean, and in Suriname too, range below the averages in the 'not yet fully decolonized' territories. Jamaica's real income diminished between 1960 and 1989, and is now below the Latin American average. This is not the case in the French *Départements d'Outre-Mer*, nor in Puerto Rico. The contrasting economic profiles in the relatively affluent Netherlands Antilles and impoverished Suriname are another dramatic case in point.

There is an equally disturbing political dimension to this equation. The group of non-independent countries is characterized not only by higher standards of living, but also by a better functioning of their democracies, and more guarantees of fundamental civil rights. Again, the oldest independent states (Haiti, the Dominican Republic and Cuba) are the most striking cases in point. In most of the former British West Indies, the Westminster-style democracy functioned remarkably well in spite of many odds. However, this part of the region has had its notorious exceptions too, in terms of both totalitarianism and corrupt regimes. In Suriname, independence in 1975 provided the conditions not only for economic collapse, but also for hitherto unthinkable political malaise: a military regime, internal warfare, and widespread corruption of the civil state. In comparison, and in spite of serious conflicts enacted in virtually all of these places, postwar politics in the non-independent nations has been characterized by more moderation and compromise, and certainly by very little violence.

In sum, in a world in which the significance of the Caribbean diminished and in which the individual countries' economic and political viability became ever more dubious, independence proved to be a worrisome accomplishment. It is therefore not surprising that the populations of Puerto Rico, the French *Départements d'Outre-Mer*, the British dependencies, and the Netherlands Antilles and Aruba demonstrate no inclination to take the final – once 'logical' – step to full independence. Moreover, as their respective metropolises do not urge them to do so, the status of 'not yet fully decolonized' may best be understood as one devoid of an expiration date. By the early 1990s, opting for the prolongation of a post-colonial liaison had become a thoroughly respectable means of exercising the right to self-determination.[3] In the Puerto Rican and Netherlands Antillean plebiscites on these islands' constitutional futures, the case for independence won less support than ever before.[4] In the French *Départements d'Outre-Mer*, the ever stronger encapsulation in metropolitan France has been translated into the virtual disappearance of *indépendistes*. Intellectual responses range from former *négritude* protagonist (now Martinican mayor) Aimé Césaire's claim to be fully French by culture, to the younger generation's praise of a cultural *créolité* (Burton, 1993). In the few remaining British territories, an increased metropolitan presence at the expense of the local political elites has produced anything but a renewed interest in independence. These are evidently worrying parameters for projects of Caribbean nation-building, as is well illustrated by the case of the former Dutch colonies in the region.

The divergent paths of Dutch Caribbean decolonization

With the loss in the immediate postwar years of its one major possession, Indonesia, the Dutch colonial empire was reduced to Suriname and the six islands of the Netherlands Antilles. Whereas the Dutch had only given up Indonesia after bitter fighting and under strong international pressure, there was not yet a significant political will on either side of the Atlantic to dismantle the remaining 'empire'. There was an awareness, though, of the need to bring relations at least somewhat up to date with the prevailing trends in a decolonizing world. In 1954, after due consultations and without serious objections in either of the three countries involved, the *Statuut* or Charter of the Kingdom of the Netherlands was proclaimed. The *Statuut* served as a constitution for the three member states: the Netherlands, the Netherlands Antilles and Suriname. In the newly styled transatlantic Kingdom, the three partners would each be autonomous in domestic administration. All parties agreed to the principle of mutual assistance, should the need arise. Only foreign affairs, defense and the guarantee of 'good governance' – including the functioning of parliamentary democracies – would remain Kingdom matters, and for all purposes would continue to be managed by the Dutch.

In comparison to the previous periods of colonial rule, the *Statuut* was certainly a progressive move. In the decolonizing mood of the day, it was certainly more so than the French solution of 1946, which had made the former French colonies overseas departments. The *Statuut* provided an acceptable arrangement for the political elites of the three countries involved, even if there was no consensus, not even an open debate, as to its status in view of a possible 'fuller' decolonization in the future. The proclamation of the *Statuut* therefore did raise doubts about the continuing asymmetry in transatlantic relations. It took some years of discrete lobbying before the United Nations consented to drop Suriname and the Antilles from its chapter on decolonization. The historical asymmetry in power relations was compounded by the weight of population figures. In the late 1950s, the Netherlands had 11 million inhabitants, as against 190,000 in the Netherlands Antilles and 250,000 in Suriname. The huge differences in demographic and economic potential implied that the principle of mutual assistance would in practice be unilateral only.

In the first fifteen years of its existence, the new-style Kingdom functioned relatively smoothly. Particularly in Suriname, nationalists urged full independence, but this minority could easily be ignored by the leading political elites. Nor did Dutch politicians think of Caribbean independence as more than a distant horizon. Yet all this changed rapidly since the late 1960s – a period of widespread racial contentions in the Americas, from Black Power in the US to disturbances in Caribbean states such as Jamaica and Trinidad and Tobago. In 1969, riots in Curaçao made the Antillean government request Dutch troops to restore order. According to the *Statuut*, the Dutch had to comply with the request, and marines were indeed sent in. The year after, political turmoil in Suriname threatened to provoke another Dutch intervention. Even if a second intervention was averted, these incidents did create an uneasy awareness that under the *Statuut*, the Dutch could virtually be obliged to engage in 'neocolonial' interventions. The fact that such interventions could well be triggered by local conflicts over which the Dutch – abiding by the principle of its partners' administrative autonomy – had no prior influence, underlined this uneasiness. The Dutch political left first urged 'full' decolonization, soon followed by the center and conservative parties. In the process, two additional motives assumed increasing significance. There was a mounting irritation over the considerable amount of development aid spent yearly without much benefit to the Dutch and without any clear sign that this money actually enhanced the economic viability of the former colonies. Moreover, Dutch policy-makers worried over the increasing number of Suriname migrants settling in the Netherlands.

The Kingdom's political agenda of the 1970s and 1980s was therefore dominated by the debate over 'full decolonization', understood as the attainment of independence in the Dutch Caribbean and consequently the shrinking of the Kingdom to its European domain.[5] This debate departed from what has long been thought of as the logical model of decolonization. Whereas the former metropolis persistently recommended independence, the erstwhile colonized West Indians were reluctant to accept the 'offer'. In 1975, Suriname did become a republic, but only half-heartedly and, as would soon become clear, at a high cost for all parties involved. There had been no referendum; the majority required in the Suriname parliament was absolutely minimal and perhaps even bribed; and in spite of the extensive development aid which formed part of the independence deal, one third of the Surinamers left for the Netherlands. Not only has the subsequent history of the country been bleak, but despite its independence, Suriname has continued to perceive the Netherlands as its most likely, if not only, partner in efforts to overcome its crises. Dutch efforts to channel the bilateral

relations through international institutions such as the European Community, the World Bank, and the IMF have so far run up against the
stubborn resistance of its Caribbean counterpart. Likewise, on an individual
level, Surinamers have continued to emigrate, legally or not, to the Netherlands. The level of migration has been dramatic enough to evoke the
perspective of a population actually disappearing.

The Netherlands Antilles, in contrast, consistently and successfully
refused to consider full independence at any stage. The second largest
member of the six-island state, Aruba, negotiated its secession from the
Antilles as of 1986, and ably managed to win the concession of being a
separate entity without complying with the Dutch request to pay the price of
independence in return. In the early 1990s, the Dutch grudgingly acknowledged the impossibility of imposing independence on the islands. However, this change of policy has implied a reclaiming of metropolitan
influence in Antillean affairs. The new Dutch policy is defended by reference to budgetary problems and evidence of mismanagement, narcotrafficking, and money laundering overseas, as well as to problems related
to the rapid rise of migration to the Netherlands. The formerly uncontested
autonomy of the islands has now become both a negotiable issue and, so it
seems, a receding horizon. The Caribbean partners in the Kingdom in turn
have felt unduly overruled. Indeed, the Dutch position has undermined
their post-1954 situation which combined the best of two worlds: autonomy
at home, combined with Dutch protection, financial and logistic support,
and unrestrained access for all Caribbean citizens of the Kingdom to the
metropolis. Increasingly, therefore, the agenda for the 1990s has become
dominated by the delicate negotiation of a new balance between the unequal
partners in the Kingdom, possibly to be institutionalized in a slightly modernized *Statuut*.

The exodus and its implications on both sides

This disillusioning trajectory of decolonization did not fail to mark the
rhetoric of nationalism in the former Dutch colonies, as will be demonstrated below. Yet in this context, it is useful to discuss first the extraordinary phenomenon of the exodus in more detail. One of the most
conspicuous characteristics of virtually all modern Caribbean countries –
remarkably, irrespective of constitutional status and economic conditions –
has been the unprecedented level of emigration. The swelling stream of
migrants has dramatically underlined the region's viability crisis, but at the
same time confirmed the 'modernity' of the Caribbean and its people's
outward-looking frames of reference (Mintz, 1989:37, 328). The exodus
served to alleviate population pressure in densely populated islands. At the

same time, however, both the brain drain and the institutionalization of migration as an economic strategy and a psychological norm have negatively affected the region's potential for development.

A cursory classification of Caribbean emigration patterns by destination would put the French and Dutch Caribbean in one category, with the British West Indies in a second, followed by Haiti and the Spanish-speaking Caribbean in a third. Both French and Dutch Caribbean migrations have been marked by a near exclusive orientation towards the European metropolis. British West Indian migration has been distinctly bifurcated, with both the New World (the United States and Canada) and the Old (Britain) attracting significant numbers of immigrants. However, immigrants of British West Indian origin in the US and Canada far outnumber those in England. Finally, migration from Haiti and the Spanish-speaking Caribbean to France and Spain respectively has been limited, focusing on the US mainly. Caribbean populations from various locales have significantly altered the face of major American cities such as New York and Miami.

The number of people of Caribbean origin in the Netherlands exceeds 350,000.[6] The sending communities are relatively small; therefore, over one third of the Dutch Caribbean populations now live in the metropolis. Ironically, one reads more about the effects of this migration to the host country than about the consequences for the sending countries, even if the share of these Dutch Caribbean immigrants in the Netherlands only slightly exceeds 2 per cent of the total Dutch population. The watershed in these migratory moves may be located in the past two decades.[7] The estimated population in Suriname was 350,000 in 1975, and it probably amounts to some 380,000 today. In the same period, the Suriname community in the metropolis increased from 120,000 to over 275,000. Most of the demographic growth was therefore concentrated in the Netherlands. Should this trend continue, the population in Suriname and the population of Suriname origin living in the Netherlands would be of roughly the same magnitude by the first decade of the next century, both totalling around 375,000. The growth of the Curaçaoan community was less dramatic in absolute numbers, but proportionally of nearly the same magnitude. Today, an estimated 80,000 Curaçaoans live in the metropolis, as against some 150,000 on the island.

The explanatory factors for this dramatic increase are manifold. In general terms, globalization and an increasing sense of relative deprivation made the Netherlands seem a more attractive place. Both economic and educational motives and an awareness of the social and psychological drawbacks of small scale induced many to leave. As mentioned above, the Suriname exodus was also linked to the attainment of independence in 1975, which implied the termination of free migration by 1980. Strong doubts – in a sad way, a self-fulfilling hysteria – about the economic and political viability of the new republic inspired many to leave before the expiration of the final deadline. Since then, legal and particularly illegal migration from the young republic have continued apace. The country's deep crisis makes people move, not just because of relative deprivation, but out of sheer poverty and despair.

The more recent, marked increase in Antillean migration, mainly from Curaçao, seems more puzzling. As both the Netherlands Antilles and Aruba are still part of the Kingdom and will continue to be so, political motivations are less relevant. Uncertainty over the outcome of the debate on independence, which was only recently settled, may have stimulated migration during the 1980s. Otherwise, the motivations of Antillean migrants seem to duplicate those of Suriname immigrants: a longing to get away from small scale, and economic and educational pull factors. Even if the standards of living and education in the Antilles compare favorably to much of the region, Dutch standards are rightly perceived by potential migrants to be even higher. In this context, an additional factor is of crucial importance. Caribbean migrations within the region and to the US, as well as the initial postwar migration to Britain, were and are primarily labor migrations. In contrast, Caribbean migration to the Netherlands may partly be explained by the pull factor of an elaborate metropolitan welfare system. The parallels with migration from the *Départements d'Outre-Mer* to France, and to some extent even with the Puerto Rican exodus to the US, are evident.

Postwar immigration has changed Dutch society. Apart from the Caribbean, the former colony Indonesia and the Mediterranean have been major senders of migrants. With some 7 per cent of its population comprising so-called ethnic minorities, the Netherlands – in spite of an endemic uneasiness about facing the fact – is definitely becoming a multi-ethnic society. As migration continues in spite of restrictive government policies, this trend will become more pronounced. In 2010, some 15 per cent of the total population will be of relatively recent foreign descent.[8]

The general situation of the ethnic minorities in the Netherlands inspires pessimism, and the specific data on Surinamers, Antilleans and Arubans seem to allow for only a slightly more optimistic assessment. The differences within the migrant population suggest that the theoretically relevant assets of Dutch Caribbean immigrants over those from the Mediterranean – a better command of the Dutch language, a somewhat closer affinity with Dutch culture – have indeed been advantageous. All the same, it is not evident whether this relative advantage will be consolidated.[9]

Researchers and politicians have increasingly argued that the Netherlands is witnessing the emergence of an ethnic underclass much along the lines of other European countries, and partly echoing the US experience. Owing to the Dutch welfare system, this ethnic polarization has so far not become as acutely noticeable as it has elsewhere. Relatively adequate housing, health care, education, and social security ensure that unemployment and low educational qualifications are not necessarily translated into substandard living conditions. Unfortunately, these benefits resulting from a long process of 'socializing' capitalism in the Netherlands have also served to conceal the ongoing marginalization of the ethnic minorities. The recent – and ongoing – major cuts in the Dutch welfare system have dramatically exposed the ethnic minorities' heavy dependence on a hand that 'gives', but may well stop doing so.

The growing presence of nonwhite migrants, many practising what the Jamaican poet, Louise Bennett, aptly dubbed a 'colonization in reverse', soon challenged Dutch self-representation as a progressive and tolerant society. The Netherlands may be a country where nationalism is hardly seen as a virtue, but intellectuals used to include specifically a tradition of hospitality among the few identifiable characteristics of the nation. This image is certainly damaged now that Dutch ethnic minorities find themselves exposed to more xenophobia and racism than the country's reputation of tolerance towards newcomers might have led one to expect.

The breakdown of the supposedly ingrained Dutch tolerance towards newcomers, especially hitting nonwhites, has inspired a host of studies reinterpreting past and present Dutch encounters with 'Others' in a grimmer perspective (for example, Blakely, 1993). The revisionist literature has its salutary function, but at the same time struggles with the explanation of the phenomenon of what is easily targeted as racism. What if we were to transplant Harry Hoetink's thinking on race relations and ethnicity, and particularly the concepts of the somatic norm and somatic distance – ideas which at the time of their conception still seemed comfortably distant from the Dutch reality – to contemporary Dutch society?

Most scholars today would concur that ethnic boundaries and ethnicity itself are constructs, shaped in specific historical processes. 'Frozen' in time, such constructs assume a self-evident quality, as if they had an imminent, unchanging quality. Thus, as Hoetink demonstrated, the emergence of different variants of race relations in Afro-America depended on a series of variables connected to metropolitan cultures, the specific sequence and character of colonization and colonial exploitation, and the resulting numerical proportions of various ethnic groups in any given locale. The resultant variants differ, not only in the way various 'races' and color groups interact, but equally in their flexibility to adjust to new developments. In Hoetink's concepts: somatic norms differ, as does the somatic distance between such norms; as does the ability to adjust these psychologically deeply ingrained social constructions to new experiences.

Historical specificity indeed seems to be the key to understanding the contrasting cases of the Netherlands and the (Dutch) Caribbean. There is no shortage of studies demonstrating the importance of ethnic boundaries and somatic norms in the Dutch Caribbean; yet the attempt to transplant such views to the metropolitan *mentalité* is complicated. Racism was part of any colonial enterprise, and the Dutch were no exception. Yet in the Netherlands itself, the small number of nonwhites and the Dutch population's general ignorance of the colonial world seem at first to have fostered no less curiosity than racist prejudice. Certainly, early and mid-twentieth century black migrants encountered an array of ignorant and arrogant reactions to their physical appearance. Yet, as many later recalled nostalgically, there was a sense of 'benevolent curiosity' which could make life rather easier.[10] There is little doubt that over the past decades, with the rapidly increasing numbers of migrants, far more tension has arisen in day-to-day interracial contacts. Yet at the same time, one cannot fail to notice the relatively easy interracial contacts, particularly between the Dutch and the Caribbean migrant population. Impressionistic though the evidence may seem, the significance of interracial mixing and miscegenation is certainly far more important in the Netherlands than in the US in particular.

One might hypothesize that initially, Dutch society did not incorporate blacks at all in its hierarchies of physical attractiveness. If there was a generalized Dutch somatic norm, it had been formulated without much serious thought on nonwhites. Once the migration processes gained momentum and contacts with nonwhites increased, there was no tradition of considerable somatic distance to fall back on. What has developed since is another assortment of evaluations and prejudice regarding ethnic minorities in which class and culture, rather than physical appearance, dominate. In contemporary Dutch society, migrants from the Southern Mediterranean seem more isolated and less appreciated than those from the Caribbean.[11] Somatic distance cannot account for the emergence of such hierarchy, whereas a stronger affinity with Dutch culture can.

Interestingly, a recent French survey disclosed a similar autochthonous appreciation of black migrants from the *Départements d'Outre-Mer* over those from the Maghreb. As in the Dutch case, affinity with the national culture is rated above somatic characteristics. Had French culture developed ideas of somatic norm and somatic distance similar to those that emerged in the Americas in a history of slavery and racial strife spanning five centuries, one could have expected a different outcome. That neither France nor the Netherlands did so underscores the historical specificity of ideas about ethnicity and race. Considerations of somatic distance may not be among the most pressing concerns of these societies – but ethnicity as defined through adhering to the right norms of behavior and taste certainly is.[12]

From another perspective, what was the significance of the exodus for nationalism and nation-building in the Dutch Caribbean? From the 1930s up to the early 1970s, migrants in the metropolis were crucial to the formulation of Dutch Caribbean nationalism, particularly in the case of Suriname.[13] There is little reason to think of today's metropolitan Caribbean communities as a continuation of this tradition. The exodus has seriously undermined the contemporary articulation of nationalism. The very existence of a large and growing expatriate community belies the belief in the former colonies' viability as independent states which underscored earlier Dutch Caribbean nationalisms. Of course, the migrant communities have remained in close contact with the Caribbean. Suriname opinion-makers and organizations in the Netherlands have influenced Dutch policies during the periods of military rule and the subsequent redemocratization in Suriname. The vital remittances in money and kind to Suriname testify to the ongoing individual engagement with the Caribbean, as do the fully booked planes to the Antilles. All the same, the focus has shifted to the metropolis.

The Suriname community in particular has gradually relinquished the myth of return. There is a sad paradox here. The contemporary presence of Suriname in Dutch society is stronger than ever, yet whereas this may be a psychological asset to the 'expatriate' community, it is of little avail 'back home'. Instead of being a source of pride and support to the agonizing process of nation-building, the stronger Caribbean visibility strengthens both the magnetizing force of the metropolis and the shock of deprivation among those who stayed behind. At the same time, the diaspora's replication of Suriname's ethnic pluralism has contributed little to a project of nation-building centered around the concept of unity irrespective of ethnicity.[14]

If one were to take the success of the annual Antillean carnival in Rotterdam as a metaphor of real life, the Antillean experience of recreating and refashioning home culture in a circular fashion seems slightly more encouraging. Precisely the non-independent status of the Antilles – and Aruba – enables both residents and migrants to engage in a personal and cultural circularity which is denied, or no longer attractive respectively, to their Suriname homologues. Circumstantial evidence indeed suggests that in the Antillean case, the cleavage between the communities on both sides of the Atlantic is not as wide, and that there is a feeling of common purpose. The absence of the deep ethnic divisions characterizing Suriname provides an evident first explanation. Most Antillean migrants come from Curaçao, are Afro-Caribbean, and speak Papiamentu as their first language. This congruence makes it much easier to identify both with the rest of the expatriate community and with the sending island. Yet as will be discussed below, the odds are that the significance of Papiamentu in the diaspora will diminish. In that case, the vital link between both communities would be seriously undermined.

Two final observations should be made. The exposure to racism experienced by the Caribbean communities in the Netherlands, coupled to the
waning of the 'ideology of return', has further stimulated the ongoing
reorientation from lobbying for Caribbean issues to negotiating metropolitan positions. Moreover, time works against the consolidation of
Caribbean cultures in the diaspora. Music and lifestyle are cases in point.
Research among younger generations of Dutch Surinamers suggests that
they place higher value on the international styles of the global village than
on 'traditional' Caribbean culture, and that metropolitan revivals of elements of Afro-Suriname culture are mainly enacted among the older
generations. Again, this shift of focus confirms the disarticulation of discourse in the various locales, leaving Dutch Caribbean projects of nation-
building ever more isolated from the diaspora.

The fading rhetoric of nationalism in Suriname

If indeed the project of nation-building in the Caribbean is frustrated by
doubts about the viability of most independent states and by the extraordinary phenomenon of the exodus, the Dutch Caribbean provides telling
illustrations. In the remainder of this essay, I discuss the trajectory of
nationalism in both parts of the former Dutch West Indies, with a particular
view as to how the divergent paths of decolonization have been translated
rather paradoxically into the rhetoric of nation-building.

The present situation of the Dutch Caribbean and its diaspora provides
no set of factors conducive to the formulation of an assertive nationalism.
The failure of Suriname's independence project; the painful trade-off between less autonomy and continued metropolitan assistance imposed on the
Netherlands Antilles and Aruba; the irreversible trend of settlement in the
metropolis, in spite of – to cite George Lamming (1984) – the lesser
'Pleasures of Exile': these sobering facts have frustrated once-formulated
aims of nationalism, and undermined the project of nation-building. In this
ideological malaise, the crisis of the Republic of Suriname continues to be
a dominant factor. The philosophy leading to the country's full decolonization
had been shared by Suriname nationalists, progressive Dutch politicians,
and a handful of Antillean nationalists alike. It implied that political independence was a necessary precondition for economic and cultural development. Breaking with Dutch paternalism, or neocolonialism, would provide
the necessary impetus for the country finally to take its future into its own
hands. Moreover, in the effort towards becoming a nation, the deep divisions of a thoroughly pluralist society nurtured by colonialism would be
overcome by a stronger sense of belonging. Indeed, independence would
enhance the former colony's viability.

Now that this philosophy has effectively been falsified by Suriname's trajectory since 1975, other perspectives impose themselves. First, there is the question of ethnicity. Pre-independence Suriname provided a classroom example of what was then described as a plural society. The ethnic composition of the population reflected a colonial history in which descendants of plantation labor recruits from Africa, India and to a lesser extent Java formed the backbone of society, supplemented with smaller groups – of Chinese, Middle Eastern, and European origin. Subdivisions mainly based on religion further complicated the picture, also in the political arena. Yet the political system as such faithfully reflected the model of a society in which ethnicity dictates political affiliation. Furnivall (1945:163–4) once stated that a 'plural society is in fact held together only by pressure exerted from outside by the colonial power; it has no common will'. Suriname nationalists set out to prove the opposite; those objecting to independence used the argument of ethnic division at least as subscript in their reasoning.

Ominously, the positions in this debate faithfully reflected Suriname's ethnic plurality. The nationalist rhetoric in the 1950s, the call for independence in the 1960s, and its translation into politics in the early 1970s had all been Afro-Suriname projects, nurtured by a small group of intellectuals and only in the last instance embraced by the leading politicians from this group.[15] On the grounds of a lack of confidence in the country's viability and concerns about ethnic relations – the post-independence experiences of neighboring Guyana were all too well-known – the Hindustani leadership strongly opposed independence. This opposition was only symbolically withdrawn, at the point of no return, when the governing coalition dominated by Surinamers of African descent had struck its final deals with their eager Dutch partners. Resentment did not wither, and the subsequent failure of independence has confirmed the earlier, bitter criticism by the Hindustani leadership and its grassroots support regarding what was perceived as irresponsible radicalism.

Since independence and particularly since the mid-1980s, the economy has collapsed. The standard of living had been relatively high at independence. The Dutch investment – a 'golden handshake' of $6000 (US) per capita – should have resulted in diversifying and strengthening the economy, but instead stimulated mismanagement and corruption. Contemporary Suriname has fallen into the category of the poorest Caribbean countries; most Surinamers live below the official subsistence minimum. Little optimism is voiced today regarding the country's economic viability. At the same time, political history since 1975 has done little to inspire the population's confidence in its leadership. The period up to 1980 left a memory of increasing political incompetence, ethnic competition, and corruption, which initially provided the military coup with a measure of sympathy. The years of military rule and internal warfare (1980–87) not only demonstrated the military's incompetence and unreliability as leaders of the nation, but at the same time cast doubt on the traditional political parties' leadership in the return to democracy. The post-1987 period of democratic rule has not put an end to economic decline, whereas the evidence of illegally won wealth amidst growing poverty continues to undermine the legitimacy of the political system. The present political leadership may well nurture resentment against the continued dependence on Dutch support. Yet, as this dependence remains in place, the electorate seems to evaluate its leadership's success mainly in terms of its ability to get the support going again.

There is a tragic ethnic dimension to the crisis of Suriname. In spite of its initial rhetoric, the military regime aggravated extant ethnic divisions. The civil war against specific groups of Maroons soon turned into derisory propaganda, confirming the worst of stereotypes. Whereas initially the military had propagated the heroic struggles of the first Maroons against colonialism as a shining example, now there was a return to tales of primitivity and brutality. As another dimension to the civil war – and perhaps partly engineered by the military – Amerindian ethnic demands have become more outspoken, confronting both the civil government and the Maroons, their competitors in the tropical forest. The transition to democracy in 1987 may have been guided by an interethnic coalition of the pre-military political parties, each with its own following. Yet underneath this veneer, ethnic affiliation and competition have remained prevalent.

Moreover, ethnic division was underlined through the workings of an economy increasingly dominated by the growth sectors of black marketing, narcotrafficking, and money laundering. Set in motion in the period of military rule, this powerful underside economy continued to prosper during the subsequent period. Not only did the military leadership enrich itself considerably in the process, further undermining its credibility, but the wealth generated through networking with successive governments – both military and civil – has particularly benefited a group of Hindustani businessmen, causing 'ethnic' resentment among the hard-hit Afro-Suriname population.

Thus, while nationalism was initiated with a nationalist rhetoric of ethnic harmony, in practice little was achieved. Perhaps the most telling case of cynical manipulation of ethnicity by the self-proclaimed nationalist military dates from the 1991 elections. The political party connected to the military faced a coalition of the major ethnically-based traditional parties headed by the Afro-Surinamer Venetiaan. In a cynical effort to win support among the Hindustani and Javanese population, the military – themselves predominantly of African origin – added their own rhyming comment to posters of *Venetiaan*: 'Stemt u op deze *baviaan*?' (Do you vote for this baboon?).

The exodus, finally, with its obvious economic and psychological consequences, has included a disproportionate share of the country's intellectual cadres. Its consequences for nationalist rhetoric are no less evident. It is more than just a passing comment on the sense of distress and lack of confidence in the country's future that the remaining intellectual and political leadership continues to send its children abroad, mainly to the former metropolis.

Not surprisingly then, the debate on the future of Suriname is cast in bleak terms, and has increasingly been influenced by the diaspora. In 1993, a group of authoritative and mainly expatriate Surinamers published a manifesto urging a referendum in Suriname on a possible revision of the relationship with the Netherlands – generally understood as a half-way or full return to pre-1975 Kingdom relations. There is as yet little reason to think that such a plebiscite will materialize, if only because most Dutch policy-makers are in doubt about the benefits of what would certainly be interpreted as 'recolonization'. Yet the manifesto itself is a telling articulation of the profound crisis of Suriname nationalism.[16] Oblique incantations of national unity and working for progress notwithstanding, the nation seems irredeemably caught in the drama of its disastrous decline and its ethnic and spatial segmentation.

The Antilles: ethnicity, race, language

In the Netherlands Antilles and Aruba, the case of Suriname strengthened the extant awareness of the perils of independence. This sensibility had of course previously inspired the politicians' successful resistance to the 'gift' of full decolonization, and had kept the Antillean electorate from pushing its leaders beyond the line, but the fate of Suriname has made the prospect of future independence even more unattractive. The absence of a serious alternative to the present status precludes a radical nationalist discourse, and leaves the Antilleans and Arubans without much room for maneuver vis à vis the Dutch. Even if the recent Dutch reinvolvement in the Caribbean is not adequately defined as recolonization, many Antilleans are apprehensive about exactly this.

In Curaçao, the main Antillean island, the political response to the renewed Dutch presence was initially characterized by indignation and a defensive attitude. Yet the political elites' attempt to play out the argument of neocolonialism stood little chance of being fully heeded in a post-Cold War international context. Curaçaoan politicians realized that the new Dutch policy, itself a devastating comment on local politics in the preceding four decades of virtually autonomous rule, left them little margin. The political parties' position was further weakened when the November 1993 plebiscite – organized by the major Curaçaoan political parties with a view to providing the final argument for breaking up the five-island state and to ensuring a separate status for their island – revealed an overwhelming majority in favor of prolongation of a federal Netherlands Antilles instead. This outcome was widely interpreted as an expression of the electorate's dissatisfaction and lack of confidence in the political system. The subsequent elections in early 1994 confirmed the debacle of the traditional political parties by putting in power a brand new party, capitalizing on its success in confronting the political establishment in the foregoing plebiscite.

Again, the conditions for nation-building and for formulating a rhetoric of political nationalism are problematic. The lack of an alternative to the present status within the Kingdom is not the only frustration. The crisis of 'traditional' politics was by definition a comment on the failures of autonomous rule. The tendency among the former Curaçaoan leadership to counter Dutch comments on what was perceived as mismanagement by referring to differences in cultural style lost further credibility when its own electorate voted for a new party generally appraised as 'clean'. Yet beyond this, there is a deeper frustration. The May 1969 rebellion has routinely been interpreted as the watershed in post-*Statuut* Curaçao. Before that date, politics was an affair of a small, predominantly non-black local elite. May 1969, in so far as it can be seen as a racial conflict, presumably set the conditions for the emancipation of the black majority, both in politics and beyond. One may well question the extent of this Afro-Curaçaoan emancipation, particularly in the economy and in private relations – in this respect too, the Curaçao experience parallels the unfinished emancipations elsewhere in the Caribbean. But indeed, since 1969, politics in Curaçao have been dominated by local black leaders, and at the same time the dividing line between the administration and its citizenry became increasingly thin – most probably, too thin. As the balance is made up, many feel that the 'new politics' have added to corruption and *clientelismo* rather than to good governance and the fair distribution of opportunities. By mid-1994, the recently elected administration seems to have firmly established the equation of the previous decades of Antillean politics with an increasing lack of morality and common purpose.[17] The record of autonomous rule apparently does not provide the strongest impetus to a sense of national pride.

Obviously, there are other and in some cases perhaps more significant markers of nationhood and ethnicity than the political ones just mentioned. 'Race' and language seem to have been such crucial markers of ethnicity in Curaçao. Yet there is a crucial difference between the two. Its unique language, Papiamentu, functions as the one element of ethnicity shared by all Curaçaoans. Race or color, in contrast, provide openings for disconcerting negotiations over who belongs to the nation. Crudely, there are two principal ways of defining who belongs to the Curaçaoan nation, both linked in different ways to history. As Römer indicated two decades ago, the local population tended to distance itself from 'newcomers'. Those groups who came to the island in the wake of its industrial modernization, that is, after 1915, were generally not taken to be *Yu di Korsow* (Children of Curaçao). Race as such was no major criterion in this categorization: Afro-Suriname immigrants were considered outsiders just as much as Lebanese, Dutch, or Poles. Yet a second, more recent, and more exclusive definition existed too. Römer reported that some Afro-Curaçaoans preferred the term *Nos bon Yu di Korsow* (We, good Children of Curaçao), relating to the black population only. The exclusion of the local whites and those of lighter complexion may be interpreted not as a denial of a common history, but certainly as a *post hoc* castigation for past centuries of slavery, and as a self-confident (post-1969!) claim to belong to a specific Afro-Curaçao culture.

Interestingly, Römer wrote that the establishing of this ethnic boundary was partly inspired by 'a poor acquaintance with the history of our island. . . . They departed from the erroneous assumption that the blacks had come earlier than the whites'.[18] Probably correct, this observation is at the same time somewhat beside the point. An ethnic group is usefully defined by a combination of three elements: a shared history (real or supposed); socially relevant cultural or physical characteristics; and shared attitudes or behavior.[19] The indistinct aspect of 'a shared history', *real or supposed*, is a clue of crucial importance, and may help to take the Afro-Curaçaoan claim more seriously. In fact, the subsequent development of a particularly *Afro*-Curaçaoan rhetoric of nation further underlined the specificity of the 'real thing'. Nor has this rhetoric been dropped since. As Broek (1994:23–6) argues, the concept of *Di-nos-e-ta* (This is ours) nurtured since the 1970s aggressively asserts this claim of a unique Afro-Curaçaoan cultural heritage which should be valued as the essence of the island's culture – a claim, incidentally, made earlier in virtually the same phrase by Afro-Suriname nationalists.[20] In the 1990s, Curaçaoan intellectuals would still debate the same issue in deciding whether the island's history should be written as the past of all of its inhabitants, or of the Afro-Curaçaoan majority (Huender, 1993). Yet there seems to be less inclination to emphasize 'race' openly, precisely because of its potential damage to the idea of one nation. Finally, in relations with the Netherlands, 'race' or color are not on the open agenda, even if always present psychologically.

In contrast to 'race', language has continued to function as the one element of ethnicity shared by every *Yu di Korsow*. As Anderson (1983) has demonstrated, definable unique languages can serve as a potent factor in the creation of the 'imagined community' of the national state, and of ethnic awareness. Both the Curaçaoan *Papiamentu* and the *Sranan Tongo* of Suriname emerged in a process in which simultaneously these very peoples, respectively one segment of them, developed. As the languages became institutionalized, they increasingly served as a vehicle for differentiation between insiders and outsiders. Yet in practice and even more so psychologically, Sranan Tongo continued to be primarily the language of the Afro-Surinamers, less so of the Hindustani and Javanese population groups. Moreover, it did not shed its image of a lower-class language. Therefore, Sranan Tongo has not reached the status of the national language for all classes and ethnic groups. Dutch continues to be the country's official vernacular, and two decades after independence there are even indications of its increasing usage in Suriname (De Bruijne and Schalkwijk, 1994: 232–3).

Papiamentu, in contrast, emerged from a history in which the language was adopted by all ethnic groups and classes, and in which it served as the central vehicle not only of communication, but also of affirming a unique identity in counterpoint to the Dutch culture introduced primarily through the educational system. The language therefore serves as the most obvious source of nationalist discourse; without even aiming to be, it implicitly serves as such as it is spoken. However, in a new social and economic context, this anthropological marker of nationality and ethnic uniqueness evokes awkward problems of social policy and individual orientation. For most Curaçaoans, their apparent bilinguality is only an appearance, masking a poor mastery of the Dutch language. One, by now classic, dilemma has emerged as Dutch continues to be the vernacular in education and a requirement for upward social mobility in local society. The dilemma is underlined by the recent upgrading of the Dutch profile in the local scene, and has acquired a new dimension as a result of the increasing migration to the Netherlands. The language deficiency in Dutch of the Antillean population in the metropolis is serious – clearly more so than was the case with the Suriname population – and provides an enormous obstacle to social mobility.

This context confronts the Curaçaoan policy-makers with a formidable dilemma. The political program of a full emancipation of Papiamentu was formulated some decades ago in the heyday of nationalism, and long before migration to the Netherlands had taken its present course. A more extensive use of Papiamentu still ranks high on the agenda of politicians and intellectuals of different backgrounds, and is certainly an obvious issue in the field of nationalist rhetoric. Yet an increased use of Papiamentu in the educational system may lead to a further deterioration of the general mastery of the Dutch language – though in all fairness it should be pointed out that not all experts agree. This policy could therefore harm chances for social mobility on the island, and certainly among the migrant population – today, one out of every three Curaçaoans. The stalemate is evident. Promoting the local vernacular is attractive, perhaps even imperative from a nationalist point of view; after all, the dictum that language is the soul of a nation certainly applies to the Leeward Antilles. Yet doing so may seriously damage the social and economic position of the individuals supposedly served by this nationalist stance.

Such dilemmas remind one of similar debates in Puerto Rico. One crucial difference is that, even if for Puerto Ricans, and certainly the expatriate communities, a deficient mastery of English may negatively effect their social and economic position, at least their own Spanish is a major language too, and has increasingly become institutionalized as such in the US. By definition, Papiamentu will never have that significance outside its natural locale. The implications should be worrying for Antillean nationalists. The Jamaican author Rex Nettleford (1990:250; 1989:22), has pointed to the social acceptance of Papiamentu as an inspiring example for the future of English creole languages. Yet one may well wonder whether it is not precisely the post-colonial status quo, with its inherent economic and educational benefits, which has so far enabled local politicians to sidestep the dilemma of either emphasizing local specificity, or preparing for optimal insertion in an ever more penetrating global economy and culture. Precisely from a nationalist perspective, the dilemma must be haunting. As Curaçao, a 'not yet independent' territory, discusses the possibility of upgrading the official use of a language spoken by less than 200,000 people, independent islands such as Dominica and St Lucia, similar in terms of scale and language situation, and equally aware of the cultural heritage embodied in the local vernacular, would not dream of taking such steps at the expense of the English language – 'Konpyouta pa ka palé Kwéyol'.[21]

These dilemmas seem to have been less prominent for Aruba, the second largest of the Antilleans, with its 65,000 inhabitants. The island negotiated its own separate status as of 1986, and has recently been accorded full country status within the Kingdom of the Netherlands. All through this process, which started half a century ago, Aruba's significant Other was Curaçao rather than the Netherlands. With their more pronounced *latino* roots and their tradition of self-representation as ethnically different from Afro-Curaçao, Aruban nationalists had an obvious case for nationalist discourse (Alofs and Merkies, 1990). Principles of ethnic differentiation actually underlie the discrepancy between the advancement of the Aruban Papiament*o* against the Curaçaoan Papiament*u*, as these had earlier on informed the segregation of the light-skinned autochthonous and the black migrant segments of the population.

Now that separate status has been achieved and the Arubans too have been confronted with a stronger Dutch presence, one wonders whether this will spark off a new, anti-metropolitan dimension in local self-definition. So far, there seem to be no clear indications that such a shift will occur. Beyond the political sphere, Aruban relations with the Netherlands remain comparatively weak. The Aruban community in the metropolis is small in numbers, and the major economic partner has traditionally been the US rather than the official metropolis. As long as these parameters do not change, Aruban politicians may have to struggle with Dutch policy-makers, but will more likely use the rhetoric of other spheres of contention to mobilize their electorate.

The latter observation holds true even more for the English-speaking Dutch Windwards, whose colonial history and postwar economic development have inserted them primarily in the Anglo-American world. As with Aruba, the renewed Dutch involvement could spark off·a new and not necessarily positive awareness of the metropolis. Before his detention on a charge of corruption, the long-term and fraudulent *caudillo* of St Maarten, Claude Wathey, indeed mobilized his following on a convenient anti-Dutch masquerade of nationalism. Yet in daily life, the context in which insular ethnicity is elaborated is far more complicated, involving concomitant encounters with the local and metropolitan inhabitants of the island's French half, a by now overwhelming number of Curaçaoan 'compatriots', immigrants from various Caribbean islands, and American and European tourists. Again, this presents a problematic context of national or ethnic self-definition.[22]

The most important challenge of nation-building affecting both the three Windward islands and Curaçao and Bonaire follows from the recently formulated policy of keeping the five Antilles together. The return to this policy responded to the outcome of the November 1993 plebiscite on Curaçao which was, among other factors, related to an awareness of the importance of interinsular kinship bonds. Whereas during the earlier oil boom Windwarders had flocked to Curaçao and Aruba, now Curaçaoan migrants form a sizeable group on St Maarten with its dazzling tourist business. The October 1994 plebiscites in the smaller islands have confirmed the will to keep the federal Netherlands Antilles afloat. It is not evident that the new policy will be translated into the fostering of a truly supra-insular Netherlands-Antillean nationalism. Yet the same migration phenomenon which has so seriously undermined nation-building in other respects may help to create a certain common inter-island purpose here.

Conclusion

Few would deny the continuing significance of 'race' among all sectors of the present populations of the Caribbean. Even so, the Caribbean contribution to 'cultures of resistance' against colonialism and racism has rightly been applauded for its – in view of the region's small size – amazing impact. From the Haitian Revolution through José Martí, Marcus Garvey and *négritude* to Fanon and Rasta, the Caribbean has had a resounding voice in the chapters of writing and fighting back to empire. Today Caribbean creole culture is welcomed by some observers as another demonstration of the region's capacity to innovate and to contribute to the global culture of the post-modern world.[23] However, it is difficult not to remark the increased fragility of these local cultures, undermined as they are by the bitter fruits of independence and the terrifying demonstration effect of the satellite age, tourism, and the nearby migration outlets. In this context, nation-building continues to be a major predicament, as is the search for a wider Caribbean identity.

Caribbean nationalisms have been characterized both by an awareness of shared Caribbean identities and by a parallel or subsequent practice of particularism and insularism. A history of divergent colonial experiences and resulting cultural differences has been of major importance here; but so have – and probably more so – the contemporary realities of differences in scale and economic potential. In spite of earlier optimism, hesitant subregional schemes, and continuing contemporary efforts such as the recent establishment of the Association of Caribbean States, the postwar period has not witnessed a decisive regional integration. The rhetoric of a pan-Caribbean identity has foundered on the sad realities of competing islands marketing the same products and services to the same clientele in a situation of cutthroat competition rather than concerted effort. The growing awareness of the volatility of the individual countries' viability has strengthened the trend to value particularistic lifelines over the insecure prospects of regional integration.

In this context, the absence of a strong pro-independence movement in Puerto Rico and the French overseas departments is hardly surprising: nor is the similar overwhelming desire of the Antillean and Aruban population to remain within the legal orbit of the former colonial power. Ever since Suriname assumed the agonizing position of providing the counterpoint to the conservative choice, the credibility of a nationalist rhetoric speaking out for full independence has dramatically diminished. The exodus to the Netherlands has only confirmed this predicament.

Dutch Caribbean nationalism today faces the exceedingly difficult task of contesting for a niche in a world increasingly dictated by a US-dominated 'global' culture, struggling on its way with an older metropolitan culture which, contrary to earlier expectations, is as strongly present as ever. The crucial difference with the earlier period of colonialism is that now the link with the Netherlands is sought after in the former colonies. This explains the agonizingly narrow limits to nationalist rhetoric and practice. Earlier nationalist rhetoric in today's context borders painfully on the obsolete. Both within the Dutch Caribbean and its metropolitan society, the future seems to lie in the eclectic retention and further articulation of cultural specificities, rather than in a wider politics of opposition to empire. This situation, which is certainly not unique in the contemporary Caribbean, will no doubt continue to inspire debates in which the older language of nationalism and its illusions of national independence and sovereignty will linger beyond its true lifetime.

Notes

1. Particularly Hoetink 1967, 1973, 1985.
2. I previously communicated some of the ideas expressed in this essay in my inaugural address as Professor of Caribbean Studies at Utrecht University (Oostindie, 1994).
3. Cf. Maingot (1994:228–49). Among the good recent overviews of Caribbean development issues and politics, suffice it to mention Clarke (1991), Domínguez, Pastor and Worrell (1993), Knight (1990), and Payne and Sutton (1993).
4. The November 1993 plebiscites in Puerto Rico and Curaçao disclosed small minorities of only 4 per cent of the Puerto Rican electorate and 0.5 per cent of the Curaçaoans voting for independence. The October 1994 plebiscites in the remaining Netherlands Antillean islands of Bonaire, St Maarten, St Eustatius and Saba confirmed the virtually complete disinterest in independence.
5. For a discussion of the changing relations within the Kingdom up to the early 1990s, see Hoefte and Oostindie, 1991. Meel (1990a, 1993) succinctly summarizes developments in Suriname since 1975. For the Netherlands Antilles and Aruba, see Reinders (1993), van Aller (1994:363–565). I discussed the specter of 'recolonization' for both parts of the Dutch Caribbean in Oostindie, 1992.
6. The statistics generally used in estimating the magnitude of the immigrant population are tellingly biased though. Anybody born in the Netherlands from at least one non-Dutch parent (in some of the calculations, restricted to a non-Dutch *mother*) is counted among this immigrant population. Therefore, a child born in Amsterdam from a Bonairean mother and a Dutch father and growing up in that city will remain an immigrant for statistical purposes. Figures used in this essay are based on Oostindie, 1988 and 1995, and Tas, 1993.
7. In the early 1960s, the total Suriname population in the Netherlands was only 13,000. The same figure applied to the Antillean and Aruban community a decade later. Whereas Suriname and Curaçaoan migration accelerated afterwards, the number of migrants from Aruba, Bonaire and the three Dutch Windward Antilles has remained modest.
8. The influx of immigrants is most clearly visible in the major cities. By 1990, the proportion of first or second generation legal immigrants stood at nearly 25 per cent in Amsterdam, 20 per cent in Rotterdam and the Hague, and 15 per cent in Utrecht. As this proportion is more pronounced in the younger age brackets, these proportions are rapidly rising.
9. In the late 1980s, the unemployment figure for Dutch labor stood at 13 per cent, but at 27 per cent for Surinamers and 23 per cent for Antilleans and Arubans. The figures for the Mediterranean groups were even more startling: 44 per cent for Turks, and 42 per cent for Moroccans. Caribbean migrants are also better represented in the middle classes. For the younger Caribbean generation, educational participation is below the Dutch average, while figures for school drop-out, unemployment and deviance are particularly high.
10. I fully concur here with the ideas developed by Hoetink on 'exotic minorities' in his *Slavery and Race Relations in the Americas* (Hoetink, 1973:177–9, 191).
11. Obviously, there is no need to think of this relative isolation as encompassing all of the

Mediterranean migrant community. Nor do we need to think of this isolation as only imposed. At least initially, Mediterranean communities have indeed been less inclined to assimilation, as is witnessed by the low degree of interethnic mixing.

12. Dutch society may be somewhat more receptive to Caribbean migrants because of an anticipation of more common ground. Yet the slow incorporation of Caribbean culture in this commonalty does underline the difficulty of expanding domestic cultural parameters. As in France and the UK, Dutch Caribbean migrants have been disproportionately successful and therefore conspicuous in one sphere of public life, that is, professional sports. But obviously, while the players may be Caribbean, the sports and the business are not. Indications of Dutch society's willingness and capacity to absorb elements of Caribbean culture proper are meagre. On the French survey, see *NRC Handelsblad*, 22 March, 1991.

13. Oostindie, 1990. This observation obviously applies as well to French Caribbean nationalism, and even, if to a lesser extent, to the British West Indian case.

14. In the Netherlands, the two major ethnic groups of Suriname (those of African and those of Indian descent) are geographically divided among distinct cities, and have tended to organize on an ethnic rather than a national basis. This applies equally to the third largest ethnic group, those of Javanese descent. On ethnic plurality in Suriname, see van Lier (1971) and Dew (1978).

15. Naipaul, in *The Middle Passage*, offers striking observations on the – with the benefit of hindsight – heroically naive ideas of the early 1960s Suriname nationalists (Naipaul, 1981:165). See also Dew (1978), Meel (1990b) and Oostindie (1990).

16. *De Volkskrant*, 29 September 1993. See also the writings of the young Suriname-born Dutch author, Anil Ramdas (1992, 1994).

17. For example, the interview with the new coalition's prime minister, Miguel Pourier, in *NRC Handelsblad*, 9 September 1994.

18. Römer 1974:53; my translation.

19. For example, *Social Science Encyclopedia*, 1985:267–9.

20. The name of the Dutch-based Afro-Suriname nationalist organization was *Wie Egie Sanie*, Sranan Tongo for Our Own Things. As these 'things' were all derived from (reconstructions of) an Afro Suriname past, Wie Egie Sanie's program failed to appeal to other ethnic groups (Oostindie, 1990:245–50).

21. 'Computers do not speak Creole.' St Lucian Prime Minister John Compton, quoted in Frank (1993:46). Cf. Frank (1993) on St Lucia, Stuart (1993) on Dominica. Alongside its tributes to local Creoles and dialects, the recent report of the West Indian Commission, *Time For Action*, equally emphasizes the imperative of continuing and even expanding the use of English in the curriculum of Commonwealth Caribbean education (West Indian Commission, 1993:269–71, 306).

22. Rummens (1991) provides an interesting exploration of cultural identity in St Maarten/ Saint Martin.

23. For example, the broad coverage of Caribbean authors in the third chapter of Said's *Culture and Imperialism* (1993); see also Clifford 1988:175–81. For eulogies of contemporary Caribbean creole culture, see, for example, Benítez Rojo (1989), Bernabé, Chamoiseau and Confiant (1989), Nettleford (1988) and West India Commission (1993:265–8).

References

Aller, H.B. van, 1994, *Van kolonie tot staatdeel. De staatkundige geschiedenis van de Nederlandse Antillen en Aruba (van 1634 tot 1994)*, Groningen: Wolters-Noordhoff.

Alofs, L. and Merkies, L., 1990, *Ken ta Arubiano? Sociale integratie en natievorming op Aruba*, Leiden: Caraïbische Afdeling KITLV.

Anderson, B.R.O'G., 1983, *Imagined Communities. Reflections on the Origin and Spread of Nationalism*, London: Verso.

Benítez-Rojo, A., 1989, *La isla que se repite. El Caribe y la perspectiva posmoderna*, Hanover: Ediciones del Norte.

Bernabé, J., Chamoiseau P. and Confiant, R., 1989, *Eloge de la créolité*, Paris: Gallimard.

Best, L., 1967, 'Independent Thought and Caribbean Freedom', *New World Quarterly*, Vol. 3, No. 4, pp. 13–34.

Blakely, A., 1993, *Blacks in the Dutch World. The Evolution of Racial Imagery in a Modern Society*, Bloomington: Indiana University Press.

Broek, A.G., 1994, *Onenigheid is een genoegen. Omtrent identiteit Beneden de Wind*, Curaçao: Amigoe.

Bruijne, G.A. de and Schalkwijk, A., 1994, 'Kondreman en P'tata. Nederland als referentiekader voor Surinamers?' in Brahim, A.J. *et al.* (ed.), *Suriname in het jaar 2000*, Baarn: Bosch en Keuning, pp. 225–41.

Burton, R., 1993, 'Ki Moun Nou Ye? The Idea of Difference in Contemporary French West Indian Thought', *New West Indian Guide/Nieuwe West-Indische Gids*, No. 67, pp. 5–32.

Clarke, C.A. (ed.), 1991, *Society and Politics in the Caribbean*, London: Macmillan.

Clifford, J., 1988, *The Predicament of Culture. Twentieth-Century Ethnography, Literature, and Art*, Cambridge: Harvard University Press.

Dew, E., 1978, *The Difficult Flowering of Surinam. Ethnicity and Politics in a Plural Society*, 's-Gravenhage: Nijhoff.

Domínguez, J.I., Pastor, R.A. and DeLisle Worrell, R. (eds), 1993, *Democracy in the Caribbean. Political, Economic, and Social Perspectives*, Baltimore: Johns Hopkins University Press.

Frank, D.B., 1993, 'Political, Religious, and Economic Factors Affecting Language Choice in St Lucia', *International Journal of the Sociology of Language*, No. 102, pp. 39–56.

Furnivall, J.S., 1945, 'Some Problems of Tropical Economy', in Hinden, R. (ed.), *Fabian Colonial Essays*, London: Allen and Unwin.

Hoefte, R. and Oostindie, G., 1991, 'The Netherlands and the Dutch Caribbean: Dilemmas of Decolonisation', in Sutton, P. (ed.), *Europe and the Caribbean*, London: Macmillan, pp. 71–98.

Hoetink, H., 1967, *Caribbean Race Relations. A Study of Two Variants,* London: Oxford University Press.

——— 1973, *Slavery and Race Relations in the Americas. Comparative Notes on Their Nature and Nexus*, New York: Harper.

——— 1985, ' "Race" and Color in the Caribbean', in Mintz, S.W. and Price, S. (eds), *Caribbean Contours*, Baltimore: Johns Hopkins University Press, pp. 55–84.

Huender, S., 1993, 'Un spil di presente/Un porta pa futuro. Geschiedbeleving en nationale identiteit op Curaçao', M.A. thesis, Rijksuniversiteit Leiden/Katholieke Universiteit Nijmegen.

Knight, F.W., 1990, *The Caribbean: The Genesis of a Fragmented Nationalism,* 2nd edn, New York: Oxford University Press.

Lamming, G., 1984[1960], *The Pleasures of Exile*, London: Allison and Busby.

Lier, R.A.J. van, 1971, *Frontier Society: A Social Analysis of the History of Surinam*, The Hague: Nijhoff.

Maingot, A.P., 1994, *The United States and the Caribbean,* London: Macmillan.

Manley, M., 1987, *Up the Down Escalator*, London: Deutsch.

Meel, P., 1990a, 'Money Talks, Morals Vex: The Netherlands and the Decolonization of Suriname, 1975–1990', *European Journal of Latin American and Caribbean Studies*, No. 48, pp. 75–98.

_____ 1990b, 'A Reluctant Embrace: Suriname's Idle Quest for Independence', in Brana-Shute, G. (ed.), *Resistance and Rebellion in Suriname: Old and New*, Williamsburg: College of William and Mary, pp. 259–89.

_____ 1993, 'The March of Militarization in Suriname', in Payne, A. and Sutton, P. (eds), *Modern Caribbean Politics*, Baltimore: The Johns Hopkins University Press, pp. 125–46.

Mintz, S.W., 1989[1974], *Caribbean Transformations*, New York: Columbia University Press.

Naipaul, V.S., 1981[1962], *The Middle Passage. Impressions of Five Societies – British, French and Dutch – in the West Indies and South America*, New York: Vintage.

Nettleford, R., 1988, 'Creolisation in the Caribbean Arts', in Baud, M. and Ketting, M.C. (eds), *'Cultuur in beweging'. Creolisering en Afro-Caraïbische cultuur*, Rotterdam: Erasmus Universiteit Rotterdam, pp. 53–74.

_____ 1989, 'The Caribbean: The Cultural Imperative and the Fight Against Folksy Exotist Tastes', *Caribbean Affairs*, Vol. 2, No. 2, pp. 18–30.

_____ 1990, 'Threats to National and Cultural Identity', in Bryan, A.T., Greene, E. and Shaw, T.M. (eds), *Peace, Development and Security in the Caribbean. Perspectives to the Year 2000*, London: Macmillan, pp. 241–54.

Oostindie, G., 1988, 'Caribbean Migration to the Netherlands: A Journey to Disappointment?' in Cross, M. and Entzinger, H. (eds), *Lost Illusions: Caribbean Minorities in Britain and the Netherlands*, London: Routledge, pp. 54–72.

_____ 1990, 'Preludes to the Exodus: Surinamers in the Netherlands, 1667–1960s', in Brana-Shute, G. (ed.), *Resistance and Rebellion in Suriname: Old and New*, Williamsburg: College of William and Mary, pp. 231–58.

_____ 1992, 'The Dutch Caribbean in the 1990s: Decolonization, Recolonization?' *Caribbean Affairs*, Vol. 5, No. 1, pp. 103–19.

_____ 1994, *Caraïbische dilemma's in een 'stagnerend' dekolonisatieproces*, Leiden: KITLV Press.

_____ 1995, 'Migrations et identités des populations Caribéennes aux Pays-Bas', in Reno, F., (ed.), *Identité et politique de la Caraïbe et de l'Europe multiculturelles*, Paris: Economica, pp. 59–80.

Payne, A. and Sutton, P. (eds), 1993, *Modern Caribbean Politics*, Baltimore: The Johns Hopkins University Press.

Ramdas, A., 1992, *De papagaai, de stier en de klimmende bougainvillea*, Amsterdam: De Bezige Bij.

_____ 1994, *Ethiek als vitaal belang*, Amsterdam: De Bezige Bij.

Reinders, A., 1993, *Politieke geschiedenis van de Nederlandse Antillen en Aruba 1950–1993*, Zutphen: Walburg Pers.

Römer, R.A., 1974, 'Het "wij" van de Curaçaoenaar', *Kristòf*, Vol. 1, No. 2, pp. 49–62.

Rummens, J.W.A., 1991, 'Identity and Perception: The Politicalization of Identity in St Martin', in Díaz, H.P., Rummens, J.W.A. and Taylor, P.D.M. (eds), *Forging Identities and Patterns of Development in Latin American and the Caribbean*, Toronto: Canadian Scholars' Press, pp. 265–78.

Said, E.W., 1993, *Culture and Imperialism*, London: Vintage.

Kuper, A. and Kuper, J. (eds), 1985, *The Social Science Encyclopedia,* London: Routledge and Kegan Paul.

Stuart, S., 1993, 'Dominican Patwa – Mother Tongue or Cultural Relic?', *International Journal of the Sociology of Language*, No. 102, pp. 57–72.

Tas, R.F.J., 1993, 'Surinaamse en Antilliaanse bevolking in Nederland, 1 januari 1993', *Moandstatistiek van de Bevolking (CBS)*, No. 41(93/9), pp. 9–12.

West India Commission, 1993, *Time for Action. Report of the West India Commission*, Kingston: The Press – University of the West Indies.

Index